Raymond Wilson was born shortly after World War II and grew up in an extended family in a socially segregated part of Salem, New Jersey. As an African-American during the civil rights movement, he found little support to help him obtain his dream of being a pilot. After college with a degree in education, he taught social studies in junior high school. He then pursued his dream of becoming a pilot by joining the United States Army in 1968, with a guarantee of going to flight school. After 22 years of service in the military, Ray retired and continued to fly as an instructor and ferry pilot for Northwest Airlines. He retired again after 15 years and for seven years flew medical evacuation helicopters for hospitals in the greater Minnesota-Wisconsin area. Ray is a mentor in the Ramsey County Veterans Treatment Court, plays trumpet in the Saint Anthony Park community band, and still flies little airplanes. He lives with his wife in Saint Paul, Minnesota.

Bruce Richardson grew up in East Providence, Rhode Island and decided to go to West Point when he was five. After graduation in 1967, he was one of the most highly trained soldiers in the US Army as an airborne, ranger, artillery officer. He served with the 82nd Airborne at Fort Bragg, the 25th Infantry in Vietnam, and the 4th Infantry at Fort Carson. He is a Wharton MBA, a former CPA with KPMG, and former CFO with Quadion Corporation. He was elected to the Saint Louis Park, Minnesota school board four times and served for ten years on the Association of Metropolitan School Districts board as chair of the Executive and Legislative committees. Bruce was a facilitator for "Echoes of War" and Veterans Voices discussion groups at the Minnesota Humanities Center, consults on leadership, finance, and strategy for RSI Consulting, and serves on the Board of the Veterans Defense Project. He and his wife live in Saint Louis Park.

To our families and those seeking a path to peace…

Bruce Richardson and Raymond Wilson

BROTHERS

AUSTIN MACAULEY PUBLISHERS™

LONDON * CAMBRIDGE * NEW YORK * SHARJAH

Ordering Information
Quantity sales: Special discounts are available on quantity purchases by corporations, associations and others. For details, contact the publisher at the address below.

Publisher's Cataloging-in-Publication data
Richardson, Bruce and Wilson, Raymond
Brothers

ISBN 9798889101321 (Paperback)
ISBN 9798889101338 (ePub e-book)

Library of Congress Control Number: 2023915744

www.austinmacauley.com/us

First Published 2023
Austin Macauley Publishers LLC
40 Wall Street, 33rd Floor, Suite 3302
New York, NY 10005
USA

mail-usa@austinmacauley.com
+1 (646) 5125767

We thank our families, our teachers and mentors, and the friends we lost for their support. Without them we might not have made it to be *Brothers*.

Table of Contents

Introduction

This story shall the good man teach his son;
From this day to the ending of the world,
We few, we happy few, we band of brothers;
For he today that sheds his blood with me
Shall be my brother;

– Henry V, Act IV, Scene iii, by William Shakespeare

Danny Glover was in O'Hare airport, and a pilot from Northwest Airlines saw him, rushed over to shake his hand, and said, "Ray Wilson, what are you doing here?" Danny Glover replied, "Who the hell is Ray Wilson?"

Ray Wilson believes Danny Glover looks like him. Bruce Richardson doesn't look like either of them. Ray and Bruce are brothers. Everyone who meets them questions that statement, because Ray is black, and Bruce is white.

We are writing our story for people who want to understand what it means to have a dream, for those who have been subjected to racism, for people who are poor, for people who cannot understand "white privilege", for those who have lost friends, or need a friend or a brother or a sister, and for students who need to find inspiration from the love of brothers and sisters who can help them realize their dreams.

Brothers attempts to make it clear that becoming brothers is more than having the same birth mother or father. All of us can be blessed with finding new brothers or sisters in our lives. There is a certain joy in finding someone who not only has been through many of the same trials by fire as you but also has discovered the bonds that really make us brothers.

Ray and Bruce tried to set up a time to meet at the Minnesota Humanities Center (MHC) where Bruce was running a series of meetings for "Minnesota Remembers Vietnam". No times worked at MHC, so we found a Dunn Brothers Coffee Shop halfway between us where we could talk. Ray was a mentor for veterans in the Ramsay County Veterans Treatment Court (VTC), and Bruce was working to bring Vietnam veterans together at the Humanities Center. We decided to have coffee together to share our stories. Between Minneapolis and St. Paul at this coffee shop at the corner of Lake Street and the Mississippi River, we discovered that we were brothers.

After the meeting with Ray was arranged, Bruce received a call from a friend at Twin Cities Public Television (tpt). She had been active in the meetings at MHC, and her colleague, Amy, was putting together a program called the "Telling Project" about Vietnam veterans. Bruce was already going to be half way to their office, so they agreed to meet at the Dunn Brothers the hour before he and Ray were to meet.

The meeting on the "Telling Project" was educational for Bruce. Amy explained who she already had as presenters and asked. "What are we missing?" The show had already recruited Navy, Air Force, and Marine veterans and a Hmong family member, so Bruce thought it was a simple answer. After he recovered from his disappointment that tpt didn't want him, Bruce said that they were missing a black Army officer. Toward the end of their meeting, Bruce told her that he was meeting Ray for coffee, so he had to put on his "USMA" hat. USMA is the United States Military Academy at West Point where Bruce had graduated from over 50 years earlier. He and Ray had agreed that since all white guys look alike, Ray would recognize him by the hat.

About that time a tall black man who looked like Danny Glover walked in the door. Amy said, "I think your guy just walked in." Bruce took one look at Ray and replied, "No, your guy just walked in!" After their original meeting, Amy recruited Ray for her project, and Ray became a star of the show telling his amazing story. Later Ray corrected Bruce's observation that he looked like Danny Glover.

After Amy left the coffee shop, we shared our stories. The similarities were amazing. Both of us had been Army officers and served in Vietnam at about the same time. We had been through a lot of the same Army experiences. We both had been commanders, both had been shot down, and both had lost close friends in combat. But the kinship went deeper. We had lived less than 300 miles apart on the East coast when we were young. Both of us were poor kids, and we both had a dream since we were five years old. We decided that our bond of brotherhood was a story worth sharing.

Bruce had been talking to high school English and history classes for a number of years. He had been invited by English teachers who were reading The Things They Carried by Tim O'Brien or by history teachers when they studied the Vietnam War. We decided that the two of us had a better story told together. We were well received by the students and teachers, and we spoke to many classes and a school assembly in front of thousands of students. We spoke to several adult audiences about being brothers, so we learned more about each other. Our thoughts on justice, equity, racism, and dreams continued to bring us closer. We decided that we had something to tell the world. With so many black and brown students struggling with their futures, so many white people misunderstanding "white privilege", and so many veterans committing suicide, we felt the world and Danny Glover needed to hear our story.

This story shall the good man teach his son;
From this day to the ending of the world.
— Henry V, Act IV, Scene iii, by William Shakespeare

Chapter 1
Dreams

A dream does not become reality through magic. It takes sweat, determination and hard work.

        – General Colin Powell (US Army, Ret.) Former Secretary of State

From the time they were five years old, Ray's dream was to fly and Bruce's dream was to attend West Point. How could two poor kids from different parts of the East Coast become brothers? Ray was black. Bruce was white. Yet they had much in common even as kids growing up in New Jersey and Rhode Island. They both had dreams.

Ray: I knew that I wanted to fly since I was five. When I told a doctor that I wanted to be a pilot, he scoffed and told me to get real. That racist basically told me that no black kid was going to be a pilot.

I had to think back to the first time I thought about being a pilot and an aviator. It seemed like I had always wanted to fly. I think I was born with that desire. My Aunt Callie told me the story. When I was about five years old, at the doctor's office getting my shots for school, the doctor, who was white, apparently wanted to be nice, so he asked me, "What do you want to be when you grow up?"

Aunt Callie said that I was very proud and excited to say, "I want to be a pilot!"

He looked at me, apparently not so nice and said, "You should try to be something that you have a chance to be!"

When I was about eight years old, I got a cast iron World War II Navy airplane for my birthday. It had folding wings and looked like a dive bomber. My backyard was part dirt and bits of grass. We lived next-door to my grandmother, so I had a very large area to play in.

I found this wooden box and a big plank of wood. I put the plank on top of the box, put some bricks on one side of the box to make it look like a control tower and with that I created a World War II aircraft carrier. I made believe that the dirt was the ocean and the clumps of grass were the land.

In my mind, it was a perfect ship just like those I saw in the movies and I was the greatest carrier pilot the Navy had ever seen. I would place toy buildings around the yard and they would be my targets. In my play, I was an ace pilot and would takeoff from the carrier and fly around the yard doing all kinds of amazing maneuvers.

I was a perfect navigator, making my way to each target. All my bombs would fall right on each one. I never missed. Getting back to my ship, I would make a perfect landing. I would then fold my wings and taxi to the parking area. I loved my playtime and flying was my dream!

I did not remember that white doctor's racist words but my Aunt Callie told me that she carried that story in her head and heart for many years. Eighteen years later, I graduated from United States Army Flight School at Ft. Rucker, Alabama.

My sweet aunt found that doctor who was retired by then. She told him that I had made my dream come true. How that little black boy from eighteen years ago was now a grown man and a pilot for the military of this country!

I remember that my Aunt Callie had a big smile on her face when she told me the story. I had to work my way through racism, roadblocks and college to reach my dream to fly.

Bruce: When I was five years old, I saw the West Point Story at the movie theater in Jamestown, Rhode Island. After seeing that movie, I was hooked. When I told people that I wanted to go to West Point, they would smile knowingly and say, "Sure, kid."

But my determination increased when I realized that my parents could never afford to send five of us kids to college. The Military Academy seemed like a good way to get a great education.

With the military history in our family, my grandfather having served in the Navy during the Spanish-American War and my dad and uncles all World War II veterans, I pictured war as gallant and exciting. I had a lot to learn. As we watched the West Point Story, my brother and I saw Jimmy Cagney become a cadet and fight his way through the system.

I decided that is what I wanted to do but even in high school when I told people that my dream was to go to West Point, they said, "Sure, kid." No one in my family had gone to West Point. Only one of my uncles had even gone to college. My dad's brother went to Brown University undergrad and got his PhD at Harvard.

He had been a Navy pilot in World War II and ran the Woods Hole Oceanographic Institute on Cape Cod. After I visited their home in Falmouth, Massachusetts, it was easy to see what education and a good job could do for a person. My uncle Bill provided a role model for me.

Late in his life, I asked my dad if he was ever sorry that he had never gone to college like his brother. He said no but he was proud that every one of his children was a college graduate and that most of us had advanced degrees. I reminded him that when I was finishing high school, he had offered to get me a job at his company.

He had pushed it and assured me that he could get me into the electricians' union but I was determined to go to college. I asked him what that was about. He just smiled. I had great support from my home, my school and my church but I had to take the tests.

I took them and passed. No one could stop my dream. I entered the gates of West Point in June 1963 when I was 17. I graduated four years later on 7 June 1967.

Together: Some people seem to enjoy killing other people's dreams. Teachers, doctors, parents and many others may try to stop us from doing what we think we were born to do. Ray and Bruce don't think anyone should be allowed to do that.

Who can stop those people? You can. When they tell you that you can't do something, don't believe them. Just go do it. Don't let anyone stop you. Do not allow anyone or anything to get in your way.

Playing games like checkers and chess as kids created insights into thinking several moves ahead—complex thinking that led us to move into more complicated worlds. Later on music did the same thing and team sports helped us learn to work with others.

Determination, guts and grit helped to dream big dreams and made them happen. In our student days, we went from elementary arithmetic to calculus. Instruction took us from simple to complex ideas by building on foundations.

How could they gain understanding? It took study and practice. You could learn to achieve whatever you want. You can make your dreams come true. Remember, only you can make your dreams come true.

We don't owe where we are today to family fortune or connections. When our mentors saw that we had dreams, they supported us. But they could not do it for us. Don't push away family members, teachers and others who offer help. That's what they are in your life to do.

Look at people as being good until they show you otherwise. Where you are from and how you were raised does not define who you can become. You do that. We are individuals. We have the opportunity to become our best selves and our best dreams, so dream big. Be patient. Learn from your failures.

Being able to withstand discomfort allows you to grow as an individual. Find alternative ways to get to that dream! Do not quit. Never, never, never give up. You are special. There is no one else in the universe like you.

Here are the three steps on the path to making your dreams come true that Ray and Bruce recommend: education, education and education.

Chapter 2
Education

Believe in yourself. You gain strength, courage and confidence by every experience in which you really stop to look fear in the face. You must do the thing you think you cannot do. The future belongs to those who believe in the beauty of their dreams.

– Eleanor Roosevelt

Both Ray and Bruce realized that to make their dreams come true, they had to get an education. The path out of being poor was to go to school. From elementary school to junior high and from high school to college, they studied, worked and played sports. For them, education was the key experience to help them take that critical step for any kid—they left home.

Ray: I grew up very poor like all the black kids I knew who lived on Hubble Avenue and 7th Street in Salem, New Jersey. We lived close to a Heinz ketchup warehouse and a large railroad yard. There were three of us—all born within three years of each other. It seemed like there were 100 children living on those two streets.

We lived right next-door to my grandparents and our lives were tied together. My brother and I were over there every day for one reason or another. One big reason was that my grandmother was a great cook and there was lots of food—more it seemed than in my house.

I remember my uncles bringing over food to help out. Sometimes, there was a quarter of a pig, a bucket of crabs and lots of vegetables to share. How poor were we? We did not go without food. It wasn't always the best food for growing boys. I remember that we got lots of government cheese.

Even back in the '50s, there was a program to buy surplus cheese from dairy farmers. Then the government gave it to the very low-income folks to help our diet. Our homes were built in the 1920s. They were just framing boards with very little insulation and no central heat, let alone air conditioning.

There was a space heater in the middle of the first floor with holes in the ceiling, allowing heat to the second floor. The other warm room was the kitchen. I remember bringing wood or coal in to start the oven in the morning in the winter.

The first adult up would start the fire in the kitchen oven to warm the place up for those who went to work or school to get ready and have breakfast. There was no bathroom in the house. We used an outhouse just outside the back door.

It was connected to the city system but without heat, being outside in winter make it very rough answering the call of nature. At night, there was a bucket in the upstairs hallway. When I was older, six or so, my job was to empty that bucket each morning.

I grew up with a younger brother. I was one year and nine months older than my brother Spencer. We shared the same room and bed until we were about eight years old. Then we got bunkbeds. We fought for the next three years over who got the top bunk. I actually have three brothers and one sister. We were all connected by our father, Ford.

The brother I grew up with, Spencer and I have the same mother. I found out about the other two boys when I was about 10 years old. Ford and Roger were 8 and 9 years older than I. They were living in the northern half of New Jersey. When they were in their last years of high school, they finished up in Salem.

It was amazing knowing that I had older brothers and they were starting to live their lives, working and making their own way in the world—deciding for themselves what is best. My sister was a mystery. I first knew that she existed when I was about 15. I think that I may have seen her but she was my father's secret.

She was born five months earlier than Spencer. This was hard news for my mother. I was 30 before my sister and I corresponded and not until 1992 when we first met in Minneapolis. I was so glad to know her and happy that I had a sister.

When I was a small child, my summers were all play. I now look back on that time and my life as happy and carefree. Of course, we were poor as hell and there was no such thing as an allowance or asking Mom or Dad for money for ice cream or go to the movies. This was the time before I got my bicycle. Having a bike in a small South Jersey town, is like a magic carpet.

You can see so many new and wonderful things but before 8 years old, I was on foot. My neighborhood, Hubbell Street and Seventh Street were filled with kids all about the same age. We were the beginning of the baby boomers. We played baseball, actually stick ball and we played in the woods at the end of the street down to the Salem River.

How did I get to the movies? The theater in my hometown had a matinee every Saturday all summer long for kids. It cost $.25. A very small amount now but big money to a nine-year-old kid. What my brother, our cousin and I did during the week was to collect rags and paper throughout the neighborhood and store them in our basement.

You would be surprised at the number of these items we could collect in a week. Early Saturday morning about 8 o'clock, we would have our treasures out on the curb piled up neatly for the Ragman. He was a white guy, very rough and looking way older than his years. The dirty bib overhauls, what looked like a gray hooded sweatshirt and a face like he had been out to sea.

It looked like a face that had been standing a lonely watch for hours for many years. He had this gravelly voice that told us that he must have smoked a pack of cigarettes a day for his whole life. He was short of stature, round in the middle and had a happy personality.

This old beat up truck pulled up and the Ragman would get out and march right up to us and examine our bundles and stacks of paper. As he got closer to the three of us, he would ask how we were doing and then get about his work, weighing each bundle of rags and stack of papers on an old big spring scale that needed both his hands to operate.

He would calculate on a piece of paper how much all the items were worth and then tell us what he was offering for our goods. He would then dole out the money to each of us. As it all turned out, we usually got about one dollar apiece. That was big money to us in 1954, enough to put $.25 away for church on Sunday and $.25 to get into the movies.

That left $.50 for treats and soda while we watched the film. I would always save about $.10 of my candy money to buy a balsa wood airplane. It had a little weight on the nose and all you had to do was slide in the main wing and instantly I had a great flying machine.

I loved the movies. They were mostly serials of the old west, Flash Gordon or some other adventure. But most of the time, it started with about half an hour of cartoons and the kids just loved that. The movie started about 11:30 and ended about 2, so in the summer, we had plenty of daylight to play in.

For me, I would find an open parking lot or field of grass and launch a little balsa airplane into the sky. With each flight, I could see myself in the cockpit doing the loops and rolls that I watched that little wooden airplane do.

When I was about nine years old, I rode my bike all the time. I had the feeling that I needed adventure—to see what was happening about my town. The streets were easy for a kid to travel from one end of Salem, New Jersey to the other in little over an hour. There was so much to see; the department stores, the library, the fire department with their doors open and men washing the trucks.

Even in the '50s, the city had a recreation center where I learned to play chess and to interact with other kids. It was an amazing time. Just outside of town on the city limits was the Salem airport. It was just a grass strip with hangers and a small office at one end.

There was a Dodge dealer nearby and an ice cream stand. I was in love as a small boy with everything that moved in the air or on the ground. When the new cars came out, I would stop by the Dodge dealer to see what they looked like. They wouldn't let me in the door but I put my face on the big window or walked around the cars that were out on the lot as long as I could before the salesmen ran me off.

I'd buy an ice cream cone and sit on the old wooden fence just off the grass airstrip. Even without the ice cream, I would sit there for hours watching airplanes take off and land. I would be amazed not knowing how those machines lifted into the air. I thought these were magical things and the men who flew them were like gods.

I knew that I wanted to be one of them, one of those who could fly. My love of science fiction and cartoons drove me and my brother and our friends to go to the matinees. Here were amazing films and movies that took us into another world, a world of adventure where we could do anything that we dreamed of doing—even fly.

My elementary school was run by a white principal with all white teachers. Except in 5th grade, we had our first male teacher and he was black. Seeing a man of color in that leadership role was inspiring. Junior High was all white teachers and a white principal. In high school, there was a change.

My guidance counselors were no help but two people in high school did support me and my dreams. The music director and the athletic director, both white men, became my mentors. I played trumpet in the high school band and the music director made me feel a part of everything. He encouraged me and said that my skills as a trumpet player were excellent.

At graduation, I got to play a trumpet duet with our most excellent first trumpet player. It was the music highlight of the ceremony and that did a lot to help my confidence in myself. Our athletic director, also the basketball coach during my four years playing high school basketball, was a mentor who helped build my self-confidence.

I was on the All-Star team for the conference for the last three years of high school. About halfway through the season of my senior year, I noticed that my coach was talking to a very tall individual who had never been to any of our games before. He watched the team play and win the game. That was unusual for us because we only won about half our games.

The stranger chatted with my coach after the game and then disappeared. In the locker room just before heading home, my coach told me that he was the basketball coach from Glassboro State. He was interested in my going there to help their sports program.

I began my working life the summer between my freshman and sophomore years in high school. Even though we were on the low economic scale for households of the day, I spent fun filled times every summer playing with the neighborhood kids and playing baseball. But after my freshman year in high school, childhood summers ended.

I'm not saying that it wasn't fun but it was just a different kind of fun. I was growing up. That first summer I worked on a dairy farm. The next summer was working on a tomato farm and the summer between high school and college, I worked construction to refurbish my high school. I met many interesting people.

Some of them were the same age as I was but most were older. On this job, I started to gain knowledge of the adult working world. I knew that I would try to go to college but none of the guidance counselors helped me with the applications. I had thought of two other schools that I wanted to attend but Glassboro was a school that was interested in me.

Early that next spring, I put my paperwork and application into Glassboro State and got accepted. I had driven the 15 miles from home to the college to see what it was like. It was a school that was founded in the early 1920s as the state teachers' college. It fit my image of what a college should look like and my 5th grade teacher was a role model for me to become a teacher.

One of the reasons I chose Glassboro over the other schools was the fact that they wanted me for athletics and it worked out that I could afford to pay for this state school. My family was in no position to give me any money to go to college, so I would have to work through school and pay for it.

I had saved enough money from my last summer job, so I could afford my first year's tuition. Then I found out that I could get spring and summer jobs with the city of Glassboro and with small loans from my local bank, I could afford to complete college.

When I first saw the Glassboro College campus, I was so overwhelmed by the idea of a higher education, I didn't see that it lacked some important things. Surprisingly to me, the thing that I didn't comprehend was that there were very few people of color on this campus. When I started classes that September, I looked around and I was the only black student in my classes.

There were a few black folks in this school but the numbers did not come close to matching the number of black people in South Jersey. I was used to being in a population where about 25% of all the people around me were black. At Glassboro, I was one of a very few black men, in a sea of white folks. I did not think that this situation would matter but it did.

I found myself feeling isolated. I only had only one close black friend and he was a year ahead of me. We met on the basketball team and on the away trips, we sat together on the bus and roomed together on overnights. There were a few white folks that were friendly and did not see a difference but the majority ignored us.

There was only one professor of color and she taught a course called *the family*. I was happy to take that course and see someone who looked like me in a leadership position. There were times when I felt overwhelmed by the loneliness. However, since I am a happy person by nature, I enjoyed my friends and the few people who were in my circle were very close.

I had one white friend who was older by 10 years, from Alabama. He was in my class. At first, I couldn't stand him. It was a time of big civil rights marches and protests and here was a guy who looked and sounded like all the evil people trying to keep us in our place. He persisted in wanting to be friends, so after a while, I decided that he was trying his best to change his outlook on people of color.

Between classes, we had some amazing, interesting, difficult conversations. He seemed open to what I had to say, so I listened and tried to understand his point of view. Eventually, we came to a middle ground and found that it was good enough for a friendship. Finally, he changed. He did away with all his learned racist attitudes.

I'm sure he fought the devil within himself for a time but the good won out. I think today, if I were a young man again, I would have gone to a school that had more black people. On the football team, a sport that I loved, I had to put up with and overcome the racial attitudes of the other players. It made a sport I enjoyed, hard to endure.

The basketball team was just as bad but there were two of us. That fact made it easier. The classroom on campus was also at times a hostile place. Then again, I endured. That experience gave me the courage to go after my dreams of being a pilot. Then no one could stop me.

When the first day of school arrived. I was happy on campus but I felt there was something missing. I had played football for four years in high school and really enjoyed the game. On a whim, I went to the athletic director, the same man who saw me play basketball and helped me get into the college. I asked him if I could come out for the football team.

It was only the school's second year of varsity football and for a small school, every person counted. They needed me, so now I was playing football on a college level and after football season, I was also playing basketball. In the spring, I applied for summer jobs with the city road and street department. I landed a job that fit my school schedule.

I did this for three years and really enjoyed it. Besides making money that paid for my schooling and kept my loans very low, I enjoyed working with the men in the street department. On my crew, I was the youngest and everyone took me under their wing to help me learn what the job entailed. Every day, they treated me with great fun and lots of humor.

As I grew up, I visited many airports to try to get someone to teach me to fly. No one would pay any attention to me until one day. There came a time when I was in college when nothing was making sense to me. I wanted to be a pilot so badly that it was interfering with my studies to be a teacher. There were days when I couldn't keep a thought in my head about school.

Between classes, I would look up in the air and hope to find an airplane flying by. I had to do something about this desire. I had this dream to fly since I was five years old, so one day I took off from class and looked at a map for airports within a few miles of Salem.

I found four that wouldn't take long to drive to. I decided which one I was going to first and then worked down the list until I found a place that would take me as a student pilot. The first place I went to was Pittman city airfield. I saw a sign that said flying lessons given and walked into a little office.

The room had a desk in one corner and a counter in another. Under the counter there were maps, knee boards and other things that pilots would need. There was a guy behind the counter. I asked him about taking flying lessons and he looked at me like I was from outer space. After a few seconds, he said they don't have any instructors that were free to give me lessons.

I asked him when they would be free and he said it didn't look like they'd be free anytime in the near future. He went back to fumbling with some papers. I took that as my cue that we were done. I went out to my car and crossed this airport off my list. I went to a second airport, found another sign that said flying lessons and went in the door.

No one seemed to be around, so I decided to wait. About 20 minutes went by, I walked around. I opened the door to the hanger. There were no locks on any doors and no one was around. I looked around the building and found every door unlocked but no one there. I got in my car and crossed that one off my list.

The next airport was almost right on the Delaware River, just west of the town of Bridgeport. As I drove up, there was a little parking lot right next to the hanger with an office attached to it. They had a parking ramp out front with three fairly new piper Cherokees just sitting out there waiting to fly. I started to get excited just looking at the airplanes.

With the possibility that I could start to fulfill my lifelong dream, I walked in the door of this bright, sun filled office. I walked up to the counter and this guy looked up at me with a puzzled look on his face. I gave him a big smile and said, "I've come here to learn how to fly."

He gave me a very long look and then after a few seconds said, "Could you wait right here? I'm gonna go and get one of our instructors to talk to you."

This filled me with anticipation. He didn't say that they didn't have any instructors with free time and he didn't say that we didn't have any airplanes. He said, "Wait right here." I found myself a seat and picked up an aviation magazine.

I waited about 15 minutes. I was starting to get a little anxious, so I dug into the aviation magazine. Then this short man with sunglasses came out from what I thought was the hanger area, stuck out his hand and said, "I understand you want to fly," as he was shaking my hand.

I said, "Yes sir, I surely do!"

He too gave me a long look and asked, "How long have you been wanting to learn to fly?"

I said ever since I was a young kid, I've always wanted to be a pilot. Marty was his name and he gave me another long look and said, "When do you want to start?"

I looked him in the eye and said, "When can I start?"

My heart was beating faster. He looked at the schedule on the board and said, "I can give you a $5, 30-minute introductory ride right now!" I looked at him with amazement. He said, "Yeah, I'll take you up and we'll see if this is really what you want. If not, it'll only cost you five bucks."

I was beside myself and tried really hard to keep cool. We walked out to the aircraft and he showed me how to do a preflight. We got in the aircraft and sitting in the left-hand seat, Marty went through the controls and the instruments. Just before we were about to start the engine, he asked me if I'd ever been in an airplane before.

I looked him in the eye and said, "No sir, this is my first time." A big smile came across his face.

He looked at me and assured me, "You are going to remember this for the rest of your life."

After starting the engine, Marty said, "Put your hands and feet on the controls and taxi it out. Remember to use your feet to steer." The excitement showed on my face as a big smile. As the aircraft slowly moved forward, I was on the controls!

We got to the run-up area near the takeoff end of the runway and Marty went through the engine run up checks and flight control checks. We were ready to go. He made the call on the radio that we were about to take off. I pointed the aircraft down the runway, thinking that he would take the controls but he did not!

Marty just told me what to do, slowly advancing to throttle to full power. "Keep the aircraft heading straight down the runway with your feet and when the airspeed indicator reads 45 knots, slowly and smoothly pull the control yoke back." And would you believe it! Within a few seconds, the nose came up and I could feel us getting light on the ground. All of a sudden, we were flying, climbing up from the earth into the sky!

It's been over a half century since that sunny afternoon at Bridgeport Airport in New Jersey. I will remember that day for the rest of my life. I will never forget Marty. I remember the look on his face and the instructions he gave me. He made me feel that he was just as excited as I was during every lesson until I left South Jersey for the United States Army. He was my mentor for accomplishing my dream!

After I had been flying for a few months, I was going up with my instructor whenever I had the funds. I enjoyed learning how to fly but it became clear that with the limited amount of money that I had, paying for flying lessons and going to college would be a long, difficult haul.

So one bright autumn day, I walked into the student union as I normally did in the early afternoon and what should I see but two rather tall men in white uniforms. I recognized them as US Navy pilots. They were setting up a projector and screen and they had a little desk set up in the corner of the student union.

They were preparing to give a presentation on joining the Navy's aviation program. I couldn't believe my eyes, here in our little backwater college, in the wilds of South Jersey, the United States Navy was looking for pilots. My ultimate dream was to be a Navy fighter pilot! I was at their table, tapping one of them on the shoulder in a flash.

He turned around and looked at me and said, "Hello, how are you doing? Give me a minute, I have to finish setting up this projector and I'll be happy to talk with you." As he finished setting up the projector and the screen, the other officer was arranging informational pamphlets on the table.

When he was done setting it up, he put on this reel of navy jets taking off and landing from aircraft carriers and dropping bombs into North Vietnam. I stood there, looking at the films and I'm sure my mouth was wide open. It was amazing.

About halfway through, he looked at me and said, "Do you want to be a naval aviator?"

I looked right at him and said, "I surely do, sir!" He started explaining to me a little bit about the school. It took about two years to get to the fleet and there were many things to fly in the Navy, helicopters, transports, reconnaissance aircraft and jet fighters.

I was sure he knew that he had me hooked right away. Then this white man said something to me that really kicked in. He told me that the Navy was looking for qualified black men to be officers and pilots. I said, "That fits me!" I cut my next class and listened to him tell me more about the training—how hard it was going to be but how wonderful it was to fly off aircraft carriers.

My desire to be a Navy fighter pilot deepened after listening to him for an hour. We set up a date to take the naval officer qualification test and the flight aptitude test. I would have to travel to the Philadelphia Naval Shipyard, which was about 30 miles away. I was beside myself for the next week.

I found the shipyard and I was amazed at all the ships that were moored to the docks in Philadelphia. I found out that it was part of the US Navy's reserve fleet. It was like walking into history with everything from destroyers to battleships to aircraft carriers. In the morning, I took the naval officers' test.

I didn't know much about being in the water or driving boats but most of it was pretty much common sense, multiple choice questions. I passed the test with no real difficulties and moved on to the flight aptitude test. That test was not easy but since I had been flying and studying for my license, it wasn't that hard for me.

I passed with flying colors—pun intended. At this point, I was excited and I couldn't believe that just a week ago I had no real idea of my future. The next thing I had to do was get through a flight physical. That would take another week to set up and I would have to go to Willow Grove Naval air station, about 50 miles west of Philadelphia.

The flight physical was the last hurdle to setting me on the path to being a Navy pilot. I left home early enough that I would have about an extra hour before my appointment time just in case I get lost. But I found the place with no problem and asked directions to the building where the physicals were given.

When I checked in, everybody was very pleasant. Since I had played sports all my life, I did not think that I would have any problem with this final check before signing up for flight school. I breezed through the blood and other tests plus the examination of my body parts. Everything was good to go. The last thing I had to do was the eye exam.

I didn't think that would be a problem, because I had passed an eye test for my student pilot's license. But this was a closer examination of my eyes. The Navy required 20/20 vision. The exam revealed my vision was 20/25. I failed.

When I was informed of the result, the medical officer told me that I was well qualified to be a naval flight officer. I asked him what a naval flight officer was. He told me it was a crewmember who was either a radar intercept officer or a navigator/bombardier. You sat behind the pilot.

I knew that that was not what I wanted. I was going to do everything I could to be in the front seat. I told him that I didn't think that that was for me and I would keep working to be a certified pilot on my own. He smiled and said that he understood and that my written test and physical would be good for 90 days if I changed my mind.

I was so disappointed on that long drive home. My imagination had me in the cockpit of a jet, taking off from a great aircraft carrier. I was not going to sit in the back and let somebody else fly. This was the one thing that I must do.

After I set my disappointment aside, about halfway through my drive home, I started planning and thinking about ways that I could make my dream come true. I was determined that I was going to be a military pilot. I continued to take flying lessons, as best that I could with the funds that I had. It meant that I was flying about once a week.

It was hard to retain the muscle memory to make the speedy acquiring of skills needed to fly an airplane. After my second supervised solo and I was cleared to go out on my own, I loved the freedom of flying myself. Flying lessons got further apart with my instructor.

I already had told Marty about my Navy physical and my desire to be a military pilot. I told him again how disappointed I was after passing all the written exams and failing by the slim margin on the eye test. Later, Marty said that he heard that the United States Army needed pilots and 20/20 vision was not required.

I looked at him in amazement—I did not know the Army had anything to fly. I thought it was all Air Force, Navy and the Marine Corps. He told me that the Army had little airplanes, some medium size twin engine and lots of helicopters. He emphasized the lots of helicopters. He said to go down and talk to an Army recruiter.

He also said you get first class training and it's all for free! I looked up the nearest Army recruiter and went to the office. The Vietnam War was in high gear and everybody was being drafted. If you were a male between 18 and 25, not in college or did not have a large family or did not have one of the jobs that were listed as essential—the Army wanted you.

There was a recruiting sergeant sitting behind a desk. When I came through the door, he looked up and asked, "Can I help you?" I said I'd heard about warrant officer flight school from my flight instructor. He gave me a long look and then handed me a pamphlet, which gave me an idea of what I was in for.

I sat down and read through it, which took me all of five minutes. I started asking a lot of questions and this sergeant was very blunt about how hard the school was and how difficult to complete. I looked him in the eye and said, 'I want to do this. What tests do I have to take?'

He looked at me again for a long while and said, "Come back on Monday and I'll have the tests ready for you." I was back in his office on Monday to take them. The Army officer candidate test was not much different than the Navy one except it had nothing to do with the ocean.

I found the flight aptitude test a bit harder but I passed it with relative ease. I had to fill out a lot of paperwork and I decided to join the Army after about six months in a program called delayed enlistment. I had to go up to Newark to do the formal interview and I was in the Army reserves that afternoon.

I got orders that told me the time and place to report to in six months for basic training and to go to flight school. I was a little apprehensive, as they were sending me to Fort Polk, Louisiana for basic. My mind was racing through all the possibilities, good and bad, of what I had signed up to do.

As you get older and look back on the things that you have done throughout life, all the hard work that got you where you are. Think about the people that lent a helping hand to the effort to get you to this day. You don't want to think about all the people who tried to hold you back—as a black man in America— there are too many of them. On the other hand, there are notable people who just want to help either through love or just the idea of doing right.

They will help you. I have to start out with a loving family. My mother's family was wonderful. They all cared for me and encouraged me to do almost anything I wanted. My mother was the most important person in those early years. She held me to a high standard and encouraged me to do lots of things—just about anything that was a betterment to me.

I had to learn a musical instrument. That was one of her rules. I had to go to church but when I was an older teen, she gave me the choice. She attended all my track meets and many of my basketball games. She thought football was a little too brutal.

When I graduated from high school, in her mind there was no doubt that I was going to college and she would not hear anything else. I wanted to learn how to fly. That was my dream and she encouraged me. When hard times hit me in basic training and it seemed like it was just too much for me in those early days, she encouraged me again stay in and stick it out.

She argued, "Because this is what you wanted. It's the path to your goal." When I graduated from flight school, she got to fly for the first time from New Jersey to Alabama to be there for me. She died when I was 27. She was just 20 years older than I and I have missed her steady presence all these years.

My Aunt Callie and my Uncle Spencer were also big influences in my life. My Aunt Callie was sweet to me from the day I was born. When I was in kindergarten and first grade, she was in high school and would walk me home from school every day.

She taught me how to dance when I was ten and told me that I was a good, young man every day. I loved her deeply back then and after my mother died, she took on a bigger role in my life. She was the one who got my letters and cards. I'd call her on her birthdays and holidays. Aunt Callie was the one I told my stories to.

My Uncle Spencer, was the jolly uncle in our family. He had a drinking problem but he was so happy and so joyful that everybody looked the other way. When I was very young, I lived next door to him and every day after work he would come over and play with me as a kid.

A great bond was formed. He played the trombone in the Army in World War II and he was in the American Legion band in Salem. When I was about 12 years old, after taking trumpet lessons for three years or so, he got me into the American Legion band where I played great musical show tunes and Broadway hits with men who had served our country in World War II.

I was part of a group of nephews and sons of these men. We all enjoyed hearing the veterans talk about their experiences! My Uncle Spencer gave me my love for music and I play in a community band to this day because of him.

Bruce: Even though our family was poor, I never realized it at the time. My mom did a good job of making sure we had what we needed. My dad worked two shifts as a union electrician to make sure we did. As kids we never had the cool clothes or sports equipment or piano lessons or braces for our teeth but we survived.

As children, we would spend part of our summers on Conanicut Island at my grandparents' home. My grandfather, a Spanish-American War Navy veteran, was a house painter and an artist. My mom was one of eight children, so there were lots of relatives, aunts, uncles and cousins, to share bedrooms. It wasn't elegant but it was fun and competitive. Checkers, chess, poker and bridge were like battles.

We would ride our bikes or walk a mile to the beach at Mackerel Cove, walk to the ice cream shop in Jamestown and take the ferry over to Newport. My dad was a World War II veteran and my parents had met at the USO in Jamestown. My dad was an Artillery NCO and was deployed to France after the Normandy invasion.

He never talked about the war. When I told people I wanted to go to West Point, they would smile knowingly and say, "Sure, kid." But my determination increased when I realized that my parents could never afford to send five of us kids to college. The military seemed like a good way to get an education—and I liked the uniforms. The military also had a lot of history in our family and I pictured war as gallant and exciting. I had a lot to learn.

In the summer, I went to Camp Crosby where we learned to swim and did all kinds of games and activities. So that no one got lost, there was a 'buddy system' where we teamed up with another kid and when the whistle blew, we had to find our buddy, grasp his hand and raise our hands in the air.

My buddy was Broadway Oris Burgess. He came from the poorest section of East Providence but since we were all poor, we went to Camp Crosby. If you were rich, you went to Camp Sharples. Oris and I were best friends for two years at camp but since we went to different elementary schools, we lost track of each other. Oris was black. I can still see our hands together raised above our heads. One black and one white hand, dripping with water, shaking with cold, warming each other.

To make money, my brother and I caddied at Jamestown's golf course. After a few years, I had some regular customers who lived in the big houses on Shoreby Hill, which overlooked Narraganset Bay toward Newport. I enjoyed seeing their big cars, great golf equipment and beautiful homes. Someday, I thought, someday I will have the money to drive big cars, play golf and live in a nice home. I never could afford to play a round of golf at that course until much later in life.

When my brother, Tom, started kindergarten, my mom walked us both to Brightridge School, which was a few blocks away. When Tom got to stay and I had to go home, I cried. We had always been at home together. Now I was alone. It didn't seem fair. I wasn't alone for long. Steve showed up within a year followed by Sue Ann and Beth.

We all went to Brightridge. In East Providence, I started mowing lawns when I was seven. I remember pushing a mower that was too big for me, so I had to push it with my hands raised above my head. After I proved I could do it, I made $1 each time I mowed that lawn. Then reality struck.

At $1 a week, there were not enough weeks in the summer to buy the Lionel train set I was saving for. There was only one solution, get more lawn jobs. By the time I was a teenager, I was mowing five or six lawns a week and working a paper route. All that work cut into my athletic career but it financed my social life.

My kindergarten teacher, Miss Harry, was a black woman and we loved her. Most of the Brightridge elementary school teachers were white women and the principal was a white man. All the principals were white men in those days. In fifth grade, there was a change. Our teacher was a man and for the first time, the guys in the class had someone who was like us.

His name was Mr. Green and after reading every book I could put my hands on, he took four of us guys who read the most books to Boston to see a Red Sox game. It was the first pro baseball game I had ever been to. Between the bright lights on the field that night and Ted Williams hitting a home run, I thought I was in heaven.

When we arrived at Central Junior High, our seventh-grade social studies teacher, Ken Walker, was a black man. We thought he was the best. There were no black teachers in our high school. This was the early '60s and the civil rights movement was just building.

My first and only, protest march happened when the state legislature said they were cutting the state scholarships. We said, hell no and marched on the state house. They did not cut the state aid to students. The world changed for many of us on 4 October 1957 when the Russians put the Sputnik satellite into orbit.

The space race was on and many of us were caught up in it—even in East Providence, Rhode Island. Some of us were put into what was called the 'math-science accelerated' group. From seventh grade on, we were pushed ahead in math and the sciences. While the academics were tough, the outcome turned me into a professional test-taker.

The grouping was based on the IQ tests that were given at the time. All my classmates in the group were white. In East Providence, high school started in the tenth grade. Most of us who started together in the seventh-grade group, went through three years of Central Junior High School and then three years of high school together too.

The students in this group were the math-science nerds. They were good kids but there were few jocks. I was a fair athlete but never lettered until senior year. I ran cross country and played tennis but I was too small for football in a 2,800-student high school. I worked and studied hard.

Between my junior and senior years in high school, a friend and I took a bus from Rhode Island to work on my uncle's wheat farm in Montana. My uncle was not the nicest man in the world. We worked like dogs. Harvesting 23 sections of a wheat farm was almost a 24/7 job and working for this uncle made it worse. But like everything else in life, it had a distinct upside lesson. The harassment of West Point and Ranger School were relatively easy compared to working for a bully like him.

I was annoyed that I had to work so hard, when others just had money handed to them. But I learned how to work and study to improve myself and I was motivated never to be poor again. One of my greatest motivators came from a snotty rich school I was considering when I was looking at colleges. This was to be a backup college in case I didn't get into West Point.

The preppy admissions director I spoke with told me point blank that I was too poor to go there and I ought to apply to a state school. For some reason, I felt shamed. Now I wish I had told him, "You were born on third base and think you hit a triple, so screw you."

I didn't. I just walked away. I would not give that guy the satisfaction of knowing how angry I was. I walked out, determined never to feel that way again. Working my way out of being poor started with a dream at age five and pushing a lawn mower when I was seven. If I thought I had it tough, I never considered how hard it was for my black kindergarten teacher surrounded by all those white faces each day.

I researched what it took to win an appointment to West Point from a U.S. Senator or Representative. I started writing letters when I was a high school sophomore. Starting the process early proved to be an advantage. One of the representatives encouraged me to take the civil service exam for the service academies even though it was a year early. As a professional test taker from my high school classes, I did well. When the test counted for the appointment, I earned it from our senior senator by getting the highest score.

I studied for my classes and worked delivering newspapers and mowing lawns and I knew what I wanted. I wanted that appointment to West Point. After I had taken the civil service exam earlier that spring, I had traveled to Montana and had forgotten about the test. I arrived home from school one fall day and received a phone call from US Senator John O. Pastore's office.

His secretary told me that they needed a recent photograph of me. I was on my way to deliver papers, so I said I would drop it off. I dug through a box of family photos, grabbed a snapshot of myself and headed for the senator's office. The secretary looked at the informal photo and asked me to wait.

She went into an inner office but came out with the picture and asked me to get a head and shoulders shot. I ran downstairs and sat in one of those photo booths that dumped out four shots of me. I ran back up to the office and she disappeared into the inner office again.

This time, a man came out and said this picture would not do. He instructed me to go to the photographer's studio downstairs, have a portrait picture taken and have it sent up to Senator Pastore's office. All I could do was stammer, "Yes, sir." This was Senator Pastore!

The next day in the Providence Journal there were pictures of those who had earned Service Academy appointments. Every other guy was in a suit and tie except me. Because I had scored highest on the civil service test, I had received the appointment from Senator John O. Pastore, Rhode Island's senior senator and 'Mr. Democrat' in the US Senate at the time.

When the news came out that I had been appointed to West Point, my art teacher cried and my English teacher tried to talk me out of going there. I had worked hard to get the grades and scores and to pass the medical and physical fitness tests to get into West Point. As it turned out, that was the easy part. My mentors, from my mom and family to my teachers and my Sunday school teacher, gave me all the encouragement any child could want.

My next step would be a big one. After graduating from high school in early June, I arrived at West Point in June 1963. I was 17 years old and thought myself ready for whatever was to come. About 25,000 men had graduated in the past and I was physically fit and fairly intelligent.

What did I have to lose? Only my innocence. Getting it back would take some time. My class entered West Point with over 800 new cadets—two were black. Institutional racism was alive and well at the United States Military Academy too.

The first few months of training for new cadets was known as 'beast barracks'. It was West Point's version of basic training for those who would become US Army officers. As I look back on it 55 years later, it was not exactly leadership training. It was a form of physical and mental hazing that was supposed to mold us into leaders of men.

We learned what every soldier learned in basic training that the spirit of the bayonet was to kill. There were many events that would shape my attitude but I had no idea of what was to change in me. A decade later, a short note from Mr. Willoughby, my high-school English teacher, started me on the discovery journey. Several lessons were learned in the ten years in between.

Part of 'Plebe Knowledge', information that all new cadets were required to commit to memory, was Schofield's definition of discipline. We had to recite on command, "The discipline which makes the soldiers of a free country reliable in battle is not to be gained by harsh or tyrannical treatment. On the contrary, such treatment is far more likely to destroy than to make an Army. It is possible to impart instruction and give commands in such manner and such a tone of voice to inspire in the soldier no feeling but an intense desire to obey, while the opposite manner and tone of voice cannot fail to excite strong resentment and a desire to disobey. The one mode or the other of dealing with subordinate's springs from a corresponding spirit in the breast of the commander. He who feels the respect which is due to others cannot fail to inspire in them regard for himself, while he who feels and hence manifests, disrespect for others, especially his inferiors, cannot fail to inspire hatred against himself."

We rattled that off without much thinking until one day, my squad leader asked, "Mister, who are your inferiors?" The answer to the question I thought he was asking, "What do plebes rank?" That question was also part of plebe knowledge.

I gave him the answer, "The superintendent's dog, the Commandant's cat, the waiters in the mess hall and all the admirals in the whole damn Navy."

But he stopped me and said, "Mister, you have no inferiors in this Army. From now on, you will use the word subordinates, not inferiors in the definition of discipline." His words shocked me. Someone was thinking outside the West Point box.

Major General John M. Schofield had given that definition in an address to the United States Military Academy (USMA) Corps of Cadets on 11 August 1879. Too bad so many officers did not heed his words and my squad leader's wise insight.

Academics were always a strong part of who I thought I was. One of my roommates had two years at Notre Dame before he came to West Point. The feeling that I was not at the same level as some of these guys was not pleasant. I realized early on that I was not going to wear stars (top 5% of the class) at West Point—a blow to my self-esteem.

But I could do other things. Tennis and cross country were my high school sports but now I could hit people. I boxed and played rugby. I'm not sure where it was coming from but there was a lot of aggression building in me. Boxing and rugby provided outlets. For some reason, there seemed to be a lot of anger. I realized that the 'spirit of the bayonet' was building. I survived plebe year.

The second year at West Point started with two months at Camp Buckner with West Point's version of Advanced Individual Training (AIT). Gary Hall, Dick Farr and I painted our class numerals, 67, on a rock on the lake where the camp was located. It was breaking the rules to be out of the barracks after taps and we were reported but we had shown leadership and class spirit.

The punishment we received, walking the area carrying our M14 rifle on our shoulders for eight hours, seemed worth it. Boxing and rugby remained my sports. Academics were tough and I settled into what we referred to as the 'indifferent middle' of my class. I almost quit. My high school English teacher helped talk me into staying.

This was the same English teacher who when I was in high school had tried to talk me out of going there. He had spent two years in the Army and we had corresponded through my plebe and yearling years at the Academy. His logic was clear—you are halfway there. Stay and graduate. I stayed.

During cow year, as the junior class was called, academics were even tougher. Electrical engineering almost did me in. My dad was a union electrician and very disappointed that I was not better with electricity. Boxing took me to the Brigade Open semi-finals against the defending champion who was a year ahead of me. He knocked me out in the second round but I was the only other boxer to make it past the first round with the defending champ.

There was a unique lesson here—getting knocked out is not the end of the world. You come to, get back up and continue to fight—the battle is not over even if they count you out. Failure does not necessarily mean defeat. That was a great lesson.

Senior, First Class, year was fun. We received our class ring in the fall, beat Navy in football and studied military history with our teachers, many of whom by now were Vietnam veterans. Our team won the rugby national championship. Our academic work included a law course on the Uniform Code of Military Justice (UCMJ).

We joked that 'military justice' is an oxymoron but I enjoyed looking at justice and law more deeply. Near the end of our senior year, we had to choose an Army branch to be a part of. Our choices were the combat arms, Infantry, Armor, Artillery, Engineers or Signal Corps. I chose the Artillery. The choice came down to a logic I heard from an Artillery officer I admired.

You joined the Army to become an Army officer. An Army officer's job was to close with and kill the enemy. Artillery had the most firepower to do that, so I became an Artillery officer. As a 20-year-old, I did not understand the implications of the power that a military commander had.

Later in my career when I was a commander, I learned some valuable lessons about power. We graduated with just over 500 of us—down from the over 800 we started with. We were excited to head off to the real world of military training, Army units and Vietnam. They were four incredible years. I grew a lot and I learned a ton. When our class joined the 'long gray line' in 1963, we didn't know where Vietnam was. Now in 1967, most of us were going to go there as professional soldiers. We thought we were ready to lead men.

Together: Rising out of poverty is not easy for black or white kids. The statistics are not necessarily good. From children to old age, poverty is not a pretty picture. As the old saw says, "There are lies, damn lies and statistics." The statistics from the Pew Research Center are ugly but they are showing some improvement and tell a story that is better than bad news for those of us who made it through college.

So how did Ray and Bruce make it? There was no magic but there were critical steps that helped them get there. We had the basics from the time we were infants—families, food, clothes, shelter and health care. We had moms and others who looked out for us. We had dreams. We had good schools with teachers and coaches who encouraged us to study and move forward to get a college education.

Bruce started wearing glasses in the fifth grade. All the service academies for many years required 20/20 vision. When Bruce applied, West Point did not see vision as a deterrent to leadership. Ray found out that the Navy would not let him fly with less than 20/20 vision but the Army would. This 'weakness' became a strength that brought us together in the same combat service to our country.

Our families were similar—both of us had four siblings. Bruce was number two of the boys and Ray was number three. The girls were all younger, so brothers were the competitive focus. We both needed to learn what to do. We both started working when we were kids. That work ethic paid dividends for us.

Ray worked his way through Glassboro State College and Bruce through four years of West Point. As cadets, we would joke that West Point was a $50,000 education shoved up your butt a nickel at a time. We both worked hard. We got through college almost debt free.

We agree with those who say college is not for everyone. With that said, we also look at the disparity in wealth between college graduates and non-grads. This book is not about money—yet, money is important for black and white students. During the time Ray and Bruce were in high school, 'the go to college for a wealthier future' argument was used.

We certainly saw it partly that way but service was more important. Ray says it this way, "If you look at what you do without thinking of the money, then you really understand what service means."

Ray started to fly and looked to become a military pilot and Bruce graduated from West Point and became an Artillery officer. That was just the start for us. With support from family, teachers, coaches and mentors, we were fulfilling our dreams. What does it mean to be an Army helicopter pilot and an Army Artillery officer? We were about to learn.

Chapter 3
Army Training

Tell me and I forget, teach me and I may remember, involve me and I learn.
– Benjamin Franklin

The transition from boys to men who were professional soldiers was not an easy one. First, they had to leave home. Then, the attrition rates at military schools like West Point and Flight School were high. Finally, Ray and Bruce were committed to stay and finish what they started. They both had to embrace the opportunity and finish the course. They both had to get totally involved.

Ray: We all have experienced fear as little kids—sleeping alone for the first time, those noises in the middle of the night and the punishment we get when we do something wrong. But what about as we grow up? I learned that fear comes in many different disguises.

That first day in the Army, I learned that I was the only one going to Fort Polk, Louisiana for basic training. All the others I knew were going to Fort Dix, New Jersey. Ft. Dix was only 40 miles from my home. There was a fear along with my excitement, as I was going down south.

In the late '60s, the South was not a friendly place for a young black man from the North! But then, my excitement was building, because I was going to fly down on a jet airliner. This was my first time on a jet, a Delta Airlines' Convair 880. When I got to my seat, next to me in the window seat was an old lady.

She was a very small woman and smoked the whole way down to New Orleans. Even though I was a smoker then, the number of cigarettes she smoked seemed unusual to me. All the way to New Orleans, this woman never said a word or even looked at me for more than a few seconds. And when she did look my way, she gave me a look as if I had just killed her dog. I thought she just didn't like black people. Welcome to the South.

Once in New Orleans, I found my way to the commuter airlines desk of Trans Texas Airlines. It was getting dark when we took off and I couldn't see any of the land outside the airplane window as we flew over Texas and Louisiana in route to Fort Polk. I was 22 years old and this was the first real fear I felt as a grown-up.

It was in the middle of the night in this two-engine airplane when we landed at Fort Polk, Louisiana. It was dark. We couldn't see anything out of the windows. I knew some horror stories about being down south. The scary things my grandmother told me came flooding back to me.

As we taxied to the terminal, in all of us new recruits the excitement and fear started to build. Then, like a bolt of lightning, two really huge men came in the front door and started yelling and screaming profanities at us all. They told us to get off the airplane and hurry up or they will do some really horrible things to us. They were our drill sergeants. The fear of the unknown took over! I had no idea that they were only playing a game and they wouldn't really kill us.

The airplane cabin was dark except for just a few lights. When I stepped out on the ramp, it was brightly lit. Two more drill instructors were there, waiting for us, yelling and screaming, acting so very aggressive. I did not know what to do, so I followed their instructions to the letter. I tried not to look in their faces.

I just did what they told me to do but the fear just kept on growing. We had to fall into line right on the runway and stand at attention. They made us get down on her hands and knees in the dark and pick up anything we could find on the apron. It was slow going. We did some push-ups and they yelled at us before we got into the terminal building. Buses were waiting and the yelling and screaming never stopped, even on the bus.

Once at the processing center with many of us only having a few hours' sleep at best in the last 24 hours and far away from home, it must have been about one in the morning. We were herded from line to line and station to station. People were calling us names. There were all these strange military people telling us to do things like line up against the wall and stand at attention.

They shouted orders in the reception station and then they took us to get haircuts. Those with beards and mustaches were ordered to shave. The fear of the unknown was on everybody's face. We turned in our civilian clothes and now wore loose fitting Army green uniforms. At about six in the morning, we got something to eat—greasy hamburgers. As they led us to our barracks, the sun was just coming up. They told us to get some sleep.

This was just the start of our first day in the United States Army. I was very fearful of what was going to happen to me. My dream was to fly but I had no idea what all this shouting and all the orders would lead. Sometimes, fear can help you focus. I was so overwhelmed by all of this harassment, nothing that I had ever thought or imagined was happening to me!

We got into the barracks and I looked around and saw a top bunk. I climbed up in it and put my head in the pillow and started crying. The guy below me asked if I was OK. I said, "Hell no!" His name was Tom Barnett. He asked me if I wanted to have a cigarette.

So we went out on the back steps and we talked about all the things that had just happened to us. After two cigarettes, we agreed that this was a real messed up place. We became instant best friends and I knew that we would be best friends forever. We went through basic training in the same platoon. Later, we would go through flight school and then went to Vietnam together.

In those first moments in the Army, I was not emotionally ready for what was happening to me. In the middle of the night, we had been greeted with harsh words and mean faces. As I look back at that night and that first day in the United States Army, the DI's (drill instructors) were mad at us all equally for just being alive and wanting to be in their Army.

We all formed friendships that first day. It was amazing that these friendships would last forever. For most of us, it was leaving our home for the first time. Our home was now in the past. All that we learned from our family and friends about other people and races would have to disappear. For some people, it would take a major effort to move past their homegrown racism.

One guy from South Carolina named Smith was a stone cold racist. He was also heading for flight school like many of us in our basic training class. He took every opportunity to make his feelings known that he did not think that I belonged in the same world with him. This nastiness was all done outside of the site and hearing of our drill instructors.

In that respect, he was a coward. But basic training was a new adventure for me. I started to understand why training was so hard and everything was repeated five times. I grew and learned to enjoy all the new things that I was learning and the friendships and closeness of my fellow new soldiers.

After being at Fort Polk for about 10 days, we were assigned to a company for our basic training. It was Delta Company, Fifth Battalion, Second Brigade. We were known as Delta dogs! There were four platoons in the company and Tom Burnett, Johnny Shuttlesworth and I all were assigned to the fourth platoon. We were a motley group, men of all sizes and shapes, from different states and cities. Staff Sergeant Green was our drill instructor.

The first week was the hardest; learning how to be in the Army and how to be soldiers. Besides marching in information about six times a day and doing physical training (PT) until you literally could not move, we got inspected at least three times a day. We had a National Guard group that was at Fort Polk for their annual two weeks training and they helped out with our initial training.

Every day, Sergeant Green would tell us to keep our things in our footlockers just like he had shown us. Two times a day, he would come through and inspect our barracks. He found it above standards and we were proud of ourselves. But the National Guard guys rated us at the very bottom of the other platoons after every inspection for that first week.

Sergeant Green was angry! He wasn't angry at us, for he had no idea why we weren't number one. Because of our last place finish at Saturday morning inspection, we were all restricted to the barracks. It's not that we could have gone home or even into town for that day and a half off but it would have been nice to leave the company area.

After all the officers and senior sergeants left the area, Staff Sergeant Green called us out of the barracks for a formation. At that formation, he told us that those National Guard assholes didn't know their butt from a hole in the ground. He was proud of us for how hard we had worked that first week. So he called us to attention, gave us a left face and marched us all to a little PX near the company area.

When we got there, he asked if anybody would buy him a beer. Every hand went up! He told us that we had two hours to drink all the beer we could. A great cheer rose out the platoon. As a group, we all went into the PX and 50 new soldiers drank beer and ate snacks together with our amazing drill instructor.

Basic training was eight weeks long and forth platoon earned number one honors for the next seven weeks in a row. That meant that from Saturday at noon, until Sunday night we were free. To this day, I think of Drill Sergeant Green, setting the tone for my leadership style for the next 22 years in the United States Army.

About halfway through basic training, I was getting used to the schedule, early morning formations, calisthenics before breakfast, classrooms to learn how to be a soldier—then more formations and more calisthenics. This was going to be our first week of learning about the tools of being a soldier, the rifle, the hand grenade, what it was like under fire.

I had never fired a rifle before, so it was all new to me. They asked who had gone hunting and who had had the opportunity to fire a weapon. Then they asked who had never held a weapon before. I was among the few who have never had the opportunity to shoot at anything. Not even a paper target.

As we went through the training and we learned all about the M 14 rifle, I became familiar with it, how it worked and how to use it. So when we went to the rifle range, I followed the directions of my sergeant and I did pretty well.

The next thing we did was the hand grenade throw. We had a class on grenades, its parts and when and how to use it as a weapon. Then we went out to the hand grenade range and again, we had our typical safety lecture. We would throw the grenade down range from a concrete pit in the ground. In the bottom of that pit was a hole lined with concrete and steel.

If we dropped a live grenade, we were told to kick it in that hole and fall to the ground. I watched those in front of me take their turn and some of the soldiers had problems pulling the pin out. There were others who did not throw it down range far enough, so there was a lot of shrapnel falling to the ground behind the concrete walls.

When it was my turn, I felt pretty confident as I headed into the pit but as soon as I got there, for some reason I tensed up. Once I held a real grenade in my hand, I started sweating and all the fear of messing up and killing one of my buddies in basic training just took over. The instructor put the grenade in my hand, instructed me to pull the pin and get into the throwing position.

I could barely get the pin out and that made me even more afraid. My hand started sweating and I felt that I couldn't hold this grenade any longer. I heaved it with all my might!

The grenade went a few feet in front of the throwing pit! The instructors screamed, "Hit the ground!" I followed instructions and no one was hurt. The instructor looked at me and yelled some profanity. He told me to get up and do it again. He put another grenade in my hand. I put my finger in the ring and when he said pull the pin, I closed my eyes and pulled.

When I heard him say throw, I threw it as hard and as far as I could. It didn't go that far but it went far enough for me to pass this part of the training. I was never so happy to complete the training as I was that day.

The last bit of fear that I experienced in basic training was on the night infiltration course. It showed me that fear could be overcome. The infiltration course was a test. It was about half of football field in length and about a football field wide. It had barbwire about two feet above the ground over every foot of it. At several places forming a line horizontal to your route in many locations throughout the route were bunkers.

These bunkers were circular areas two feet high made of sandbags and inside the bunkers were explosives. They were set off to simulate Artillery fire. At the very end of this course were three machine guns mounted on top of platforms and they were firing about four feet above our heads.

The objective of this training was to overcome fear—fear of being shot at. Until this point, we had done all the shooting. Now we would get to know what it felt like to be shot at—or in this case shot over. We first looked at the course and had a class there during the day. We were all assembled in a trench just like the days of World War I. Our drill instructor would yell, "Roll out!"

All of us would roll over the side of this trench and low crawl with our rifles and our packs. Ft. Polk was forever muddy and we were going to get dirty. This training was show us that by staying low to the ground, we could make it to our objective. By using what we learned, we could survive and get close to the enemy.

During the day, it wasn't scary. It was like much of the other training that we had been through. But the training wasn't over yet. They trucked us back to the barracks, for dinner and a little rest. Then they trucked us right back out to the same range after sunset. As it got dark and it was very dark in Louisiana, the whole company got into the trench.

Since I was in the fourth platoon, we were going to be the last ones to assault the enemy lines. Now it was about 10 o'clock at night when the first platoon rolled out. Just before they did, the machine guns that were on the platforms opened up! Back in the trench, you could see the tracers going overhead. In an ammunition belt that feeds an M60 machine gun, every fifth round is a tracer. The back of the round has a dot of red phosphorus on it that lights up the track of the bullet, so you can see where you are shooting in the dark.

The sound of three machine guns can really energize your soul. As first platoon moved over the lip of the trench, the fear started building. About a minute after they moved over the wall, it was time for the second platoon. By this time, my heart was beating faster than a rabbit could run. Then it was the third platoon's turn and before I knew it, I was right up against the edge of the trench waiting for the command to move out.

By this time, I thought my heart was going to beat out of my chest! I was so scared I didn't think I could move my legs. The noise was so loud and the tracers going over our heads were so bright, it seemed like I could reach up and touch them. Then came the command to roll out. To my great amazement, my legs worked as well as my arms and before I knew it, I was crawling on the ground underneath the barbwire.

It seemed like it was going to take forever. And right in the middle of taking forever, I crawled next to one of the bunkers with the explosives in it just as it went off. The ground shook below me and I felt like I was bouncing up and down. I almost peed my pants! Just as I thought that it would never end and it felt like I'd be low crawling all the way back to New Jersey, I looked up and the barbwire had ended.

Just over my shoulder and now behind me, the machine guns were blasting away. As we have been told to do at this point, I stood up and let out a war cry and ran with my rifle with fixed bayonet to the finish line. I met up with Steve, Tom and Johnny and we congratulated each other on making it through the course.

We climbed into the trucks that were going to take us back to our barracks and shared a cigarette together. We were excited, the adrenaline high was wearing off and we knew that because we were up past midnight, we would have an extra hour to sleep in.

Near the end of basic training, those of us that were going to flight school had to take another flight physical. Being the only black man, I had to take a sickle cell test. None of us knew what this was all about and we wondered if we'd all have to take the test. A medical corpsman came by and we asked what this sickle cell test is? He told us that it was about different shapes of blood cells and that only black men were required to be tested. Smith jumped on that.

He went over the top and with a loud voice he said, "See there, you people can't fly! You are inferior to white folks just like I always knew." The other guys told Smith to shut up, that he was an asshole and they didn't want to hear that crap anymore. I was heartened by the number of white men in my basic training company that would stand up against racism. They were my best friends.

Going to Texas to attend the first part of flight school was an adventure in itself. I had to wait a week after basic training, so there could be enough of us to fill a bus. Once filled up, off we went. It was about a five-hour trip from Fort Polk to Fort Walters Texas. We drove through the flatlands of East Texas, very green and very lush. Then we got to drive through Dallas and Fort Worth, big cities.

After that it was the desert or as far as I was concerned, it was a desert. Before long, after going through small town after small town, we reached Mineral Wells, Texas. There the bus went through the gate with helicopters on each side. I was excited! I was finally at flight school. When the bus pulled up in front of the barracks, onto a large parking lot, there were four training officers waiting to meet us.

I thought this was going to be different from basic training but starting off, it was not. They yelled and screamed at us they made us get out of the bus and stand at attention. The only thing different was they didn't use foul language. They told us that only about 25% of us would pass the course. Then they made us turn our duffel bags upside down and dump out all its contents. They kicked through it and asked us dumb questions, like what is this for or why do you need that?

Then with all of us standing at attention, they got into everybody's face screaming. They asked, "Do you want to quit now and spare yourself all of this heartache?" To my surprise, about five guys actually stepped forward and quit on the spot. I said to myself, not me! I am here and they're going to have to kick me out. I will not quit!

It took time to get all 200 men together to form a new training company. We were in what is called the holding barracks for about 10 days. I got to know more of the men that I was going to train with. Tom Barnett and I got closer and formed a friendship with another guy from Texas, Johnny Shuttlesworth. But even these close friendships did not stop my fears from growing.

Being in the deep south in Louisiana brought back all the frightening stories my grandmother had told me. The news on TV had stories about sit-ins and lynching's. I formed an image of this part of the country and the people who lived here. Also, some other recruits, white guys from the deep south, were not friendly at all to me or any other of the black man in flight training— even though we were theoretically fighting for the same country.

At Fort Walters Texas for preflight and basic flight training, there was a lot of classwork. I did well with all the subjects. I was excited about being at the controls of a military aircraft. It was my dream. But in normal Army fashion, the powers in charge were late and getting me my flight glasses.

I would go out to the flight line with my class but I had to stay in the briefing room and watch them all go out and fly. And then when they come back, I could only listen to all the tales of all that they had done.

After about 10 days, my flight glasses finally came and I started flying. My instructor was a retired Air Force lieutenant colonel who had been in helicopters all of his military career. He was a large man with an easy smile and he gave me every bit of knowledge he had to give in a short period of time. My learning curve was about straight up. But time was running out.

On what could have been my last day with my class, if I did not solo this day, I would be sent to a class that was two weeks behind us. My instructor was hammering me with everything that I was doing wrong, I couldn't do anything right for him.

It seemed to me that I was going to be set back. Near the end of that session, he got very angry and told me to hover over to the pad under the tower. It was a cold windy October day in Texas. I had my head down, just looking at the instrument panel as he was telling me all the things that I needed to do. Then, all of a sudden, I felt that cold wind coming in the door.

I looked over and he was halfway out of the aircraft, still talking to me. He looked me in the eye and a big smile came over his face. Then he said, "Can you take this ship around the pattern three times?" I said I could. He just waved and walked away.

The first time around the traffic pattern, I was a little scared. It seemed like the aircraft didn't fly the same. Of course, it was at least 200 pounds lighter! The second and third times around were pure joy. When I completed the third circuit, I hovered over to the tower. He got back in for the ride back to the main helipad. On the way back, we chatted about everything and anything. When we landed, he shook my hand and he said, 'Very good job!' With that I was the last one in my class to solo.

Mineral Wells was a backwater town. It didn't have a lot going for it except for the Army Aviation Training Center. I would learn later when I got a pass on the weekends, that there were no outward signs of racism. The town depended upon the fort for their livelihood, so there was no resistance or negative reaction to black soldiers. Each military post was made up of people from all over the United States.

The Army and most of the military had integrated by President's Truman's order in 1948. Some commands fought the policy of equal opportunity but by 1969, the Army had integrated. That integration forced people to see all other people of color as equals for the most part.

I went to flight school right after basic training. Going from college and civilian life into the Army was a shock. To be yelled at and treated like you didn't know your butt from a hole in the ground was degrading but that was the Army's method to tear a person down and then build him back into the soldier they wanted you to be.

After completing Army basic training, I had a mindset that nothing was going to keep me from graduating from flight school. There was a steady outflow of candidates who just couldn't meet the standards in the time the Army allowed. Some just decided to give up and go back to something more normal in the Army.

As we moved through the training, it became clearer to me that I was working toward my life's dream and this is what I was going to be. Our numbers steadily dwindled. As time went by, there were just 100 of us left and that number now had only three black men remaining in the group.

I hardly noticed their leaving, as we were so into our own heads, trying to push in facts and information at an amazing rate. At graduation from Basic Flight School, I looked around and saw only three brown faces. Out of the 200 men who started, only 85 of us graduated.

After that we went deeper into the south, into the heart of the Confederate States of America, to Fort Rucker, Alabama. Even with the tolerant nature of Texas, Alabama still caused fears to come over me again. In Texas, I could explore the area around Mineral Wells but in Alabama in 1969, I stayed close to the post.

After graduation from Fort Walters, primary flight training was over. Fort Rucker was advanced training. There we were treated more like the officers we were going to become, so we had more freedom. I bought a car and wanted to explore the lower half of Alabama and the panhandle of Florida. But fear crept on me again.

One Saturday, I was out driving the roads of Alabama and I stopped to look at some shacks. They looked like those that housed slaves before the Civil War and sharecroppers after the war. As I was looking at them, an older white man drove up in a pickup truck. He got out and in a loud voice said, "Boy, what do you want around here?"

I told him that I was just driving through the neighborhood and that I was a soldier learning to fly at Fort Rucker. He looked at me for a short time and said, "You just better get along the way." I got into my car and drove the other way. I glanced into his pickup and saw a rifle hanging on the back window. I couldn't get back to Fort Rucker fast enough.

Outside of the gate at Fort Rucker was the town of Enterprise, Alabama. The big thing about this town is that it is the peanut capital of Alabama and it had a statue to the boll weevil. Sometime later after discovering this oddity, I found out the history of the statue. That voracious insect came through in the early 1920s and ate up almost all of the cotton in the area.

People were faced with bankruptcy but at Tuskegee Institute, a black man named George Washington Carver discovered hundreds of ways to use the peanut. He convinced the area white farmers to plant peanuts instead of cotton. It was a great success and the area thrived. Instead of honoring George Washington Carver, a black man, they became the only town in America to erect a statue to a bug!

In Alabama, I saw all the things that reminded me of what I had seen in movies about slavery and what I had read in the history books. I got to Atlanta a couple of times while I was at Fort Rucker but I was afraid go too far afield. One of my classmates, Steve, was married, so he and his wife could live off post. On weekends, Tom and I would go over to Steve's house and study our butts off, getting ready for the next week. It was nice getting away from the barracks.

We had more freedom at Fort Rucker than we had when we were in Texas. I choked back my fear and with my little car, I explored the area a bit more. The local white folks seemed very distant to me and they gave me some very hard looks. I thought they were warning me not to get too close. They seemed to be saying, 'This is 1969 and if you go too far, we're going to hurt you.'

I was very uncomfortable and felt I was not welcome there. Racism was alive and well in Alabama. On post, there was no racism that I could see. I did not have to find a different place to get a haircut. We all went to the same club and whites and blacks were treated the same. It was not the same outside the gate.

I saw signs at water fountains saying this one's for colored and that one is for white. The laws were all changed but the signs were still there. They had not taken them down. The feelings and the intentions were still there. As a New Jersey Yankee, I found a new view of America that I had not known before.

I wondered what it was like for black folks during World War II and the Korean War. They trained down south, getting ready to fight for this country. Having those signs all over the place was disrespectful to them. What a powerful will they had to live their dreams and fight for their country under those conditions. The signs were still disrespectful to me.

In advanced pilot training, I loved every moment of flying and learning new things. Learning how to fly on instruments was a challenge and so was getting into the UH1 helicopter. It was the first jet powered helicopter that I flew—the others were piston powered. I would fly this aircraft for the next 15 years all over the world.

When I was about halfway through Fort Rucker and everything was leading up to my graduation, things got pretty relaxed. They stopped treating us as warrant officer candidates and started treating us as the officers we would soon be.

My mother was also at this time getting into making her own clothes and traditional African clothing. She made me a very beautiful multicolored *dashiki*. My roommate at the time fell in love with it and wanted to wear mine. I told him that my mother would make him one. The next time I talked to her, she agreed and two weeks later, it came. He was delighted.

I flew my mother to Fort Rucker for the flight school graduation ceremony. Many times, she had given me the courage and support to keep going and work harder. Her prayers helped me through basic training and flight school. Her thoughts and prayers would bring me safely through my year in Vietnam.

This was her first time in an airplane and her first time south of Washington DC. She loved the adventure and the excitement. I could see where my spirit of adventure came from. At the ceremony, we got our appointment as warrant officers and family and significant others got to pin on our bars.

The pride and joy in my mother's face when she pinned on my warrant officer's bar and then my wings put a tear in my eye. My roommate did not have any family there to pin on his bars to show his achievement, so he asked my mother to do it for him. My mother was overjoyed. From that moment, she had two sons to be proud of.

During one of our last formations after we knew that we were all going to graduate, our training officer told us that we had all received our orders and we were all going to Vietnam! Then, he told us something that really changed our thinking about going to war. Almost as an off-hand comment, he said that if you want your buddy to get out of Vietnam for a while, go home and tell your mother or wife that if you get killed, you want your buddy to escort your body back home.

With that thought, going to war took on a new dimension. I was standing next to Tom, my good buddy and best friend for the last year. Looking at him, I could see no other person that I would want to be with my mother from the Army if I died! I could see in his eyes that he felt the same way. So at that moment, we said to each other, almost at the same time, 'I'm going to tell my mom that you were going to be my escort officer.'

It was like the most natural thing for Tom and me to do. We had faced so many challenges together. We had met each other's families and we knew each other's darkest fears. We had shared the same feelings about going to war. His love of flying was the same as mine; a deep, abiding love for the adventures of being a pilot. Even though we were from different parts of the country, he was white and I was black, none of those things mattered."

Bruce: After 17 years of schooling, including four years at the United States Military Academy, I was ready to go to work. West Point was the start of my military education but real Army training followed. As plebes (freshmen) at West Point, we had to qualify with the M-14 rifle—that is, we had to take it apart, clean it, put it back together and shoot it.

I had never fired a weapon before, so it took a while for me to become a 'marksman'. That's the lowest rating that still qualified—you kept shooting until you qualified. The process involved shooting at stationary targets to set the sight on the weapon and then shooting at pop-up targets shaped like the head and torso of a person.

The military had learned in World War II that only about 20% of the soldiers in combat shot to kill—so by the Korean conflict, soldiers fired their weapons at above 90% to kill. Pop up targets that were human-like replaced bulls-eye circles. That was part of the psychology of overcoming the resistance to kill. We learned.

Advanced Individual Training (AIT) was the focus of our 'Yearling' or sophomore summer at Camp Buckner not far from West Point. One part of the training was bayonet drills. Taking an M-14 rifle and attaching a knife or bayonet to the end of it was all part of becoming a trained killer. To think that a 17-year-old kid from East Providence who had never hurt anyone was screamed at, "What is the spirit of the bayonet?"

And we all screamed back, "To kill, sergeant!"

The command was "fix bayonets" and we would click the knives into place at the working end of our weapons. The training was a choreographed, intricate dance of death and we would complete a 'vertical butt-stroke series' consisting of several steps and lunges, ending in sticking a man-shaped dummy with the bayonet—growling all the time.

We were admonished to get it right with 'Pay attention, gentlemen, this could save your life—or your buddy's life.' When the enemy came at you, his charge was parried with footwork and a block with your rifle. Then you brought the butt of the rifle up until it was vertical and smashed him in the face and brought the bayonet down in a slashing motion and stabbed him in the chest.

To make the drill more realistic, we practiced with pugil sticks and lacrosse helmets to simulate combat on our classmates. Pugil sticks are the length of a rifle with padding on each end. We had a contest and after a series of elimination rounds, two guys were left in 'the pit' where we trained. One was a baseball player and an excellent athlete and the other a smaller cadet who came to West Point through the Army.

I thought the athlete would win easily and for the first minute or two, the smaller guy fought defensively and frustrated the jock. The ball player stayed aggressive but the military guy got in a good lick and pissed the ballplayer off. He took his pugil stick like a baseball bat and swung it for the fences—but he missed. In a beautifully executed vertical butt stroke series, the little soldier took down the jock. The training really worked!

Between our second and third years at West Point, we were assigned to Army units and treated like junior officers. My assignment was to an Artillery battery at Ft. Carson, Colorado. We got to do everything a lieutenant would do including teaching classes to guys who were twice my age. Here I learned a great lesson.

The 'Chief of Smoke', a senior sergeant first class, took me under his wing and showed me how to act in an Army unit. The officers' command and the good ones led the troops but the NCOs ran the unit. The lessons were valuable for the future.

After our junior year as new seniors, we toured the country, visiting each of the combat arms headquarters. Our tactical officer was Artillery, my dad had been an Artillery NCO and my focus was pretty clear. The firepower demonstrated at Ft. Sill; Oklahoma confirmed my decision. I reasoned that as an Artillery officer, if the Army's objective was to kill the enemy, didn't it make sense to kill as many as possible with the most firepower?

So when the time came to choose my branch after four years at West Point, I choose the Artillery to kill as many of the enemy as possible. This was a very different person from the kid who left East Providence four years earlier. Basic training or Beast Barracks at West Point was not exactly like basic training in the regular Army.

When we arrived that first summer, we were arranged into 'New Cadet' companies and the companies were broken down into platoons and squads. From day one, we were drilled on how to march as a squad, a platoon and a company. The squad movements for parades were complex and dated to the Civil War.

They were designed to bring units from a company mass formation into skirmish lines. For cadet companies, these drills were used for parades. We also learned practical military skills like cleaning and shooting weapons. This was not my strong suit.

But like everything else in the Army, they broke the steps down into the basics and even a 17-year-old could master shooting a rifle. The requirement was to pass the test and you would stay as long as required to pass. I was part of the 'late show'. Eventually, I passed. You qualified as an expert, sharpshooter or marksman. I was a marksman.

The trouble was not entirely my fault. An M14 ejected the spent cartridges to the right side of the weapon. It was made for right-handed soldiers. Since I was left-handed, the casings would eject into my face. Not a pleasant experience. It probably influenced my decision to become an artilleryman.

Inspections covered everything from weapons, to uniforms, to rooms and lockers. There was a prescribed way to do everything and you either did it that way or you were gone. We learned very quickly to follow orders and do things as instructed. I found it easy to get along with my classmates and by working together, we survived.

We called it 'cooperate and graduate'. We started with over 800 New Cadets. By the end of the summer, there were only about 650 of us left. Between the hazing and the strict discipline, it was not what some people wanted to do. I had decided that it was what I wanted and nothing could make me quit.

We finished 'beast barracks' and our class was accepted into the Corps of Cadets. It was a proud moment. We moved into regular cadet companies and the academic year. The hazing didn't stop but as everyone settled into the academic grind, it let up considerably. When I was there, cadets did not have majors but I was determined to take every English course I could.

Even in English class, 'a cadet will recite every day in every subject'. Math was six days a week. Sports were a big deal—especially football. The Army-Navy rivalry was legendary and in the four years I was at West Point, we never lost to Navy. The other big deal was that plebes (freshmen) did not go home for Christmas, so my family came to West Point for Christmas dinner. Their support never wavered. The class of '67 was the last one to stay there for Christmas.

At the end of the first year for those of us who made it, we were 'recognized'. We stood in formation after the graduation parade and shook hands with all of the upper classmen in our company. From then on, we were on a first name basis and we could behave almost like real people.

After summer leave, we returned for Advanced Individual Training and exposure to the combat arms at Camp Buckner. It was great fun to build bridges, drive tanks, shoot big guns and see West Point as an adult—and not a plebe.

Sophomore or 'Yearling' year was relatively easy but I started to question my commitment to the military. I played for the rugby team during my plebe year and got to be friends with some of the upper classmen. Clair Thurston was a model cadet and a great guy. He was also the first person I knew from the class of '64 who was killed in Vietnam.

They started announcing the names of the men from earlier classes who had died. When I heard his name, I couldn't believe it. It was near the end of the academic year and that was a big choice for each one of us. The Academy told us that with the investment the Army had made in us, they wanted us to graduate and serve as officers. If we stayed, we would graduate but by this time, we were down to just over 500 of us.

For the first time in two years, I considered quitting. That was when my family, my mentors and my classmates supported me. The family assured me that they would support me either way. My high school English teacher who originally tried to talk me out of going to West Point, made the case on why I should stay and graduate. My closest friends were staying and I stayed. For me, it was the right choice.

The next two years were tough academically but a great learning experience. West Point has the greatest military history courses in the world. All the great battles from Napoleon through the Civil War to World War II. I also had the best Shakespeare course taught by Colonel Richard Burton.

Between our Yearling and Cow (junior) years, I was assigned to an Artillery unit at Ft. Carson, Colorado to get some real Army experience. The summer between the junior and senior years, I was part of the detail to bring in the new cadets, the class of 1970.

All this time, the losses in Vietnam of people I knew from previous classes continued to grow. But now there was no longer any fear of losing friends. Now I was committed to do something about it. When we started at West Point in 1963, the US combat losses for the entire year totaled 122 KIA.

In 1967, the number was over 11,000. We had the motto of the Military Academy, 'Duty, Honor, Country', drilled into our heads from the first day as plebes. Now, most of us felt that it was time to do our duty, with honor, for our country. We would 'march to the sound of the guns' and not wait to be called up. We would volunteer. But there was more to learn before we could go.

The Artillery Officers' Basic Course at Ft. Sill, Oklahoma, was followed by Ranger School and then airborne training at Ft. Benning, Georgia. Ft. Sill in the summer is hot. My 'ranger buddy' Mike and I had lots of classes together and became competent Artillery officers. What that meant was that we were trained in fire direction center operations, calling in Artillery fire and shooting the big guns that supported our troops.

Since most of the guys in our Artillery classes were our West Point classmates, it was like being back at the Military Academy except we were in Oklahoma. It was worth noting that West Point training is largely strategic. We did have some map reading training during plebe and sophomore summers at West Point and the training at Ft. Sill included some map reading—when you are shooting eight-inch shells, it is important to know where you are.

So as we headed to Ft. Benning, Georgia to become Airborne Rangers, we thought we knew what we were doing but we still hadn't differentiated between the strategic and tactical. Map reading was tactical. Ranger School came in three parts. Phase one was at Ft. Benning near Columbus, Georgia south of Atlanta.

There we got up close and personal with the red clay of Georgia. Our class was known as 'frostbite five' because it took place in October and November when temperatures could fall below freezing. That had no impact on the training—rain or shine. The misery of low crawling through that red clay was compounded—being cold is bad.

Being wet and cold was really bad but being wet, cold and covered in red mud was true misery. The big deal in this first phase of training was the map reading course. You couldn't operate in the military, especially in the Artillery, without knowing where you were. If you didn't know your location, you could kill people—your own people.

Mike and I got hung up on the map course—literally hung up. The vegetation around Ft. Benning included some nasty stuff called 'wait a minute' vines. These vines had thorns on them and they seemed to jump out and grab you as you moved through the woods. As you tried to untangle yourself, you would call out to your squad, 'Wait a minute.'

The map course had ten points that we had to find by map navigation and compass directions—we found one. They brought us up in front of a board of officers who were to determine whether or not we could remain in the Ranger program. They allowed us to stay with the provision that our map reading skills improved by being point men on patrols—*every* patrol. We became map reading experts.

By the time we completed the mountain phase of the training in north Georgia, we could not only tell you where we were on the map but we became good at nailing the time it would take to get over the rough terrain of the southern Appalachian Mountains. In military operations, knowing where you were was important and knowing how to get to your objective and how long it would take to get there on time was equally important.

Military maps showed contour lines. The closer they were together, the steeper the terrain. North Georgia had some difficult mountains to climb or get around with abundant rivers and streams to really make it interesting. Our last big obstacle was Yonah Mountain. We never saw the top of it, as the weather was foggy and cold. Then it started to snow.

When we got off the mountain, at the lower elevation it was only raining. I was exhausted, so I just laid down on the ground to sleep. Before I dozed off, I heard some rustling around our area. Mike had gotten up and dug our rain ponchos out of our packs. He covered us both and we slept soundly and mostly dry. That's what Ranger buddies do. We survived the mountain phase of Ranger School and headed for Eglin Air Force Base in sunny Florida.

This next and last phase was three weeks in the Florida swamps. Map reading in the mountains was relatively easy with all the valleys and streams to orient yourself. But the swamps of Florida provided new challenges. Keeping track of distance was more important on the relatively flat terrain. The weather was so much warmer and the biggest obstacles were the swamps, rivers and snakes. This was much like the terrain of Vietnam, so we paid close attention.

One night, we were attacked (by the cadre) and my job was to call in a fire mission. I had already plotted our position on the map and set up where I wanted the Artillery. But the attack from the cadre was so realistic with automatic weapons fire and flash-bang grenades going off, when I got on the radio, I stammered, "This is R-r-r-ranger 43, f-f-f-fire mission." All the noise and confusion actually made me afraid. I wasn't criticized but I was disappointed in myself. I vowed that this fear would never control me again.

We finished Ranger School with a 25-mile forced march that was the final test. If you didn't finish the march, you did not get your Ranger tab. We started before dawn with full packs. With all that gear, it was tough going but we had already walked over 250 miles, so we were not going to let this pace stop us. There were two Navy Seals in our squad.

At about mile 20, one of the Seals had a problem with his feet. We solved the problem by splitting their gear among the squad and one Seal carried his

Ranger buddy for the last five miles. Those guys were tough. We finished the course and our whole squad made it. We were Rangers and Mike and I were experts on map reading in any terrain.

Airborne school was easy compared to Ranger training. We had just walked over mountains and through swamps for almost 300 miles, so the morning runs and physical training were a lark for us. The five jumps out of C130 aircraft were a rush. In three weeks, we were Airborne and Mike and I were headed for the 82nd Airborne Division at Ft. Bragg, North Carolina.

I took some leave and went home to Rhode Island for the Christmas holidays. I was treated like royalty and enjoyed seeing my family and a few old friends but it was becoming obvious that I had changed. In January 1968, I drove south to Fort Bragg, North Carolina, to report to my first Army duty station. I crossed the state line from Virginia into North Carolina and there by the side of Interstate 95 was a huge billboard with a rearing white horse and a Klansman holding high a burning cross.

The billboard sign read *Fight desegregation! Impeach Earl Warren!* I realized that I was entering a whole new world. The military may have desegregated in 1948 but 20 years later, it was obvious to me that North Carolina had not. For this Yankee, it was a shock. Welcome to the South! As a white man, I didn't fear the South but as a Yankee, I didn't always feel welcomed either.

I reported to Ft. Bragg, found a place to live with some West Point classmates and settled into the routine as an Artillery-battery executive officer (XO). When the North Vietnamese Army (NVA) launched the 1968 Tet offensive, we observed the Vietnam War on television and were amazed to see how strong the NVA was.

Out of the combat zone, military units train every day for combat. There was a line attributed to General Patton that went, 'The objective of war is not to die for your country. It's to make some other son of a bitch die for his country.' We focused on our training, so my life was routine and fun— shooting big guns, jumping out of airplanes and chasing local women.

When the Assistant Division Commander needed an aide, I applied for the job. I interviewed and won the job by being the closest thing West Point had to an English major and I was a fair tennis player. I read the book, *Blackburn's Headhunters* by Col. Russ Volkman and would ask General Blackburn about it.

The stories were incredible. Some of the local guerillas he trained and worked with hated the Japanese so much that they did not take prisoners. They would decapitate them. He said that he disapproved of the mountain people who took Japanese heads but it happened and he did not discourage it.

He also told me that through the four years after the escape from Baatan, he kept promoting himself and his officers—he wanted to promote himself to general but thought it was a bit too ostentatious at age 27. He was the youngest full colonel in the Army after WWII.

At one point as General Blackburn's aide, his old friend Ferdinand Marcos, President of the Philippines, appointed himself president for life. General B had me compose a congratulatory letter to him. I worked on the letter and had him sign it over his usual signature block. As I was walking out of his office, I looked at his signature and turned to him saying, "General, this letter is to President Marcos, you cannot sign it 'Don'."

He smiled at me with the usual twinkle in his eye and declared, "I can."

Ft. Bragg was the closest active military post to Washington, DC, so the dignitaries often visited to learn what was going on and to show their support for the troops. The 82nd had a firepower demonstration called 'Brass Strike', which showed the firepower our training could deliver.

Many congressmen and Pentagon officials attended. The demonstration started with one infantry rifleman and grew from that single person to the squad, the platoon and finally to a full infantry company. Each group increased the firepower as they shot downrange, the noise and the tracers, plus Artillery, airstrikes and a battalion airborne jump from Air Force C-130 aircraft were all impressive.

At one of the firepower demonstrations, there was a table where drinks were served and I was getting General Blackburn some water. As I turned from the table, I almost bumped into the man behind me. He was taller than I and all I could focus on were the three stars on his collar. I almost dumped the drink on a three-star general! He backed up to avoid me and I apologized. He stuck out his hand and said, "Hi, Davis here!"

I knew who he was and shook his hand. BO Davis was an Air Force lieutenant general who had graduated from West Point in 1936. His story was amazing. He was only the fourth black man to graduate from the Military Academy since it was founded in 1802. Even more incredible was that from his first year there, he was 'silenced' by white cadets in an attempt to drive him out.

He was accused falsely of violating the honor code but a board of officers allowed him to stay. He stayed but no cadet was allowed to talk to him except in the line of duty. He lived alone, ate his meals alone and studied alone for four years. I was honored to shake his hand. I'm not sure I would have had the courage to stand up to that harassment.

General Blackburn was from Savannah, Georgia and graduated from the University of Florida. He was no ordinary man. He was a highly respected Special Forces soldier and was nominated for his star by General WC Westmoreland, then Chairman of the Joint Chiefs.

My time as an XO of an Artillery battery was good small unit training. As General B's aide, I saw the Army from division level. It was an amazing view for a young Army officer. But on April 4, things got crazy. Dr. Martin Luther King, Jr. the clergyman and civil-rights leader, was shot at the Lorraine Motel in Memphis, Tennessee. The television reported that Dr. King was rushed to St. Joseph's Hospital but died that evening.

The 82nd Airborne Division not only had a war mission but also had a mission to keep the peace at home. An event happened when we were preparing to go to Washington, DC during the riots after Dr. King was assassinated. Gen B and I were having breakfast and watching the television news.

At one point of the reporting on the rioting and looting the news film showed a black man walking out of a store with a television set in his arms. Gen B said, "They ought to shoot that son-of-a-bitch."

I'm not sure where it came from inside of me but I said to him, "General, you don't shoot a man for stealing a television." The room got very quiet. I couldn't believe that I, a lowly lieutenant, said that to my boss, a general officer.

After what seemed an eternity, he looked at me and said, "You're right. Let's go."

What was I thinking? Perhaps it was the influence of Mr. Walker, my 7th grade social studies teacher or my friend Oris from camp or Miss Harry, my kindergarten teacher—but I was becoming a new, stronger individual. Three days later, the 82nd's first brigade loaded onto C-130 aircraft at Pope Air Force Base and flew to Andrews AFB outside of DC. Police departments today could learn a lot from how these soldiers conducted themselves and restored the peace.

My West Point class had two black cadets. Black cadets had not fared well historically at the United States Military Academy. After West Point, I found that in the real Army black soldiers made up more than 20% of the enlisted troops but less than 5% of the officer corps. Institutional racism was alive and well at West Point and in the military.

The Army was bad but the Navy, Marines and Air Force were even worse. I was beginning to understand why the whole civil rights movement was literally catching fire. Dr. King's murder was the lighted match that touched off an explosion.

A historic view of the Army's role in unrest in America in a *Fayetteville (NC) Observer* blog by Drew Brooks was posted on 14 August 2014. In the article entitled *Fort Bragg Report: Paratroopers no strangers to civil unrest*, Brooks described how the Airborne and Special Operations Museum in downtown Fayetteville hosted an exhibit.

That exhibit was titled 'Supporting Civil Authority: An Era of Domestic Unrest' and looked at paratroopers responding to riots and protests between 1955 and 1971. In 1968, following Dr. King's death, the 82nd and 18th Airborne Corps were again called upon, this time to protect Baltimore and Washington, D.C.

The exhibit included several photographs of paratroopers in action, riding jeeps or marching along streets. One of the photos shows an 82nd airborne paratrooper standing in front of the Washington Monument. Others show soldiers outside the U.S. Capitol Building, directing traffic and even talking with passersby.

From the ASOM: 'Airborne soldiers involved in civil-disturbance missions received training in riot-control techniques. But their primary mission was to maintain peace and to ensure compliance with federal law.'

The 82nd Airborne Division was prepared to quell riots around the country with 'Civil Disturbance' training with fixed bayonets if necessary. As aide to the Assistant Division Commander, I visited with police and mayors around the country with General Blackburn. Most of them welcomed his input and help, as he had been commander of the Military District of Washington after he came home from the Philippines.

Things settled down for us after the DC riots in 1968. We were not deployed to Los Angeles when Robert Kennedy was assassinated or to Chicago during the riots during the Democratic National Convention. Chicago police overreacted to that situation. Perhaps police everywhere could learn from how the 82nd Airborne Division acted in DC with discipline and military precision.

General Blackburn would occasionally wear his Military Assistance Command Vietnam, Studies and Observations Group, combat patch on his right shoulder. He said that he never liked the patch—a skull wearing a green beret. He thought it gave away what they did. Part of my duties included handling secret information, an assignment for which I obtained a top-secret security clearance.

One day, the General handed me some documents labeled 'TOP SECRET' to put into the safe. As I took them, he warned me not to let anyone else see them and added, 'If Congress ever got hold of them, they might question the Tonkin Gulf Resolution.' That resolution had been the basis for increasing the bombing and troop-strength against North Vietnam in 1964.

There were rumors that the action which precipitated the US response had actually not been initiated by North Vietnam. Some observers believed that the fire supposedly from North Vietnamese gunboats had come from other sources—such as US Special Forces commanded by then-Colonel Blackburn, who was in charge under General Westmoreland as part of MACV.

When General Blackburn was reassigned to the Pentagon, I went to Vietnam but not before I checked with a New York psychiatrist I knew. I asked him if he thought I was crazy for volunteering to go to Vietnam. He said, 'No, you are a professional soldier and you have to find out if all that training works.' I arrived in Vietnam in March of 1969. I came home 364 days later as a very different person who had witnessed firsthand that Army combat training worked.

Together: When we walk into a classroom of diverse students, we have something to say to the black, brown and white students. Yes, we are different but we shared similar experiences and we are brothers. We do not glorify war or the military but we try to present military service as an opportunity—especially for kids looking for opportunities to serve.

We tell about times when we were afraid. Handling fear is a part of growing up and training. Fear of the unknown may be one of the worst fears we faced. But fear may also have a benefit. A young black man going into the deep south may be afraid and if that fear keeps him out of danger; that is a good thing.

The same situation can apply to combat. Fear can heighten our awareness of the dangers around us—also a good thing. We both feel that our training gave us a sense of confidence and control that allowed us to stay calm in moments of extreme danger, fear and stress. This sense probably saved our lives more than once in Vietnam.

Explaining the training for combat and then telling combat experiences go hand in hand. How did we survive the training and actual combat when so many of our friends did not? The answer is that we do not know. Call it luck or the prayers of our families or fate.

The fact is that we both felt that serving our country was a higher calling than just earning a living or making a million dollars. Ray created a definition of service that Bruce appreciated. He said, "True service is when you follow the call to do your duty and the money doesn't matter."

As we wrote this part of the story and discussed the fact that we were both airborne soldiers, we started singing a chant we used to sing as we ran in formation, "I want to be an Airborne Ranger. I want to live a life of danger. I want to go to Vietnam. I want to kill some Viet Cong."

The memories and the military training still have a hold on us. People in the coffee shop must have thought we were crazy but were we brainwashed? We say that we were highly trained professionals. When we hear the word, 'brainwashed', we think of those who are programmed to do something without consideration for the people around them.

We were not trained that way. We were trained from our early youth to care about others—both family and friends. Empathy is a quality that brings others closer. When they know you care about them, most often they return the favor—even in the military.

As professional soldiers, we had to consider the lives of those soldiers we impacted every minute of the day. So our answer is simply, no, we were not brainwashed. We were soldiers. We were there to control fear, protect those young soldiers around us and do our duty to protect our country as leaders.

We each had a dream and found help from family, friends and mentors to make that dream come true. We did not let anyone stop us. By the time we got to our goals, we were both in our early 20s, college educated, trained professionals and ready to serve our country.

Both of us worked hard. We made good grades, worked jobs, played sports and saw the military as a path out of being poor. We sometimes asked for help when it was needed. We took an oath to serve and we took our leadership seriously. We were both strong, physically fit, had played team sports and had family, friends and mentors to support us.

We were not perfect but we set goals and achieved them. Still with all we had accomplished, we had more to learn. Ray had to deal with the color of his skin from the day he was born. Bruce had to learn how to lead both black and white soldiers. The Army's 'we don't see color' was not the right answer.

As we developed our reasons for creating this book, we decided that we wanted to share our story with those who had dreams. All the fights that we had to go through to get where we are today reinforced our idea that we are two former soldiers who needed to speak out. We came to the realization that we would go back and do it all over again.

It's working long hours for what we want to do in life. For us, our story shows that hard work and dedication to our dreams help us live the life we had envisioned for ourselves. Both of us had people tell us that we weren't going to make it and our dreams were foolish. We should do something less difficult, more into the role society had outlined for us. We said, "No."

For Ray as an African-American, it became an obsession for him to make his dreams of becoming a pilot reality. There may not have been loud voices telling him that he could not succeed—some of those voices were soft, persistent and determined that black folks just didn't do these things. Ray's determination was not for the greater good of poor and black people, to show them that there is no limitation to one's dreams.

That did not come until later in life. Seeing the looks people's faces at an airport, as he climbed out of his aircraft gave him real satisfaction. But in the beginning, it was that dream of being a pilot. To see the world in a new way, to be among the clouds.

For Bruce going to West Point fulfilled his dream. Then he had the opportunity to be a leader in the Army and in his community. He was learning how to lead men but he still needed to learn how to work with other leaders.

He wanted to serve his country and find out what combat was like. He needed to learn firsthand how to do that. He thought he was ready. Bruce and Ray joined together. Bruce needed the support.

In training: Ray in flight school

In training: Bruce at West Point

Part Two:
Being in War

We few, we happy few, we band of brothers;
For he today that sheds his blood with me
Shall be my brother;

– Shakespeare

Chapter 4
Vietnam

No bastard ever won a war by dying for his country. He won it by making the other poor dumb bastard die for his country.
– General George Patton addressing the 6th Armored Division on 31 May 1944

The Vietnam War may have been a mistake. We may have supported the wrong side. Power hungry politicians may have used their positions to put soldiers on both sides in a terrible situation. Ray and Bruce did their duty to protect and defend the Constitution of the United States and their brothers in arms based on the oath that they took. They thought their desire to serve was based on honorable and justifiable reasons. They both came home.

Ray: During one of our last formations after we knew that we were going to graduate, our training officer told us that we had received our orders and we were all going to Vietnam. Then he told us something that really changed our thinking about going to war. Almost as an offhand comment he said that if you want your buddy to get out of Vietnam for a while, go home and tell your mother or wife that you want him to bring your body back home if you are killed.

With that thought, going to war took on a new dimension. Graduation from flight school was moved up two weeks early because of the casualty rate of chopper pilots in Vietnam. This added another dimension to our going into combat. As I think back about becoming a warrant officer candidate, I remember an interview.

After I passed all the tests and the physical examination, I had an interview with an officer, a major. He was a white guy, slender with the bearing of an officer in the military. He seemed very relaxed and very positive about our encounter. He only asked me a few questions about going to war and did I understand what that meant? But the oddest question was, did my mother know that I had joined the Army to fight in war?

He had my records in front of him and there was my age, 22 ½. I told him that my mother did know and she had nothing to say about it, because I was old enough to make my own decisions. Then he asked me if I had a girlfriend and what did she think about my serving in the military? I told him again that I was my own man and this is what I wanted to do.

Plus, we were not married, so she had nothing to say about it. He thought about this for a few seconds got up right from his chair, started signing my papers and said, 'You are going to make a fine warrant officer.'

After graduation from flight school, we all got 30 days to 45 days leave. Since I was last in the alphabet, I got 45 days at home. I took the long drive home from Alabama to New Jersey, because I had just bought a new car, an MGBGT. I left late in the afternoon, after putting my mother on an airplane headed back home and I drove north.

I got to Atlanta just as it was getting dark. The city lights were beautiful. I made my way through the maze of the highway system, found my way to I-95 and started the long trek home. I went through Georgia then South Carolina and North Carolina before I even knew what was going on. Washington DC was the first place that I had some remembrance of.

Then as the sun was coming up, I got to Maryland and drove into Delaware. Only the Delaware River now kept me from being in my home. My mother had gotten home the night before and I pulled into my driveway about 10 in the morning. She was waiting for me. We had breakfast and talked about our trips and then I went to bed. After 45 days, I was rested and relaxed but it was time to go to war.

On the day I departed, my mother took me to the airport in Philadelphia. We were very quiet on the way and in those days, you could see people off right at the gate. We got there early and we sat down and chatted for a while. She looked at me and the sadness was all over her face.

She said, "Take care of yourself. You know I love you and I want you to come back." She stared into my face and looked deeply at me. I'm sure she just wanted to remember every feature of my face and hold in her thought who I was.

When they called my flight and the time had come to get on the airplane, she gave me a big and tight hug like the ones I remembered from when I was a little boy. We said our goodbyes and I could see tears in her eyes as I walked down the ramp. On the airplane, my seat was right by the window and I could see the gate area with my mom in the window, holding up her clinched fist. I could still see the tears running down her cheeks. I flew from Philly to San Francisco.

I was excited. I was a military pilot and I was living my dream going off to war. My dream was not to kill people. The whole idea was to test myself and my training. This idea filled my thoughts. I wanted to be like all the men that I had seen in all the movies as a little kid about combat. I was going to defend my country.

The gentleman sitting next to me started to chat. I was in my Army uniform with my wings on and he said that he was a Navy pilot during the Korean War. Right away, I felt lucky that he started talking to me. He gave me insights about what war was like—at least what he thought war was like for him and those around him.

He didn't put fear into my heart. His sense of duty confirmed what I believed I was supposed to do. My job would be to do everything possible to safeguard the guys on the ground. He was talking to me about that great feeling you get when you were helping your fellow soldiers survive a difficult situation.

It was an interesting phenomenon that all of us who had gone around the world to fight for our country were brothers. When we arrived at San Francisco airport, he shook my hand and said, "Good luck to you." We went our separate ways. I got a bus to Travis Air Force Base, checked in for my flight to Vietnam and went to the officers' club.

There I met classmates and other officers heading off to the war zone. It made you feel like you were part of a more important group of folks. We were off to do our duty for our country and to give this effort all that we had to give. We were now all on the same schedule heading off to war. We boarded a contract airliner.

It was Seaboard World Airlines, normally a cargo airlines. We settled in for at least a 24-hour flight to Vietnam. Our first stop was Hickam field in Hawaii. I had an uncle in the Air Force who was stationed there. He came over and met me at the Air Force passenger station. He brought me some food from home and we sat down and chatted until I had to go. He wished me goodbye, good luck and be safe.

The tension in my stomach grew with every hour that we got closer to Vietnam. We had one more stop in Guam for refueling and we were finally on our last leg of the flight. To counter the fear of going to a war zone, I dwelled on the excitement of this great adventure. My father, uncles and teachers from high school had all gone to war. I was going to prove to myself that I was a man equal to all of them.

After Guam, we headed for Bien Hoa Air Force Base just north of South Vietnam's capital, Saigon. There were many places that a soldier sailor or airman could enter country. For the United States Army, Bien Hoa was the biggest port of entry. As the plane got closer to landing, I sat by the window and could see the ocean grow lighter in color. Then the white sandy beaches came into view.

After the beaches came the green of the Vietnam countryside. The beauty took over my thoughts. It was around noon when we entered the traffic pattern for landing but I still could see no sign of war that had been going on for the French and now Americans for many years by then. As we got lower, the fact that I was really going to a war zone now took over my thoughts.

On final approach, you could see what the war was doing to the land. Trees were gone and big holes from bombs were half full of water. Then to make the situation hit home harder, two cobra helicopters flew in formation with our airplane until just before we touched down. They gave me another insight that this was a real war.

When the airliner taxied to the terminal, there was a big sign over it, *Welcome to Bien Hoa*. I was seated in the middle of the aircraft. I moved toward the front door and I could see the sun lit up everyone as they walked through the door and disappeared. I made my way forward, excited to get my first view of the country I was going to defend for a year.

I stepped through the door into the sunlight and left the cool of the airplane behind. The heat hit me in the face. The flight attendants were all at the door wishing us good luck, giving us a big smile and saying, 'See you on the way home, soldier.'

We walked down the stairs onto the ramp. Then a bus took us to the reception center. I was overwhelmed by the sights, sounds and smells. I was barely in country more than 10 minutes and wondered if I would ever get used to all of this. But I was on my way to find out where I was going to be stationed and what unit was going to be my new home.

After leaving the terminal area with duffel bags over our shoulders, this whole airplane full of FNG's (f**kin' new guys) was bused off to a large room with a giant map of South Vietnam on the front wall. The lower ranked enlisted men were sent into another room. All the sergeants and officers were in this one big room with the map. All the sergeants sat on one side of an aisle and all the officers on the other I was seated in the back on one side, next to the sergeants.

We got a welcome to Vietnam and a short briefing on what was happening in the country over the past few weeks. I was impressed with what little had happened before I got there. I thought there would be battles happening every day. As I looked around, almost everybody seemed very relaxed and unconcerned about what they had just heard, so I decided to play along with this game.

Some of the folks were on their second tour in Vietnam and a few were on their 3rd. I decided to show a very cool attitude even though I was excited and apprehensive. I thought acting with a cool attitude like I could handle anything would be good.

The briefing officer got around to all the units in country and the procedures for which we were going to be assigned to a unit. It wasn't complicated. We had five choices with the needs of the Army having the final pick. With the form in hand to make my choices, I looked at the big map. I felt confused about what I should do and it must have shown on my face.

Across the aisle that separated enlisted men from officers, a senior NCO leaned over to me and said, 'Sir, pick all five of your choices in III and IV Corps.' South Vietnam was divided into four corps or military areas. One of these military areas, IV Corps, was in the far south and the other, III Corps was around the capital of Saigon.

Since this guy obviously knew what he was talking about with all those stripes on his arm and the fact that he was likely to be on his second or third trip over the Pacific Ocean, I decided to follow his advice. Since I did not know my butt from a hole in the ground, it felt like as good a plan as any to me. The briefing went on for another hour and we went off to the replacement center bachelor officers' barracks to find a bed.

The next day, our assignments were posted on the bulletin board just outside of our barracks. I found my name and I was going to the largest brigade in the United States Army, the First Aviation Brigade. I had another briefing that afternoon and there I heard about the mission of my new unit. I learned I would be going to the 145th Combat Aviation Battalion. By the end of the day, I found out I would be part of the 118th Assault Helicopter Company known as the Thunderbirds.

Just an hour later, I was given my written orders and told to be ready to travel with all my belongings to my new unit. I watched as other new pilots got on helicopters to go to their new outfits. My new adventure started an hour later when a private first class picked me up in a jeep and drove me 20 minutes to the headquarters of the 118th, my new home!

The driver never said a word of welcome or anything about my new company. It was SOP not to be friendly with FNG's until they made it through the first week. If they made it through the first week alive, then it was ok to talk to them.

It seemed to me that I had been inside a building for my whole two plus days in Vietnam. From the door of the airplane to the terminal was the only time I was outside, feeling the sunlight and the heat of the day. Now for the first time, I was seeing the people of this land, as we drove through Bien Hoa from one side of the village to the other to get to the Army airfield known as Plantation Army Airfield. I was amazed at the smells and the bright colors of the shops and the clothing of the people.

I found myself staring at all the people on the streets as we drove by. We went through a marketplace and I was almost overwhelmed by the sounds of the people's conversation. It was like music. I had never imagined how different a language could sound to my ears. And the people were small, with unusual clothes and large, weird hats.

It was like nothing I'd ever seen in New Jersey. I also got the feeling that they were staring at me. I started to feel a little fear. Were they good guys or the enemy? How could I know? I was so new to this land and to war. How long would I last?

When we arrived at the company headquarters, I got my bag and went into HQ to check in. Like any other FNG, I had questions about procedures, where to sleep and what to do now. I was greeted with a smile, a big welcome to the

Thunderbirds, assigned to the first platoon and shown to my room. It was a small cinderblock building with five or six rooms in a row.

They housed two officers each. There were only two black officers in my company and John from North Carolina was my roommate. He told me I could take the top bunk and helped me settle in. He answered all my questions about what it was like to be here, where we ate, when the meal call was and about the small officers' club—all basic things that an FNG needed to know right away.

We got into a conversation about where in 'the world' I was from. The world was our reference to the United States. When it was time to go to the mess hall, I thought we would be eating local food. No, we were eating food that I would call hospital food. It wasn't good but it was filling. I felt apprehensive that first day but was very excited about what was going to happen in my first flight in Vietnam as a combat pilot.

All through basic training and flight school, we had to march in formation to build discipline and sing songs to foster comradeship. The songs in cadence to our steps and the words were like, "I want to be an Airborne Ranger, I want to live a life of danger, I want to go to Vietnam and I want to kill the Viet Cong!" I would sing along, not knowing and not feeling what it really meant to kill.

There was a picture of me, the first one in my new unit. When I look at that picture today, I see a young man not sure of what's going on and how he was going to handle it. The picture was taken in my room and as I look back at that person then, he's a little scared but ready for the adventure to come. When that picture was taken, I had been to the head, taken a shower, found my bed and discovered the food was OK.

I liked my new roommate but missed home, my mother and even my little brother who was 20 years old at the time. I laughed to myself, "Raymond, you are not in New Jersey anymore!" I had been 'in country' for less than a week, so I still wasn't used to all the sights, sounds and smells, The odd feel of the earth, the hot air and even the sky. Everything was different.

I never had the thought in my head that I might die. I thought I could get hurt or something—maybe even wounded but never that I would die in Vietnam. I felt that my skill as pilot would get me through it all. The enemy would not get me. I also felt it was just not worth the time to worry about what might happen.

I was excited about being a military pilot living the dream and the adventure that I had dreamed about all my life. What I was afraid of was messing up. 'Don't fuck up' was the mantra everybody used when we were in flight school. Now it meant life or death.

I needed to make new friends but the Army was a mirror of American attitudes. The people were friendly but still standing off this FNG. My roommate was a black man who could be very funny. He and I got along well but he was a short timer meaning that he had about three months to go.

He was what we called a two-digit midget—that is, he had less than 100 days left in country. I was brand new and had a whole year to go. I wondered what would happen and what kind of a roommate I would have when he departed Vietnam.

In flight school, like playing sports, we blended together to get through whatever we had to face to win the game or survive. Here, the groups fell into the same pattern since there were so few black officers in the Army. They seemed to keep us separate with those ancient attitudes still on the surface. It had only been 20 years since the Army had integrated and the Air Force and the Army started training black pilots.

I had seen many war movies where the new guy, the FNG, was teased all the time but also was made to feel welcome. There was always a shortage of pilots in every unit. I was determined to make them see that I was good pilot and a good officer—trustworthy and fun to be around.

By nature, I was a happy person, open to all people and that attitude had served me well but at times it was hard to ignore some of the racist crap that might come out of someone's mouth. So I stayed away from those I saw as just plain racist assholes, the ones who didn't like me just because I was black. They existed everywhere—even in the Army.

I wanted to feel what it was like to fly in combat, carry troops into battle and see the enemy in the jungle behind the trees. Would I be brave or would fear take over? The fear of being shot was just a small item in my mind. The sights and sounds of war were fueling my imagination.

My fear was that I would not do my job at the level of my expectations or that my training would not kick in. What if no one would want me to be in the cockpit with him when the chips were down? I made up my mind to face every situation remembering my training and my desire to prove myself. I did not have long to wait.

My first flight was my in-country orientation flight. I had been with the 118th assault helicopter company for about five days. They weren't going to waste much time getting my name on the schedule. I got a briefing with one of the other new guys on our mission in the AO (area of operations) we would be flying in. I had been issued my personal handgun, a very old 38 caliber.

I also got my survival gear, which was a vest that had a survival radio, first aid kit, about 100 rounds of ammunition and a shoulder holster. It did not make me feel that I could defend myself against the enemy but now I looked like a combat pilot.

I came to my unit with the same helmet I had when I went through flight school. A friend of mine, who spent some time in the Navy and was an art major in college, painted the head of a frog with a mask and a cowboy hat on the back of it. Some months from now that would be my unofficial call sign, The Lone Frog!

My in-country orientation flight started out by meeting one of the company's instructor pilots. He seemed friendly and we went on to go through all the little things I needed to know about the airfield and radio procedures. He gave me some maps of the area and had me work out how to fold them so they fit in my bag.

We went over the maps and operations of all the airfields in the area including all the places where I could get fuel. When we got to the assigned aircraft for this training, he looked at me with a smile and said, 'Don't worry. As long as you don't kill me, you'll be on the schedule tomorrow morning.'

It was a bright and sunny day perfect for flying. It was hot but not so that you would have to worry about how the aircraft performed. I did the preflight as my instructor strapped in the seat and proceeded to start the helicopter up. The helicopter was parked in a revetment with sandbags up to almost the height of the aircraft on each side. I smoothly moved the ship out of the revenant and to the taxi way.

Everything went well and with my performance, he seemed to relax. I hovered out to the runway where we had about 10 tasks to do. It was fun after almost two months without flying. I love being in control of a five-ton aircraft. We did some emergency procedures and a slope landing from a hover. When that was done, we called to the tower for takeoff.

We flew around the traffic pattern doing more emergency procedures. It was like I was back in-flight school near the end of my training and I remembered how to do everything correctly. After that was complete, we went out and looked at the area. It was my first time out into the countryside and it was just beautiful. The light and the colors were like nothing I've ever seen before. The beauty was intoxicating.

It took us about an hour and a half of flying around to do everything that we needed to complete. We talked about everything but the war. We talked about what my home was like. My instructor had never been to New Jersey. He asked if I were married and where I went to school. In the Army, you always asked these questions to find out if there was an extra connection between you and the other person.

We were both from the East Coast and that was good enough to like each other. After landing and engine shut down, he told me of the duties of the copilot post flight inspection and helped clean out the ship after the mission. As we filled out the forms and walked to operations, he smiled again and said, "Welcome to the Thunderbirds!" With that I was a combat pilot, now a member of the team, just waiting for my first mission!

At 23 years old, I was starting my war. Vietnam was now my war. I was not the oldest pilot and for sure not the youngest. There were guys just 19 years old. You had to be that old just to get into flight school and go to Vietnam. Until you had a few missions under your belt, the aircraft commanders didn't trust you. They treated you like a dumbass little boy, no matter how old you were. That is the Army way of training in FNG's but looking back, I knew there had to be a better way. Hazing is not leadership.

The morning came early that day. I was in operations meeting my aircraft commander and finding out where we were going. We were on a direct support mission, which meant we were going to do supply trips, carrying messages, mail and everything else back-and-forth. We also carried people who needed to get from one place to another. Had it been about a year earlier, we might have carried a young Lt. Bruce out to Cu Chi but by this time, Bruce was fighting new battles at Ft. Carson, Colorado.

Our mission was to fly for a signal company that was in a base camp called Cu Chi. We were going to carry new radios and other equipment, code books and personnel to all of their locations for the whole day. My job as copilot was to do the preflight of our ship and make sure that we had everything we needed for the mission.

All this took about 40 minutes, my pilot was getting all the paperwork together and I went out to the aircraft started my preflight checks. I introduced myself to the crew chief and our door gunner. Both of them had been in country for many months. I wasn't their first FNG, so they didn't pay a lot of attention to me. They just wanted to make sure I did everything on the preflight correctly.

When the aircraft commander showed up with the codebook and frequencies, he asked how did the ship look, was it ready to go? I told him the ship was ready and so was I. He got into the 'loveseat' (the command pilot's seat on the left side of the helicopter) and I got into the one on the right.

The crew chief helped him strap in but I had to work my straps myself— again, because I was the new guy. We got the aircraft started and were just about all ready to go and the pilot said, "You got a grease pencil with you?"

I said, "Yes, I do." The procedure for all copilots was to mark on the windshield in grease pencil the number of sorties and what we carried.

Then the pilot said, "Don't touch the controls unless I tell you to. Keep your mouth shut and just look around." I gave him an odd look and nodded my head in the affirmative. After doing all the checks and making sure everything was ready, we got clearance from the tower and off we went on my first mission.

My aircraft commander was a Chief Warrant Officer 2, so he outranked me by a grade. He had been in country for 10 months and one of our company procedures was to have your first flight with a pilot that had been in country for a long time. They figured that the old guys could handle us FNG's and still get the mission done. In the first few minutes of our flight out to Cu Chi, he mellowed out.

On that 30-minute flight, I learned that he was from Iowa and married with a little boy. The crew chief and door gunner also told me about themselves like where they were from and what they were going to do when they get back to the world. After that they got around to asking about me and my history.

We flew toward Cu Chi and all I had to do was look at the scenery. Not having to navigate was a real joy. Then I got to fly—I was told to stay at 1500 feet. That's just outside of small arms range but not too high that you can't see the terrain around you. The land in this area of South Vietnam is flat and lots of small rivers and streams with rice paddies in all directions. There was one major road that had a hard surface with two lanes. It was called Highway 1 and it was heading right where we were going, easy navigation.

I was amazed at the beauty of the land. The rice paddies had many small villages nestled in groves of trees. I could also see the people working the fields. On the highway were lots of people on motorcycles, small cars and buses. In my head, I thought, 'Where is the war? These people do not seem scared. What's going on?' But I would soon learn that no one travels after dark. At night, the war can pop up anywhere.

The sky was clear with small clouds as white as Florida beach sand. I felt so comfortable flying over this place being a part of this ship. I thought we had plenty of firepower, an experienced crew and an aircraft commander who knew what to do if things got crazy. Being a part of this group gave me confidence. As I flew more, feeling the controls in my hands, I knew that I was the master of this machine. The training was paying off.

Flying straight and level was so natural to me—it was like breathing. I love the feeling of the controls and the movement of the aircraft. It was doing what I wanted it to do. The sounds of the engine and transmission, all these high-pitched noises is a sweet sound coming through my helmet telling me that everything was normal. I learned to trust those sounds. They would give notice if anything was going wrong.

I also had the instruments that would tell me how everything around me was doing. Above all this was the sound of the rotors hitting the air, giving us the support to stay up in speed and direction to get where we wanted to go. Here we were almost to Cu Chi, my first experience of flying over this amazing country filled with such beauty. The newness of it all was almost overwhelming.

I was trying to show my new aircraft commander and crew that I could fly this 10,000-pound helicopter smoothly and look cool doing it. As we flew near, our destination was a very large mountain, Nuit Ba Dinh, the Black Virgin Mountain. I was taught in flight school even when I was not navigating, to study the map and memorize key points before we departed.

This mountain was north of our destination. It was so large, it seemed to come out of rice paddies like magic. As it got bigger, I knew we were getting closer to the airfield. When we got about 10 minutes out from the airfield, the aircraft commander called the signal company operations and told them how many minutes we were out and how many hours of flight time we were going to give them.

That time was assigned to them and they could use it anyway they needed. Signal companies support all the other combat arms communications. He then called the Army airfield where we were going to land and told them that we were just a few miles to the south. Most of the approaches were straight in. We would go directly to the airfield and make one turn onto final approach into the wind.

This was different from flight school where we always entered the traffic pattern from down-wind and made two turns for final. We weren't in Fort Rucker anymore and you did not waste any time getting from the air down to the ground. I learned that the first day.

I did a brief landing check from 1500 feet and at 500 feet I turned on final, down to the center of the short runway and then hovered over to the signal company pad. I must humbly admit, it was done very smoothly and I was proud of my first flight. We shut down the aircraft and a waiting jeep took us to operations. The crew chief and gunner took care of the aircraft, refueled it from a fuel truck and did their checks on it while we were gone.

After meeting with the operations officer, he told the aircraft commander as I listened in, what he wanted us to do a courier run in the morning and in the afternoon do a re-supply to all his little bases. Now I really was on my first combat mission and I was excited. It was not like we were flying into the teeth of the enemy but we were heading into the Iron Triangle, a hot AO, also called a 'free fire' zone.

We met our couriers, three guys with a big box of codes and other classified information, heading to a small communication center west of Cu Chi close to the Cambodian border. These were Special Forces camps and they monitored enemy troop movements on the Ho Chi Minh trail.

My duty on this sortie was to navigate. By taking this responsibility, I was learning the company operational area. I talked on the radio, got our clearance to takeoff and told the aircraft commander which way to head. It was obvious that he knew the area like the back of his hand but I was still giving directions and he followed them.

I got him to the first two sites without any problems. I realized that I was good at this. I also made marks with my grease pencil on the windshield, noting how many passengers and cargo per sortie we carried. On our first stop, the helipad was near a small hamlet and next to it was a pond. As we approached, I could see small kids, half dressed, fishing with large nets.

When we landed, a Special Forces sergeant met the aircraft and led the three guys into a small underground bunker while we waited. The crew chief and the gunner talked more about where I was from and formally introduced themselves. I now started to feel like I was a part of this crew—just like I had seen in those World War II movies.

After about four hours of flying to these little outposts that were guarding the roads and rivers to Sargon, we went back to Cu Chi for lunch. We always carried a case of C rations. That's combat rations with eight meals inside. There were four different kinds' ham and eggs, beef patties, spam and turkey. Each had a small package of three cigarettes in a pack, a dessert type cake, fruit and a chocolate bar.

I learned that the chocolate bar was called a John Wayne bar. It was thick and heavy chocolate. It had so much energy in it that after eating one, you could take on a company of NVA. Our aircraft commander decided to eat in the signal company's mess hall. We had hamburgers and French fries.

They were OK but not at all like what I got at home just 10 days ago. I started wondering if those C rations were better—not! Through my year of flying in Vietnam, I would learn every place I could go to get a good hot meal. I would never go hungry when I was in country.

After lunch, we were in the aircraft and off on the afternoon sorties. A sorti was a take-off to the next lending point. This time, it was re-supply runs to a half dozen communication sites. These were radio intercept stations and re-transmitting positions. We carried batteries, new radios, parts, food, water and ammunition. We would take a load to one place, come back, reload and fly to the next place.

One was on top of the mountain and the others near small villages. Some were all American units and others had advisors to the South Vietnamese Army, known as ARVN. We also carried men from place to place, some going on R and R, other FNG's going to their new units and others going home. We also carried the mail. I found it fun and hard work.

This was the longest time that I had ever sat in a pilot seat and my butt hurt. After eight hours of flying time and about 10 hours away from our base, we were heading home. I never thought that I would get used to the pain in my ass but I did. Soon that would be no problem at all and there would be longer days and nights to fill my logbook.

We got back to our base, refueled and parked the ship in our assigned revetment. The AC went to operations to turn in our classified material and I helped the crew chief and gunner clean the aircraft of all this day's dust and dirt. I was done with my first combat day and I was excited. At dinner, I relived what I had done and then went to the officers' club for a few drinks and comradeship.

I was asked by the other pilots what I thought of my first day. I said it was pretty good—with a big smile on my face. I was now a member of this company. I was a combat pilot. After a few drinks, I went back to my room and wrote to my mother about that first day.

The combat support missions, better known as ash and trash missions, were really varied. One day, you would carry supplies and people around the country. The next day you would be working for Special Forces, doing reconnaissance of their area, bringing food and ammunition to outposts on the Cambodian frontier.

Also, there were those missions working for the Red Cross and special services. We would fly 'donut dollies' out to visit the troops at forward bases and fire support Artillery bases. There are also missions to take sports stars and other celebrities out to visit the troops.

The other mission was that of carrying troops into the face of the enemy. This is what everybody saw on TV and in the newspapers. During the first half of my tour in Vietnam, we worked mainly with American units. From time to time, we did work carrying Vietnamese soldiers. We would fly about two or three days of combat assaults for each week.

They would range from four aircraft to as many as 15 or more. We would all come together early in the day and get a briefing on who we were working for, where we were going to pick them up, where we were going to take them and what was the strength and nature of the bad guys. We would also be briefed on our support. There were times when we had a big formation a command and control (C&C) aircraft would help us find the landing zones (LZ's).

The C&C ship had an overall view of what was happening and could help coordinate support. We would have helicopter gunships on almost all our combat assaults. From time to time, we had fighter aircraft from the Air Force and anytime we wanted or needed it, we had field Artillery.

The mission would start out from our base going to a pick-up zone (PZ). The first assault I was in had 10 ships. We were going to haul two companies from the 9th Infantry Division. We could carry about seven troops on each aircraft. With those numbers, we were going to do many sorties to get both companies to the landing zone (LZ).

At the PZ, the troops were all lined up, waiting for each helicopter, in the correct number for each trip. We landed in line right in front of each shock. I was not flying, as I did all the checks. Once we were on the ground, I looked at the faces of the soldiers getting into my ship.

They were fully loaded with backpacks lots of ammo and their weapons. Our crew chief got out to help them in and place them orderly around the cabin area. For combat assaults, we took all the seats out except for the crew chief and door gunner.

I was amazed at what I saw in those young men. Some men looked very determined; they had their war face on! Others showed no more concern than getting into a car going down to the corner store. I did not see anyone that had what I thought was fear in their eyes. I was told later that getting to the LZ was what concerned the veterans.

They would say that there isn't any place to hide in the sky. Once we got our load on board, we would take off in line and then move into our formation that would be good for the LZ we were going into. That was determined by the shape of the LZ. We would fly in at echelon left or right or a V formation and sometimes trail formation.

As I looked about once we were in formation, the power of 10 aircraft flying together came over me. A flight of 10 helicopters meant that we had 20 machine guns, our door gunners with M60's. We also had four helicopter gunships, with rockets and heavy machine guns. When we were about 30 minutes out, the Air Force fighters came in and bombed and worked the LZ over with machine guns. We also had field Artillery pounding them.

As we flew toward our LZ, I could feel the excitement build in my chest with all the ships around me and all the fire power we had, I felt protected. I wondered, "Who could stand up to all this?" The field Artillery rounds came in, shot from miles away. The large rounds started hitting the tree line all around the LZ. Then they started hitting a little back in the trees.

When we started on short final, they stopped. My heart was beating harder now, my eyesight sharpened and the colors of the jungle around me got brighter. Then the gunships played their part. They fired rockets and machine guns into the tree line right next to where we were going to land.

I had never heard such noise before—my head was rocked by the waves of sound! The last rocket hit the ground just before we cleared the trees and at that moment, the crew chief and door gunners started opening up with their machine guns. Our machine guns fired about 500 rounds a minute and the noise added more intensity to this first combat assault for me.

By this time, the troops were all gearing up to get out of the helicopter. When we were about a foot off the ground, they were ready to jump out. Some were standing in the door and others seemed to dive out for the ground. Once all of the troops had exited our helicopter in maybe 10 seconds from touchdown to takeoff again.

The crew chiefs and gunners open fire again and the helicopter gunships started working a little further back in the tree line. After we got off the ground and headed back to the PZ, I had a cigarette to help me calm down a bit. In about 15 minutes, it would be my turn at the controls.

When we landed in front of our line of troops, my aircraft commander looked at me with a critical eye. I could also feel the eyes of my crew chief and door gunner looking at the back of my helmet. Jim said in a low voice, "It's your turn, you have the controls."

I looked at him and said, "I have the controls, sir!"

He came right back with, "don't call me sir, you f**kin' new guy!"

I quickly looked at the troops getting on board and then stared at the ship ahead of me, knowing that I must keep my place. No more than 5 feet behind and 3 feet to the left or right. With only a very few minutes on the ground, we did a pre-takeoff check and we were off with our seven troops in the back. The troops were sitting in the middle of the helicopter or sitting in the door with their feet dangling out.

As I settled into the process of controlling my aircraft and flying in close formation, my aircraft commander would tell me from time to time to get closer or stay in position. He was urgent about these instructions but it was only to move a few feet up or back. I felt that I was doing OK this first time out.

The trip took 15 minutes from takeoff to touchdown and things started happening almost right away. Everyone got ready to face the enemy once again. The door gunner and the crew chief charged their weapons and the troops settled in, ready to start fighting as soon as they exited the helicopter. I was starting to get excited but the task of flying kept my mind and thoughts focused. This kept me surprisingly calm.

The troops on the ground were in contact with the enemy we wanted to kill. The radio was alive with calls for aircraft to attack positions and asking how far out we were. Gunships where working an area to our right and the smoke and noise was once again amazing!

On short final, some of the NVA turned their attention to us. I could see out of the corner of my eye tracers going below our formation but none hit us. Our fire made it hard for the enemy to concentrate.

Just before touchdown, I could feel the troops moving around the back of the aircraft ready to jump off as soon as the skids touched the dirt. It was a smooth landing not soft but firm. No more than 10 seconds, maybe less, we were back in the air, still in formation, heading back to the PZ for another load of grunts. Then it hit me. My legs shook but only I was aware of it. As we got to about 1,000 feet above the ground, everyone relaxed.

A thought came to my mind, "Wow, we have to do this again!" But I also had a smile on my face—I did pretty well for an FNG. There would be a few more weeks of combat assaults before I could get comfortable with all the noise, the smoke and people trying to kill me.

As I landed, the aircraft commander said, 'I have the controls.' I let go and marked on the windshield the sorti and number of troops that we had carried. As a third load climbed in, I got a cigarette out and made it ready for when we got back in the air.

It was a clear day, an amazing day and it was the time that I was scared half to death. I never thought that I would be hit either in my body or my helicopter. But the laws of war, the numbers game, finally got to me. I was on a resupply trip to a fire support base north of the city of Tay Ninh which the grunts called 'Rocket City'. It was an add-on mission at the end of the day.

After completing a full day of moving cargo and people around the south part of Vietnam. I had gotten back to base early in the evening and was refueling my helicopter when operations called on the radio. There was a need for a hydraulic hose at a fire support base and they wanted it right away. Since I had a full bag of gas, I was sent over to the big supply depot at our base to pick up the hose.

It was an hour and 15-minute flight to Tay Ninh, so we stopped for gas in route. Then all we would have to do was drop off the hose and fly home. It was starting to get dark but I had been in the area earlier that day and felt that I knew the way. When we got there, I made calls to operations and they put a couple of lights on the landing pad.

It was an easy approach, all the trees had been cut down for a couple of hundred yards around the base. When we landed, I shut down the helicopter. We talked to one of the officers, as they unloaded the hose.

This Artillery officer was thanking me for coming all the way up there with the hose. They needed it because they had fire support missions that night and they wanted all their guns ready. As we were shaking hands, I heard a whiz in the air and looked over to the other side of the fire support base and rounds were impacting. I didn't even say goodbye and ran back to my helicopter.

My copilot and I started and were just about up to full power. We were taking off when we heard rounds from a machine gun hit the right rear of our aircraft. We were barely at a hover when all the emergency lights came on, telling us that the engine was hit. With no power to the rotor blades, we settled back into the LZ.

There was no hesitation. We all jumped out and ran through the gate into the base itself and looked for cover. One of the sergeants on the perimeter directed us to the base operations. They asked for our call signs, so they could call and tell everybody that we were OK and send someone to come and get us. The four of us, not used to being on the ground and not wanting to be on the ground, started wondering if we would have to fight to stay alive.

They told us that all this action firing at the base was not unusual. It happened about every other night and our helicopter gave them another target to shoot at. I didn't think of it that way. I had been flying in country for seven months and this was the closest that I had come to getting hit.

We were on the ground for about two hours when another helicopter from our battalion came and picked us up and took us back home. We got there about midnight. When we got back, I went to operations and gave them a debrief of what happened. They told me that my aircraft would be picked up the very next day.

The medic in our unit checked us all and said we were OK. The operations officer asked me if we were good to fly the next day. I said sure. I went over to the mess hall, had myself some late-night scrambled eggs and then to my quarters for a couple of beers. I fell asleep right away, knowing that I would be flying in about six hours.

One big thing that I learned when I was in Vietnam, my first combat zone, was that letters from home, were so very important to how you felt each day. The person that I wrote the most was my mother. She was always worrying about me, from the time I was a little kid until the day she died. When I was learning how to fly that first day, the first lesson, I told her I was going to go flying and taking my first trip in an airplane and I was going to be the pilot.

She had a noticeable, apprehensive look on her face. She got real close to me and said, "When you get to the airfield, call me and when you land, call me again, so that I will know that you're safe."

When I got to Vietnam and settled into the replacement company, I wrote her a nice long letter, telling her about my trip over the vast Pacific Ocean and that Vietnam was such a strange place, hot and with very little people dressed in very strange ways. Then when I got assigned to my unit, I wrote to her again. Then when I was assigned to the company and got my quarters, I wrote to her and told her all about the jeep ride, my new unit and my new roommate.

I did write to other people. I had a girlfriend at the time and I wrote to her. My Aunt Callie, my brothers and my father, all got letters. After about three weeks in country, I got my first letters, four of them and they were all from my mother. I felt really good that she was writing to me and telling me all that was going on at home.

And for the rest of the time there, I got a package a month, mostly sweet things, cookies, meat in cans and sometimes, some sort of clothing. My mother was getting into knitting and low and behold, came a box of her first efforts. A box of wool socks! I thought she knew, as I told her in almost every letter how hot it was. She thought that I needed them, so I wore them.

All the other letters kind of trickled in. I never got a letter from my dad. My Aunt Callie and my dear cousin Marcia would write but my girlfriend stopped very soon after I got there. I felt great comfort in getting the Sunday newspaper my mother would send with the packages of food and news of the family. So what did I tell my mother?

I told her about my daily life, about what we had for breakfast, lunch and dinner, about all the cities that I was flying to and about the times that I carried loads of troops. But that was it. As far as the hard times, being shot at, the faces on the troops that we landed in the hot LZ's and the long hours each day of flying all kinds of missions around Vietnam—she did not hear about it.

I felt that I could not burden her with all that I was going through. I couldn't shower her with the times that I was so scared that my legs shook. I couldn't tell her about late afternoon missions that ran to midnight and flying home in the total darkness that was Vietnam.

It's not that I wanted her to think that I was just having a good time flying around this small Asian country but I just did not want her to worry about me every day and have that fear take over her life. I knew if something happened to me, she would find out within hours.

As I think back on it now, I wrote my mother at the end of the day and I tried to write three times a week. Normally at the end of the day after we've flown for hours after post flight in the aircraft, then to dinner in the mess hall and then maybe a movie and a few drinks at our small officers' club. I feel that the reason I didn't tell her things was that I was coping with them myself.

This was a time to push all that stuff that happened to me and the things that I did out of my mind. I remember that after writing to my mother that I felt relaxed. Then I would fall asleep and the next day would seem brand new.

The thing that I must say was that writing letters is a lifelong joy for me. There's an old saying that you have to send letters to get letters and there was status in your unit for people who had letters coming to them. They were seen as lucky individuals. They had people who cared about them and were never alone.

When I was very new in Vietnam, flying almost every day, with a day off in between long stretches of flying, my company got to work with the Fifth Special Forces Group. They controlled all the special operations in the southern half of Vietnam. We had been doing combat assault for the Ninth Infantry Division and we completed about 10 sorties that day.

It was about midafternoon when we got the word that we had completed that mission and four out of our 15 helicopters were put on standby for another mission we were briefed for. The other helicopters flew back to base and we refueled at a nearby airfield. Then we waited in our helicopters for the word to go pick up some Special Forces troops.

After about an hour of sitting in our cockpit, the word came down that we were supposed to fly over to this village and pick up the troops. When we arrived, we got a load of about five of the most oddly dressed soldiers I'd ever seen. When we landed, we were told to shut down. We were to wait for our takeoff time.

We landed in a line formation and shut down our helicopters. I was in the Trail End Charlie. Our five soldiers got on board, made themselves as comfortable as possible and started doing inventory on their equipment. They didn't have helmets. They had scarves tied around their heads. They were not clean shaven and some had pretty good beards. Their uniforms looked kind of dirty and there was nothing shining on them.

After about 10 minutes on the ground, we got the word that we were going to takeoff in about 20 minutes. We got the location and my aircraft commander marked it on the map. As we settled in for the 20-minute wait, I looked back at this rag tag crew, they had this faraway look on their faces. It was not like they were scared or anything but not like they were really there.

They were concentrating on what they were going to be doing. Two out of our five were sharpening the biggest knives I'd ever seen and the other three were cleaning rifles, AR 15's. In my thoughts, I started wondering what we were going to be doing and where we were going. I asked the aircraft commander and he said that we were going to a village where intel reported a suspected party headquarters for this district and our mission was to capture as many VC as we could.

As we got closer to the takeoff time, I started really getting nervous, I think that I was in country for just over a month on this day. My mind raced through all kinds of scenarios, all of them scared me to death and I had never done this before.

Two minutes before takeoff time, we started engines, everything was ready to go and precisely on time, we took off. I was told to stay very low and follow the aircraft in front of me but we didn't fly as close as we normally did in combat assaults. The village that was our target was only 15 minutes away.

We came to the village from the east and the first two helicopters landed on the north side and second group landed on the south side. On short final, our five troops were standing on the skids and before we touched down, they jumped to the ground and charged into the village.

We immediately took off and got back into trail formation. We went about three miles to the north and did a left-hand orbit. Within 10 minutes, we were called back in to pick up the troops. We all landed in a line on the north side of the village. As soon as we touched down, the Special Forces guys ran to the choppers with five prisoners. They pushed them onto the helicopters. We got one of the prisoners along with our five special ops guys.

This older man was the first suspected VC I had seen that close. He was a small man and looked very scared. Once we took off, they put a blindfold on him and we settled into the 20-minute ride to base. When we landed, two light trucks met us at the airfield and the Special Forces and their prisoners got off and quickly climbed into their vehicles.

As I watched them leave, I could see that their faces had changed into broad smiles. That was my indication, besides the fact that we didn't get shot at, that the mission had been a very big success and the stress relief was clear on everyone's faces.

I was out on a mission in October 1970. It was a support mission day and things were going well. I had not really thought about Tom for a couple of weeks. We had talked on the phone when I had duty officer and things with Tom and I were both in good shape. He was Flying Cobras and excited about that fast, new helicopter.

I got a call from operations late in the day, telling us to come back right away and that I was going to be an escort officer. I looked at the other pilot and asked, "What the hell is an escort officer?" He gave me a puzzled look and the rest of the crew didn't know either.

I had forgotten about the promise that Tom and I made to each other those many months ago telling our moms that we want one or the other to bring our body home if the worst happened. I had no idea that either of us was going to get hurt—let alone get killed. We were 23-year-old pilot warriors. We thought we were invincible.

When I got back to base, I was told to go talk to the operations officer. The first words out of his mouth were, "Do you know Tom Barnett?" I said that I did—we were classmates. He handed me orders, as he told me that Tom had been killed and I was to take his remains home. It didn't click—I gave him the deer in the headlights look. He said, "Ray, you have 30 minutes to pack a bag and catch the airplane back to the States."

As I think about that time, I can't even remember what my thoughts were. I ended up in an airplane with everybody else who had just finished their tour, going back to the States. My head was filled with all the thoughts that didn't track. What did his remains look like? Was his body all in bits and pieces? I've never been an escort officer. How do I know what to do? For a while, I panicked. The long flight back was filled with memories of all the things Tom and I had been through.

When we got to San Francisco, I showed my orders and I was taken to the mortuary unit at the Presidio. It was early in the morning. I was fitted with a new uniform. Then I was given orders to escort Tom's remains back to his home. I was given the tickets necessary to get the two flights that would take us back.

I went to a class where with four others, we were taught how to be an escort officer and what our duties were. Three of us were escorting soldiers from Vietnam and one was from Korea. When the class was finished, I was driven to the San Francisco airport cargo ramp where I found the shipping crate with Tom's coffin. I checked to make sure the paperwork was correct and I was given an American flag, which I spread over the coffin.

Then came the time to take it to the airplane's cargo hold. I watched men put the coffin onto a truck and we drove to the airplane. When we got there, I stood at attention and saluted the flag draped crate as it was loaded onto the airplane. When it was secure, I sat inside the plane.

I had one transfer in Chicago to get to Tom's hometown in Tennessee. During the transfer, I had to stand by the cargo door as it offloaded the casket. As soon as it was out of the plane, I ordered them to stop and I put the flag on the casket again. I stood at attention and saluted it all the way down.

During this time, the whole ramp could see what I was doing. Some people didn't seem to care and others looked away. I felt alone. This is how it was when we transferred to the next airplane and when we finally reached our destination.

A few years ago, I saw a movie called *Taking Chance*. It was about a Marine lieutenant colonel who took the remains of a Marine Corps private back home during one of the Gulf wars. The film was about all the people that this colonel met along the way getting this young Marine from Dover Air Force Base to his final resting place in Wyoming.

Along the way, people would praise him for what he was doing, say thanks for his service and offer prayers and affection toward the man that he was taking home. They weren't really making this trip alone. Everybody they came in contact with was helping him carry this young Marine home.

In 1970, the Vietnam War was not popular. My experience was not at all like that of the escort officer in the film. America at the time did not care about their military. They wanted it all to go away and stay far away from them. Tom had the bad luck to be killed in a war that the country just wanted to end. Tom and I paid the price on that journey home. Not only would people not look at me and not talk to me but also I could see in their eyes, they weren't even seeing me. Bringing Tom home was the toughest duty assignment I ever had.

In Tom's hometown, Parallel, Tennessee, the family undertaker met me at the airport and I went through the whole ceremony again, putting the flag on the coffin and saluting it until we got it into the hearse. When we got to the funeral home, the funeral director opened the crate and took out the casket.

The funeral director opened the casket. He asked me to examine Tom's remains to make sure he was presentable to his family. It was a hard thing to look at my best friend. He was a good man, a happy-go-lucky man, now lying there in full uniform, dead.

I was driven to his mother's home to a very tearful reunion. I had met his mom several times and she had accepted me as a second son. We had laughed and joked about Army training and what the future was going to be for us. Now she was in tears, holding on to me, asking me how this could have happened to her son. I remember telling her that I did not know, how a good man like her son could die in war. This was what war did to families.

The next day, we prepared for the funeral. The nearby reserve base sent over an honor guard and I talked to them about what we were going to do. I was the officer in charge and I would lead the ceremony. I sat in the back of the church and listened to what the minister and all his friends had to say about my dear friend.

After the service, there was the motorcade to the cemetery where the honor guard was waiting. We went over to the gravesite, there were more words about the heaven that was waiting for us all, the 21-gun salute, taps and the folding of the flag.

The folding of the flag by the coffin was a tradition that went back to the beginnings of our republic for those who had served in the military. The flag was crisply folded into a triangle with only the stars showing. It was handed to me after I saluted it. Then I walked to Tom's mother, knelt on one knee and handed her the flag.

I told her that this was a token of gratitude from a grateful nation for the sacrifice of her loved one. She cried, taking the flag and with tears in my eyes, I stood and saluted her and that flag. When the funeral was completed for my dear friend, Chief Warrant Officer Tom Barnett, I spent another day with his mother and shared my love as a brother for her son. I told her about all the events that made us so close. She seemed really grateful and with many heartfelt hugs, I knew that I had helped her start the grieving process.

All these many years later, I often think about him and wonder about the adventures that we would have had as young and then old men! The family stories that we would have had and the good and bad times we would have shared. We would have been good friends, brothers in arms, in life or death forever.

I was given a week's leave to go home to see my family. When I got home, my mother was visibly shaken by the fact that someone so close to me and someone she knew so well had been taken. My mother and I talked for the day and into the next day about family and what I was doing in Vietnam. I did not tell her about the close calls and the fact that people were trying to kill me. I told her about flying every day and the good people that were around me.

Those seven days went by quickly. On my third day home, I went up to McGuire Air Force Base, only 30 miles from my home and booked my flight back to Vietnam. On the day I left, my younger brother drove me to the base and hugged me goodbye.

When at home, I saw many friends and lots of family and no one ever asked me to stay home or not to go back. I would not have entertained that thought anyway. I had come to feel that my place was with my unit and the men that I had bonded with. They needed me. Besides, I wasn't going to show anybody that I was afraid.

Without hesitation, I climbed aboard that big airplane and flew off to our first stop in Anchorage, Alaska. The plane was full of soldiers from the East Coast heading to Vietnam for the first time and for many the second and third time. I settled into my seat and the next thing I knew, I was in Alaska. I was in my summer uniform and when we got off the airplane in October 1970, it was cold!

After a short layover where we walked around the terminal, got snacks or made phone calls home, we got back on that big bird and headed for the war zone. Again, I slept all the way and the next thing I knew, we were landing in Vietnam. When I got into the terminal, I gave my unit a call. They came and got me right away.

I checked into operations and they said they would give me a couple days to get used to things again and put me back on the schedule. I went to my room, unpacked my bag, sat on the end of my bed and talked to my roommate about what the world was like for a couple of hours.

At first, I was surprised that I felt so comfortable being back in Vietnam right away. It was like this place was my real home, the reality of my life. It wasn't like being at home in New Jersey. It wasn't all my friends and all the familiar surroundings. It was this reality of war and all my brothers were here now. They were fighting alongside of me and I finally realized what the term 'brotherhood of war' really meant.

When I had about two months to go in Vietnam, I was flying almost every day. This was my world. Getting up early in the morning, going out to the ramp, preparing my helicopter to go and taking off for a full day of flying. I grew to like this crazy life, not the war but the challenge of completing each day's mission.

Word had come down from higher headquarters, that everyone who was not 'volunteer-indefinite' but were reserve officers, would be discharged from the Army as soon as we got back to the world. I thought about this and came to a decision. Civilian life did not hold anything for me as a black man. I loved flying. I didn't know about flying jobs outside of the Army, so I thought another few years would help me work that out.

On one of my few days off, I went over to personnel to fill out my paperwork to stay in the Army and pick my next assignment. I got to the battalion office and I was assigned a senior NCO to help me fill out the paperwork. When we got done with all I needed to do to stay in the Army, he said it would be approved right away. Then he asked me where I wanted to go. I said I wanted to be stationed near my home at Fort Dix, New Jersey.

The sergeant leaned back in his chair and said, "Sir, do you like Vietnam?"

I looked him dead in the eye and said, "Hell no!"

He came upright in his chair and explained the facts, "If you go back to the States, you'll be back here in 18 months. I suggest that you go to Germany. The beer is great there and your assignment is for three years. Then they have to send you back to the States. That's 4 ½ years out of this hole in the ground and this war will be over by then!"

A smile came over my face. What great advice! My head was running through all the things about Europe I had heard when I was in school. I looked at him and said, "Sergeant, sign me up!"

Like everyone who had spent time in Vietnam during the war, you did a countdown of days till you were heading home. When we were in the 300s, we didn't pay too much attention to the number of days we had left but we did mark it off on our calendars.

I had one in my room and I marked those days off. I didn't start telling anybody how many days I had left when asked, until I had around 200 days to go. When I got under 100 days, I would tell anybody who looked at me, that I was a two-digit midget!

We walked around saying, "Short!" There were jokes about not being able to look over your boot tops, drowning in the shower or being too short for anybody to even see you. For me the real excitement about going home came when I had 30 days to go.

Before that I was just thinking about one day at a time, the next day's mission or if I was going to get any mail from home. Then I still had a lot of days to go but now thinking about going home became an obsession.

When I had about a week to go, I got my orders and started handing in all my equipment with no more thinking about the next day's missions. I really started thinking about what was it going to be like at home in the middle of summer. I never really thought that I was going to be killed but there were some scary times where that ugly thought snuck in my brain for a second. But now I knew it was going to happen, I was going home.

About five days out, I went to the replacement company and turned in my orders. I sent my travel uniform to the cleaners to get pressed and settled into a routine of going to check the flight list every day to find out if I was on the next flight out. As the song went, my bags were packed and I was ready to go.

But it took some time. A couple of flights were canceled and the backlog started adding up. When my name finally made the list, I was booked on a flight back to the world! That day marked 366 days in Vietnam.

When we loaded on the aircraft, everyone was very quiet. I was lucky to be seated by the window and I looked out on a foggy, rainy morning at Bein Hoa Air Force Base. As we taxied to the runway, it was so quiet inside the airplane, it was spooky. When we got to the end of the runway and started the run for takeoff, it seemed like all the tension in the world was released.

As that 707 lifted off the runway, a collective sigh of relief came over the aircraft with a great cheer that was deafening! As we settled down, people were now talking to each other. When we cleared Vietnamese air space, another large cheer erupted.

Our route home took us to Japan to a United States Air Force base in northern Japan. There we stretched our legs and looked around for an hour, as the airplane took on fuel. The next thing I remember was flying across the Pacific Ocean to Travis Air Force Base. We were all too tired and too excited about getting home to do any cheering about the takeoff from Japan or the landing in the United States.

We were hustled off to customs. It was about two in the morning and we were the only people around except for the inspectors. I got through customs with no problems and the customs inspector asked me where I was going. I told him back to Philadelphia, because I lived in New Jersey. He told me to get to the airport before eight in the morning. I gave him an odd look and he said, "You'll see why when you get to the airport."

I got there at about six that morning and went up to the USO airport facilities, where I took a shower, changed clothes into my travel uniform and got a little rest. That facility was on the top floor of the airport just inside the entrance.

When it was time to go to the gate for my flight, I saw outside the main entrance that about 100 or so demonstrators were yelling profanity, spitting on and generally trying to degrade all military people trying to get into the airport. I was so happy that that inspector had warned me—welcome back to America!

When the flight reached the Philadelphia area on final approach, I could see all the things that I remembered—the Phillies' baseball and the Eagles' football stadium, downtown Philadelphia, the Delaware River. Then I knew I was finally home!

When I got off the airplane and went into the terminal, the first person I saw was my mother waiting for me with open arms and tears in her eyes. I was so happy to see her. With tears in my eyes, I cried in a loud voice, "Mom!" We hugged and told how good it was to see each other.

I got my bag and we went down to the parking ramp. My mother had driven my sports car to pick me up. I climbed into the driver's seat and carefully drove out of the ramp onto a very crowded highway. As I tried to merge into traffic, a taxi driver almost ran into my car. I was so angry, I wound down the window and called him everything but a child of God!

Then I remembered that my mother was in the right seat. I looked over her with a sheepish grin and she said, "Raymond, your language has changed." From then on, I decided to watch my language. That started my healing from being in a war zone. I was happy to be home.

Bruce: With all the Artillery, Ranger and Airborne training I received after West Point, I was a professional soldier, trained by my country. I was prepared to fight in a war when duty called.

Leaving for Vietnam involved a series of goodbyes with friends and family. My dad had served in World War II in the Artillery, so he knew what possible assignments I could take on as an Artillery officer. Before I left, my mom handed me a yellow legal pad and said, "Write each day what you are doing."

My letters on these pieces of paper became the 'yellow pages'. In March 1969, I was 23 years old when I left for Vietnam. I had assured my mom that as a senior first lieutenant about to make captain, I would get some desk job out of harm's way. The desk job didn't quite work out. In fact, things got pretty crazy but I had some great jobs with good leaders—and some not so good.

My mother saved the 'yellow pages' and gave them back to me when she moved to Georgia in 2000. Audrey found them in 2018 and she typed them for me in 2020. I wanted them preserved for our children, Molly and Jon, so they would know what I was like as a soldier, some of the history of Vietnam and what I wrote to my parents and siblings.

The yellow pages started on 1 March 1969 and ended in November 1969, when I left the field and moved into the CuChi base camp. I became a REMF (Rear Echelon Mother F**ker). There are a lot of things that I cannot believe I wrote to my mother. They were the words of a 23-24-year-old professional soldier serving his country in a war zone.

Out in the boonies, we mocked the REMF's with their starched uniforms and polished boots but to keep one of us in the field, it took about 10 REMF's in the base camp. They ran the finance, admin, supply, maintenance, intelligence, helicopters, hospitals, command and control to make life almost livable out in the nasty places where we operated.

I ran a desk for my last 75 days in Vietnam keeping track of body counts—enemy soldiers killed by the 25th Infantry Division. The yellow pages had turned brown around the edges now but the words were still legible. The words I wrote home are in quotes below—I'll edit most of the boring stuff but it was exciting for me to read my story 50 years later.

"1 March—flew (5 ½ hours) from Boston and 3" of snow to sunny California. I included a poem by Rod McKuen. It began, 'You won't believe this but I'm going off to war.' So here I was on an airplane headed to Vietnam.

"3 March—Today began while in the air and it'll never end in 24 hours, as somewhere before we get to Vietnam, we cross the international date line. We will stop in Hawaii and Okinawa. The people going are all kinds. They make life pretty wonderful as usual. Life always has been good though. Maybe that's why I volunteered to go; America has always been so good to me. I sometimes wonder if war is the best way to be of service and I guess it is if that is what we need at the moment. The future should hold opportunities for service in other roles."

The next day I wrote, "stopped in Honolulu and it was really beautiful even at midnight. We are now going to stop at Wake Island because of the headwinds. We should get there in about 4 hours. Seems better than going 10 non-stop. Wake wasn't exactly a tropical paradise but the 30-minute stop was good for a stretch. The sun has finally caught up with us and it is really a beautiful sight. Okinawa looked interesting from the air and now 3 ½ hours to Bien Hoa."

As I looked back, we had flown through WWII history. The battle of Wake Island was part of the start of the war. The Japanese attacked the island and took it over. At the end of the war, the Japanese commander was hung for atrocities he ordered. Okinawa was the scene of some of the bloodiest fighting near the end of the war.

The American losses were so great, the President Truman made the decision to use the atomic bomb to save American lives that would have been lost had we invaded Japan, then on 4 March 1969, we landed in Vietnam.

Over the next nine months, I continued to write home. "Since my assignment wasn't up at 0700 this morning, I guess I might get the 173rd. I'm still hoping for it. I slept like a baby last night. I didn't think I would and yet I guess the plane ride tired me out more than I expected. There was a lot of chopper activity just outside the wire and some bombing far off but no mortars around here. War is hell.

"We flew over the country from Frisco to Bien Hoa over Cam Ranh Bay in a TWA 707. Rode a bus from there to here, had hot meals, movies, booze, music, hot showers, etc. since we arrived. Things can only get worse they tell me. Interesting that while I'm feeling so secure as we rode from BH to LB during the day, at night the ride requires an armed escort as the road is VC controlled.

"My assignment came down last night and I'm going to the 25th Infantry Division at Cu Chi. I was disappointed not getting the 173rd but the 25th was a good outfit. They came here from Hawaii, one brigade a few years ago and the rest last year. During Tet they got hit pretty hard, so that's why I'm going there. It's wonderful to be needed and I'll have a new home this afternoon. (Later) The new home is nothing to write home about but I have run into old friends.

"The Division Command Sergeant Major is CSM Howard Brosseau who was Sergeant Major USCC while I was at West Point. Paul Cline is General Prear's aide, he has 4 months to go. Anyone who is 'short' (less than 100 days to go) rubs it in." Captain Haywood was General Williamson's aide. I met him when he was an instructor in Ranger School.

"Orientation School got canceled today; the S3 said it was a waste anyway and assigned me as a forward observer (FO) to A Company, 2/34 Armor. I spent the day packing and getting 'ma shit in order' as the old sarge would say. A pleasant surprise in reporting to A 2/34. Art Schulz is the CO. He was a year ahead of me at WP and in my company, B2, when I was a plebe.

"Must get ready to go out tonight on my first night laager. The recon Sgt. is SP4 William Smith and the RTO is PFC Clarence Murchison—Smitty and Murch." Smitty was white and Murch was black.

The first time we got into a serious firefight and I called in my first fire mission. Our fire direction guys were surprised I was so calm. I wasn't but that's when the Ranger training kicked in. I was confident that I could do the job and protect these guys. A pattern developed and defending yourself and your troops became a daily part of life. Killing enemy soldiers was also a necessary part of it. You could see the pattern.

"The plan was for A Company to act as the reaction force for the FSB, so we set up a night laager just off highway 8A with 3 tanks and 7 APC's and 2 Jeeps. Of course, we surrounded ourselves with claymores and Artillery. I planned and shot my first fire mission in Vietnam at 2037 hours 14 March 1969. The perimeter was pretty light.

"To shoot in my targets, I just called in one I had preplanned and asked for Willie Peter (white phosphorous or WP so I could see it in the dark) on the deck by base piece with 2 guns in adjustment and 2 in effect. Once I saw the WP, I just moved the rounds around a bit. I didn't sleep well last night.

"Today, we moved into FSB Crockett about 0700. I visited with Carl Bowen, a classmate and had lunch with him; the Artillery had hot chow. We didn't. When I went back to see what events were transpiring, I found Smitty sitting on a track already.

"A LRRP had found some VC activity and along with some ARVN (Army of the Republic of VN) popular forces, not exactly crack troops. We were going to sweep the bad guys out. I ran over to the TOC to plan some fires; it wasn't too hard, as the activity was 600 meters north of where we had spent last night!

"We swept the area and it was heavily booby trapped and tunneled. I got to call in some more fire and worked the rounds up a stream. Charlie had grabbed his hat and made it. We didn't find him but I learned a lot. Clearance for fires is difficult to get and occasionally the battalion FDC screws up and doesn't clear the right ones; that is what happened to my blocking fires, so when the Armor asked for them, I couldn't deliver.

"Clearing them requires both military and political permission to fire; necessary but time consuming, if in contact with the enemy, they speed up and the process, I'm told we shall see.

"The guy I replaced was pretty popular and I felt some problems working to fill his shoes. I worked on it to make shoes of my own to become a part of the unit. They refer to the former FO as FO, (pronounced foe.) People are beginning to call me FO. I consider this a compliment.

"The days may have little activity, as we do most of our shooting and fighting at night. I get busy from about 1800 on clearing fires, plotting ambush patrols and planning H & I fires for the night and clearing defensive targets for tomorrow; for the next few hours, we just wait for some action. I created a direction finder for the tower at Crockett.

"When we had some movement on the perimeter the other night, the grunts on the 40-foot tower called me and asked me to shoot at it. I asked them for a grid and a direction and they gave them to me. By talking on the radio, we couldn't get the rounds where they wanted them, so I put on my steel pot and climbed up the tower.

"No wonder they couldn't hit the target, their grid was off 1,000 meters! I adjusted the rounds and went to bed. To solve the problem, I developed a pointer system much like the forest rangers used to use to 'fix' a fire. After explaining to the guys how to use it, I haven't had to go back on the damn tower in the dark and they have directed fires pretty accurately with it.

"Last night, the village down the road about a mile got hit. We cranked up the tracks and Smitty and I went clanking off into the night on the back of a tank. I was praying to beat the band and fortunately, we did not get hit. It was a wild experience. The next day, one of our tanks hit a 100-pound bomb mine on a RIF (reconnaissance in force)—no one was killed but it rang a few bells and burst some ear drums.

"We have been running sweeps all day and laagers all night and that leaves about one hour in the morning and one at night to eat, shower and shave. We have been on the go all week. I guess most significant about the operation was that I finally ran into the North Vietnamese Army (NVA) with the guts to stand and fight."

I wrote down my thoughts after these NVA troops played the AK boogy over my head. "Observations, 30 March: Today at about 1015, I ran into my first significant contact with the crack thump of AK47 fire and an RPG (rocket propelled grenade) landing close. I get the feeling that in combat there is such exhilaration and death could come so swiftly with apparent indifference, that this is the only reason a person can withstand the pressure."

I was finally in a war after years of working to get into West Point, four years there, studying everything from Shakespeare to military history, strategy and tactics, a year plus of training and preparation. After one month of being tested. I was tough, strong and was not about to let any enemy get the better of me.

The days started to reveal a pattern—seek out and destroy the enemy. When we found VC or NVA troops, we would back off and pound them with Artillery, then move in and kill as many as we could. My job was to protect those grunts around me. I was good at what I did but just moving in the bush with booby traps, mines and enemy fire, the pressure was intense.

"April 1969: We ran into more VC again today. In last night's contact, I must have fired $5,000 of Artillery and illumination rounds over the battlefield. I fired some 155 at a light we had outside the wire. It was a lovely sight and a loud bang. When the battery fired for effect (four guns, six rounds as fast as they can fire), it sounded like a freight train going overhead. I checked the results of my fire last night and found nothing.

"The other night when I shot the two missions at the same time, there is a good chance I got him moving out but there is no real evidence to be sure. They seem to be as good as we are at getting their dead and wounded off the battlefield. Body counts here are pretty accurate, in the 25th at least and Charles and the NVA have taken a hell of a beating in this area.

"I really don't understand why the enemy sticks around. Every time he masses, he gets blown away. The 2/27 used some classic Artillery when a convoy got hit 'VC in the open, VT fire for effect' and they killed 88 out of 100 with a battery six rounds—that's six guns (105mm howitzers) shooting six rounds as fast as they can.

"If you are in the open, VT (variable time fuses) blow up about 10 feet off the ground and send shrapnel all over the place. If the 88 out of 100 is true, that is a very efficient kill ratio. Later in discussion with a Vietnamese soldier, he explained it this way. 'To you, it is a war. For us, it is our country'.

"Happy Easter. The Bible says, 'Jesus died for our sins.' I wonder why so many are dying here. We went from Crockett to Trang Bang and then escorted a tanker to the Go Da Ha Bridge on the Quan Hien Thein (River). The tanker had to leave its fuel with the US Navy installation beneath the bridge, so they invited us to stay for chow. It was great and the Navels really know how to live. I met Jack Young, USNA '67 and we worked up a bet on the Army-Navy Game.

"After escorting the tanker back toward Trang Bang, we went to FSB Hampton where I was greeted by Mike Cox, battery commander of the 155's there. There were really quite a few fine people there from the arty and the ¾ Cav. I shot in my DT's at night and brought one into within 200 meters. I knew it was close when I heard schrap metal falling all around. Only took one incoming tonight.

"Mike has had some bad times with his battery. For four months, they did a good job but in the last month, his world turned black. One of his men was killed when a bunker collapsed on him. Then one of the guns fired out and the VT round landed in the middle of Go Da Ha, killing five and wounding many. I kept my defensive targets (DT's) a little further out tonight.

"I was in the middle of shooting my DT's and in the process of making a correction when I heard a voice behind me, '33 November (my call-sign) you don't know what you're doing.' Of all the people in the world to show up at this firebase, it was Gary Carlson.

"His wife had just had a baby girl and he was a happy man. We talked until one o'clock and it was really great to see old Gary. Apparently, he had done a fine job in the ¾ Cav and has been nominated for two silver stars. He'd take command of 'B' troop soon.

"Flew two hours today on convoy cover in a LOH (light observation helicopter). In talking with the Artillery, I found out how much human life is valued over here—we pay $40 for killing a civilian and we pay $200 for a rubber tree. On the second day at FSB Hampton, I finally figured out why my DT's came so close that first night.

"The LNO who just left had our position plotted 300 meters out! Thus, when I plotted the target 600 meters away, naturally it looked close, because the first round was only 300 m out. I dropped 100 m and got all that splash on the wire again naturally, because now it was only 200 m out. Mistakes like that get people killed. Fortunately, I didn't.

"We RIF-ed (reconnaissance in force) through the Filhole Rubber Plantation today in the NE corner where a stream fed the Big Blue (Saigon River). The VC dede-ed to the other side. In the meantime, four eagle flights of ARVN Marines were landed in front of them. The shooting was hot and heavy for a while but the VC apparently decided they'd rather fight the Marines than us. We got five of them with one ARVN killed. If all the Vietnamese units were like them, we wouldn't have to be here.

"Not much sleep. The company planned 'road runner' operation on highway 8A because a mine blew up a truck, killing the driver and wounding a passenger. We had to patrol from Mule Skinner gate at Cu Chi to the Phu Cong Bridge. The day found us never having gone to bed from the night before. We searched for more bodies, got some breakfast and went out on a short RIF. I was really tired.

"If I weren't a Ranger, I'd have told someone where to go. We were a blocking force for some ARVN PF's. They didn't get anything and we didn't get back into Cu Chi until late. Then we went out to our night laager. It hit the fan just before my radio watch started at 2200.

"The ARVN compound at Trung An started taking incoming and our CRIP platoon got hit. We moved SW across a cemetery, as I called in illumination. We reached the village, much of the firing stopped and then it started again big time.

"We went racing west down 8A and then turned south. After moving SW for 1000m, it got really quiet. As the CRIP platoon swept the village, we then moved east. That was when it hit the fan from the north. All hell broke loose and the fire was intense. We backed off and called in air strikes; those Cobras tore 'em up.

"The CRIP moved down and killed one. Where the rest went, I don't know. As we went back to the night laager (NL), we got hit again; nine got away but one didn't. In this war of the 'unseen enemy', this body count did morale a lot of good. It is sad to lose people to mines and booby traps without any action to take.

"When Charles gets caught, he is a dead man. I felt no sympathy for this guy. I tried to keep this thing impersonal but Lee Preston was killed here last month. It was a relief to see that little bastard lying dead in front of me. As we moved out to pursue, we got about 1,000m south and the NL got hit again. We went back, circled up and I called in Artillery. The sniper kept shooting until I walked 155's around to the N and NE. Total body count was three.

"We RIF-ed south of Trang Bang in an NVA infested area. We had contact but they didn't want to fight. They ran. I took the night laager out and got it set up south of Trung An where the contact had been the night before. It was a good experience for me, as I am learning to employ tanks and APC's.

"Tonight in Trung An, we had a nasty firefight and there were three probable enemy WIA and one water buffalo KIA, probably VC. In that action last night, there were AK holes in a metal chaplain's case we had on the track in front of me. The case was a foot from my head where I was talking on the radio.

"We went out at 1830 and set up a night laager with only one tank and 5 APC's. Some ARVN troops were supposed to be with us but rather than keep them on the perimeter, the CO told me to set them out as an ambush. I put them 100m. to the north as an AP, gave them a star cluster as a warning that they were coming in if things got hot and told them quite explicitly with sign language that I personally would shoot the 13th man to come in.

"They had twelve troops. The tankers said I must have scared them, because even when I shot in the arty, they stood up but didn't run. They were awake all night. We had a sweep in the Filhol and ran across some new bunkers with rice left out and fresh water just drawn. Also, there was an APC that had hit a mine and Charles had used a hack saw blade to cut through 1 ½ inches of aluminum armor plate and carried the pieces off to fortify his bunkers.

"You just can't help admiring the ingenious bastards. 2,000 meters north, we caught up with three of them and put an end to their ingenuity. On the way back, we hit two mines but fortunately there was no damage. Today was the first time I had done any Artillery shooting from a chopper. I called in the mission on the ground and halfway through, I got to go up in a chopper and finish it in the air.

"Things are really different from up there and while it was easier to adjust the fire and see my corrections on the ground, it is quite different when you have been used to shooting from the ground. Originally, what I saw as bunkers on the ground just looked like normal land formations from above. That's how good Charlie and the NVA are at camouflage.

"When you are in a combat zone and in enemy contact on most days, you don't pay a lot of attention to politics. You also quickly lose the idealism you came with. Part of 'Duty, Honor, Country', the US Military Academy's motto, was the first thing to go. I was not fighting for my country anymore. I was killing the bad guys, so our guys would survive—that was my duty.

"There was honor in that duty of protecting the troops. Also, my attitude toward the people was changing. My respect for the NVA soldiers was growing as was my disdain for the ARVN. During this time Buddhist monks, a minority religion in South Vietnam persecuted by the Catholic majority, were setting themselves on fire.

"What was that about? I was getting the distinct feeling we were supporting the wrong side. At the same time, we were losing our soldiers with over 1,000 KIA in April, down from last month but still 1,000 too many for a war that should have ended.

"I was assigned as F.O. to an infantry unit protecting the Go Da Ha Bridge. Larry Burrows from Life Magazine was at the bridge today, shooting a story on a Chu Hoi who claims to have been the guy who blew the bridge last year. What this guy says conflicts with the way the engineers theorize it was done.

"A lieutenant who was here when the bridge was blown got pretty disgusted with the whole idea of giving this guy so much publicity. How can you tell how much good it does? They tell us that one Chu Hoi is as good as ten dead VC, a POW as good as five. Try to remember that when someone is shooting at you!

"I was wondering why I was out on the bridge where to me there didn't seem to be a great need. When I went back to CC, I found out. The command track had hit a 155 mine and everyone was either killed or wounded except the CO. What gets me is that the sergeant who took my place in the company while I was on the bridge got hit pretty badly. That could have been me!

"One boy lost both legs below the knees and three were killed. Anyone of them could have been me. That was sobering in itself but the other aspect was just as bad. If I had been there, perhaps it wouldn't have happened. Anyway, someone up there was protecting me but the loss of those people was hard to take.

"Incoming M79 and 60mm put us on 100% alert tonight and got me calling in illumination. The arty clearances came through in five minutes. The infantry 81 mm were ready in two minutes but couldn't get near the target. The night continued. It appeared that the 81's aiming circle was about 1000 mils out; fortunately, we were only shooting illumination. He could have killed people.

"Got off the bridge today but before I leave B Company, 2/14, I should note some of the people I've worked with. Captain Boyle is really good. He commands and has excellent discipline. Some of his lieutenants do not. First Sargent Holbrook is one of the best NCO's I've seen. He has quite a history with the 25th and in particular with this company. What a character!

"When things weren't going right, every other word was profane and 'bricka-bracka-bullshit' covers whatever was happening. He was colorful to say the least and on a first name basis with most of the newsmen who visited.

"The Vietnamese here are an RF company and Dhi Hui (Captain) Minh is outstanding. RF and PF forces are comparable to the National Guard in the States and like the Guard, some units are good, some not-so. Minh wants his men to meet our standards, so he runs a good outfit.

"They have a long way to go as do the rest of the ARVN forces but with people like him, perhaps there is hope. Except for the Marines and though some improvements have been made, the majority are still thieves, stealing anything that isn't nailed down. We left Trung An last week and they must have taken every chicken in the village; not our standard.

"Last night was my first in FSB Emery since we first laagered there two weeks ago. It is pretty secure now with two rows of triple concertina around it and all the outside bunkers finished. Back to the war—laagered on good old 8A and nothing happened. Since this is the time of the May offensive, everyone is on alert but things aren't supposed to start popping until 19th, which is HO's birthday and the NVA have vowed they will spend it in Cu Chi.

"This night will live in my memory for a long time, for it shows just the simple lesson how letting down one's guard for one night can get your shit blown away. After my radio watch, I took a quick look around the perimeter, decided everyone was awake and went to sleep at 2330. At 0145 I heard the sound of that first RPG slamming into the track next to ours.

"Several more followed, about 15 total, plus a lot of AK and 51cal fire, all coming in. Then I saw the most heroic action I witnessed in the war. Sgt. Brock dashed across the laager, jumped up on a tank and cranked up the 50-caliber. The ca-chink of the first round being chambered is a beautiful sound. The noise that machine gun makes was musical—and deadly.

"The track which took the first RPG exploded and burned but we finally managed to beat off the attack, starting with Sgt. Brock's heroic act. As incoming fire subsided, I got the medics working on the wounded while the CO called in the Dustoff (med evac choppers) to get them out. I went running around getting litter teams organized and got everyone ready just before Dustoff came in.

"I got my Artillery clearances, so I began shooting them in. All this occurred in a hail of exploding ammunition from the burning APC. We had three pretty seriously wounded and ten evacuated. After the airstrikes and arty finished, we swept to our north but didn't find much.

"I got hit with shrapnel from an RPG. It was a small piece in my hand, so the doc patched me up. I asked him not to write it up and he said, 'Hell man, this will get you 5 points on a civil service exam!' The benefits of combat.

"Last night, we were fortunate that no one was killed but then we didn't kill any of the enemy. We began sweeping the area once it got light and found some food, which we destroyed. We then acted as a blocking force for the two companies of the 2/14 as they were 'eagle flighted' into the North. They swept toward us and ran into some VC who killed one of our guys. But they also captured one of them and he sang like a bird telling us where they were.

"He told us that the guys who hit us last night were not VC but NVA and were about two platoons strong. He pointed where the platoons were. The infantry moved in on the hedgerow and the fire got intense. They moved back and everything came down on that hedgerow, gunships, Artillery, airstrikes and the tanks even shot it up.

"We eventually got 29 of them. Not bad for a day's work. We had a combined operation that night with the 82nd around Tan Tan Dong and after a few hours' sleep, we were off again. We moved out at 0045, laagered for a while and then moved into position at 0200; we didn't have any action all day, as we were on the outer cordon-the inner circle got about 80 or 90 VC suspects, including 16 or so who were black-listed.

"I did get down to the HQ to see LTC Jim Irons who was the G-1 at Bragg. He is the BN CO and I think I'd mentioned how great that family was to me while I was at Bragg. I then went back to Emery with the company and there to greet me was my replacement.

"Major Eggleston, our S-3, clarified my new position as liaison officer of the 2/34, which included $110 per month flight pay. LTC Tague, the battalion CO and I talked and we were both on the same frequency. Still getting squared away in the new job. I had two new people who I could break in and work just the way I wanted them to.

"They seemed like good guys and they worked well together. I'd got the LNO job mostly under control and had been working to get equipment, personnel and targets straightened out. I had had the opportunity and worked out several complicated problems, especially one in human relations with an FO who wanted my job.

"He really fought against my every plan at first but now he had come over to my team. He saw some of the problems I was having and last night, he sat down with me and really helped me straighten them out. He has had a lot of experience over here, four months more than I and his help has been invaluable.

"Dan Putman left yesterday after helping me break in two brand new FO's. The two FO's are young Artillery second lieutenants and there aren't many of them in Vietnam. I have been working to get the final details of the new job cleared up. LTC Tague leaves in a few weeks, so I'll get to work with a new colonel, one who will use his Artillery better, I hope.

"I have nothing bad to say about LTC Tague except that he doesn't use me enough. I got Smitty back to work for me. He was just pulling details around the battery, so I asked for him and to my surprise, got him. He is a great guy; a hard worker and I feel I owe him his last three months in country in an easy job.

"I was trying to understand what makes men fight. I suppose leadership has a lot to do with it and the factors of a man's personal duty concept, social pressure and some form of patriotism but if enough guys just said, 'We ain't goin!' There probably isn't a whole lot that could be done. Mutiny over here would have to be severely dealt with or it would run wild.

"How do you tell a man, 'well, we've got a new operation today in the Hobo Woods after you've just spent five days in the Filhol?' These kids bitch but they go and they fight. They really are great. Bill Moore (not the classmate) got both legs blown off the other day. We talked and he didn't even seem bitter (as I'm sure I would have been). All he wanted (and got) was a CIB (Combat Infantryman's Badge). He was the scout platoon leader.

"Today is Buddha's birthday and a ceasefire. We had A Company in a hell of a fight yesterday. Task Force Bobcat killed 59 VC while losing one and having several wounded. The cease fire ended today at 0600 and we had no violations around us. A Company caught two yahoos trying to lay a mine in 8A as they were on their way to the bridge. These two idiots must have been really stupid to be caught by tanks in the middle of the road."

"May 1969 was the most I have been shot at since I arrived. This month the US lost over 1,400 soldiers and Marines KIA. Since I have been here, almost 4,000 guys have died. That's lower than the almost 5,600 last year but still a crime.

"First Sergeant Holbrook who I wrote about earlier, was on patrol and stepped on an AP mine that blew his foot off. He told the medic, 'Hurry and shoot me up (with morphine) Doc, I'm going back to Hawaii to be the first one legged surfer!' The courage under fire of these guys is amazing. Casualties are up because of a battle to our north that the journalists called 'Hamburger Hill.'

"This month after all the shooting, I caught myself using derogatory terms for the VC and NVA troops. That is something I said I would not do and I'm embarrassed. In combat, standards can slip even for a good kid from East Providence High School, Mr. Docherty's Sunday school class and West Point.

"The NY Times reported the secret bombing in Cambodia. Though it was illegal, it wasn't stopped until the following year. AF General Curtis LeMay bragged that we were going to 'bomb them back into the stone age'. Where do we get people like that? Clearly a member of the 'Greatest Generation'. At one time, I said that I was here to put 10,000 holes in Vietnam. I did that in under 60 days of combat. Perhaps, I'm no better than a General LeMay.

"I adjusted some eight-inch guns in on a VC bunker complex and it was fun from 1,500 feet. Those big guns really make a bang and they are accurate as a direct fire weapon. They were shooting 15k's or about ten miles. I called for a grid on a road and the rounds were exactly where I called for them.

"Yesterday, I took the day off and went to Waikiki East, the new division pool for 45 minutes. I felt like I was AWOL. It was just like the pool at any officer's club anywhere. All we lacked were females—just a few were around, nurses and donut dollies.

"We had an operation involving four ARVN companies and our A Company. We controlled it from the C&C ship. The eight choppers from Hornet swooped in with white, whirling blades, while the gun ships from Stinger raked the area with mini-guns. All the activity made beautiful patterns in the rice paddy grass.

"They landed and took off and we were on the ground for a while. I fired a mission, dropping the first WP round right in the middle of the Saigon River. Then I went to work on the riverbank with HE. War is ugly but it does have a grotesque beauty.

"While I was shooting up the countryside, my Artillery battalion called me and said, '62 (my new call sign), you will report to this location prepared to spend the night, with a clean uniform, shined boots and lots of money.' That meant that my promotion to captain came through. I was happy for the confirmation.

"We finished up the operation and flew back to Cu Chi. They held a rehearsal for the change of command of 2/34 and had a steak dinner afterward. Then I went over to 1/8 where everything was extra special but not *just* for me. They had also invited the CG to the Saturday night steak dinner. General Williamson showed up and promoted me. I bought the bar and it was $35 well spent. Two steaks in one night is typical of this experience, when it rains, it pours.

"With all the coordination I have to do in this job, it seemed to be a thankless task—until yesterday. My FO with HHC was out in a laager and the CRIP platoon sprung their bush. We had coordinated the arty ahead of time and as soon as the ambush hit, we had illumination out there. The next day Captain Lewis, HHC C.O. thanked me for the quick response.

"Then a chopper went down near the Phu Cong Bridge. LTC Smith and I flew two hours of cover for it while the infantry secured it. Four hours of sleep, breakfast and I was up in the air again, this time for three hours for A Company in contact.

"The afternoon brought three more hours and a total of eight for today. In the afternoon, we fired 202 HE on an area just a little bigger than the Kelly's lot. We put in air strikes and napalm and got 8 VC. We had one ARVN KIA with one WIA.

"This afternoon, the battery screwed up a target number and they blew part of a village away with 30 rounds. So far, two killed and 13 wounded and five hooches burning. The fire direction officer is a good guy and feels terrible. Killing innocent civilians isn't what any of us signed up for.

"During the operation, they shot 202 rounds for me in close support, sometimes not more than 300 meters away and one miscalculation ruins the day for all those people. The air strikes and napalm were like watching a movie. The green of the terrain set off by the colorful marking smoke made it look almost festive. But it isn't. Its war and the jets were deadly accurate. It was something to see.

"This evening, the Colonel and I went flying to the Phu Cong Bridge. General Black was on the chopper with us and when we got there, we saw that the guys who were trying to repair the mine boom weren't having much luck, so Colonel Smith and I swung into action. He jumped into mud and started moving toward the boats; he turned around and I reached down to help him out.

"He said, 'No, I want you down here!' It was shades of Ranger School, waist deep in mud. He was great and with his leadership, the boom got put back together. I helped but it was miserable. That mud stank! The next morning, I got a shock.

112

"A call came from my S-3 and he said, 'I've got a new job for you.' My thought soared to a Battery/Command! Like WOW! Like no. He changed me from liaison officer (LNO) 2/34 to LNO 1/5 Infantry (Mech). It is a compliment that he picked me for the job (it is more challenging than this one and more action) but LTC Smith paid me a bigger one when he fought to keep me.

"He took me aside and told me that he thought I was outstanding, that he had put me in for another bronze star for the action on the bridge the other night. The first was from the action with A Company as their FO. He also said he'd written a letter to LTC Cooper and told him how he felt.

"I got out to 1/5 fire base the next day about 1600 and by 1800, after talking to LTC Bob Kureck, we were up in a chopper, flying counter mortar for FSB Stuart. The RIFs today gave me a good chance to put my stuff in order. We got mortared, 13 rounds of 82 mm, so I fired up a storm of Artillery around us. The bad guys didn't shoot back.

"We had a good operation today working with one of our companies, one 2/12 and one 2/27 (Wolfhounds). The 2/27 company is commanded by Jim Kotrec (USMA '64), an old friend. We got a couple of VC and I got a good opportunity to know the people I'll be working with in action.

"1/5 has two fire bases, Patton to our northeast and Devins (between CuChi and the Cambodian border) where I stay. We have two mech companies and two 'leg' types, so I'll have my hands full. Today was 13 hours in a chopper. My usual day begins at 0600 with an hour 'road bust' where I fly over highways 1 and 8A in our AO.

"Then I usually fly convoy cover thru our AO and it can finish any time. Today at 1030, the major and I took a visual reconnaissance to the area where we were to put in two companies. At 1200, we got in the C & C ship for the insertion which went in and 10 minutes later, we got a change in mission to the Hobo Woods, which is west of the area called the Iron Triangle. Nasty place.

"Everyone formed up and we choppered north. Then we put down again and swept the area while Artillery and airstrikes went in. We got ready to extract them and then it started the when the NVA shot down a chopper. It landed and was able to fly out under its own power. The next lift wasn't so lucky. Another ship got shot down and couldn't fly and by this time it was getting dark.

"We put three ships of troops in to secure the downed chopper. By this time, the chopper we were on was out of fuel (for the 3rd time), so Colonel K and I went down to the people on the ground again. By now, it was dark. We got back up in the air and a hook, a flying crane helicopter, came in to lift out the chopper—we finally got all the troops out and got in at 2100, a long day.

"Tonight has been the busiest night I have seen so far. The battery must have put out 300 rounds in the last hour. The engineers have been running clearing operations in our AO, so we had to secure them. They level hedge rows with a 60-ton chain about 50 meters long. Two bulldozers pull it around each side of the hedge row and then just parallel one another and knock down everything in their way.

"It is really cool to watch all that destruction! Busy is the word and it appears that such is how life is going to be for the next eight months. We took two KIA from booby traps today, so we plunked about 400 rounds of arty into the area. We react to mines and booby traps just as we would to actual contact and blow the hell out of the area.

"We took another KIA today from a booby trap and to top it off, the company got mortared; we pumped about 700 rounds 105-155 into the hedgerow complex. There must be something in it they don't want us to see. The sweep found a mortar tube and some ammo. The days have been busy too.

"That same hedgerow complex acted up again today. This time some AK fire. We shot more arty in but the sweep didn't find much. We got some intelligence from a Chu Hoi of a VC hospital complex about 10K's north of here in the Hobo Woods.

"June 1969 was a month to remember with a new job, promotion to Captain and more medals with 'V' for valor. What is valor? The dictionary defines it as 'great courage in the face of danger, especially in battle.' I am not sure that my actions rated that definition. I was doing my job protecting those kids. If that was valorous, OK, because I hated to see them get hurt. US KIA in June were just under 1,400 including some close friends I didn't learn about until later.

"I have to say something about LTC Kureck. We hit it off from day one and he listens. He uses the Artillery the way it should be employed. He came out of the Korean War as the most highly decorated enlisted man in the Army. The troops love him and I couldn't ask for a better boss.

"Nixon announced his plan to Vietnamize the war. The big losses last month sparked increased protests in the States, so Nixon reacted. They say the plan called 'Vietnamization' of the war was in the works long before May's numbers were in. The ARVN would now be responsible for combat operations—ready or not—and US troops would gradually withdraw.

"Henry Kissinger was also cranking up peace talks in Paris. These were good ideas but there was no honor in them. The peace talks were started by Lyndon Johnson but Nixon interfered with Johnson's peace efforts. Nixon only cared about himself and being elected self-interest is not honor. It's cowardice. 'The greatest generation' strikes again.

"Up at 0600 in a chopper at 0630 and we air-mobiled two companies into the area. The NVA didn't even have time to set their booby traps and the Chu Hoi led the troops right into the complex. They took three POW's right away and another refused to come out of his tunnel, so he came out the hard way via frag grenades.

"The Stinger gunships got another three-body count and we found a big cache of food and medical supplies (2,000 cans of mackerel, 1,600 pounds of rice and extraneous junk). Later, we got two new AK-47 rifles but the NVA had suddenly turned into innocent farmers tending their fields. The trouble is there are some civilians (none of them are innocent in this area), so we can't just blow the hooches away.

"We have to receive fire from them first. While two companies were going through this village, we put another company in an area to the south of where the Rome plow operation was going on. I had four FO's working out and it was fun to keep track of them all. The area was so lucrative for the two companies we were with, we planned to go back tomorrow.

"We had an interesting operation. The same Chu Hoi who showed us to the caches and holes a few days ago was back in action again. This time, we found 2 NVA radios and a couple of POW's. That Chu Hoi so far has netted about 4 AK rifles, 4 SKS pistols, beaucoup medical and food supplies, the radios and 5 POW's plus a couple we had to kill who wouldn't come out of their holes. Apparently, he came over to our side because another guy had been messing with his girl.

"A message came down from HQ that no fireworks (flares, star clusters, etc.) would be used tonight, the 4th of July. The troops missed out on the word, as usual and it was gorgeous. After it got dark, all the fire bases just lit up.

Charlie tried to ruin it all by ambushing one of our tracks, so the Colonel and I went flying.

"The fire bases looked like jewels on black velvet; it was really quite beautiful. A 51 caliber anti-aircraft position in the center of Phuoc village made life rough on the choppers flying around, fortunately no one was shot down.

"We had a 2/12-unit op-con to us and they went on what was to be kind of a routine intelligence reaction mission. They took some fire as they landed, so I shot some arty into the tree line on the stream. Things quieted down. The rest of the day stayed quiet until we went to pick up the troops. They were PZ-ed just north of highway one, so it looked easy until they got mortared.

"The ARVN outpost on the road saw the tube flashes and I had the first rounds on the ground in 2 minutes. For the three rounds they shot at us, I shot 172 back not a bad ratio.

"We had another airmobile operation and used the mech. Today, it was the mech who found the gravy. Another VC Chu Hoi-ed and showed us to a cache of 82 RPG's. I'd much rather buy them than fight for them. They were found about 200 meters from where I had shot in all the arty yesterday. Also, the company stuck some C-4 into a hole to blow it.

"They moved back about 50m but the local farmers all began to take off. The hole blew and made creator the size of what a 500-pound bomb would blow. There was no schrap but the tracks were all covered with dust and dirt. It was pretty funny. The Rome plows are still working and they had another bad day with one KIA and five WIA from booby traps not funny at all.

"Today started off right. I shot a prep that was so effective, the chopper pilot said it was about the best he had ever seen. To make things better, it was a classic air mobile insertion and the choppers were on their final approach, as I gave them, 'tubes clear, rounds on the ground.' It really looked good. I went back to Ch Chi to get some finances straightened out and got to talk to LTC Crowe.

"Apparently LTC Smith had written the letter he said he was going to and it had been pretty effective. Crowe said that if he kept hearing and reading things about me the way he had been, I'd have little trouble getting the battery. I have been working with 'C' battery commander on how to be a B.C. and he has been a great help. The LNO job is great but I do want to work with a battery. A combat command would be the highlight of my time here.

"This morning, the VC ambushed our 'road bust' off Highway One. The tracks just rode on through it and fortunately no one was hurt. My Artillery section is pretty well settled now and I think it is pretty good. I've had two F.O. changes in two weeks, which leaves me with 3 F.O.'s all of whom I have worked with before and their recons and RTO's are all good. Bill Owen and I came in country about a week apart and he's a solid guy and a Ranger.

"Mom, this is a hard thing to tell you but I just found out yesterday that Gary Carlson was killed on 19th June. He was buried at West Point on July 2. If you'd remember me to Mrs. Carlson and tell her how sorry I am, I'd appreciate it. You've met Gary's family from Massachusetts. Gary's wife just had a baby and when I find out her address, I plan to write. They are somewhere in NY. CSM Brosseau told me about it and Father Kelly confirmed the news tonight. What a loss.

"This was an extremely profitable day. After a beautiful prep, B Company, 2/14 air-mobiled into Sa Nho, which is a real nasty area in the Hobo Woods. We must have caught the NVA asleep, as we took several prisoners including an NVA captain and a bunch of weapons and ammo, a good haul. Then things slowed down for us.

"The 15th was supposed to be the start of the big offensive but nothing happened. The evening of the 16th every fire base but ours got mortared; we've been pretty fortunate. The 17th was the first airmobile we've had in a while, this time C Company, 2/14 went into an area north of Sa Nho and the prep was again beautiful-330 rounds but they didn't find much.

"LTC Kurek and I went down to visit the company. I talked to the F.O. (who I had chewed out for not calling in as soon as he landed) and found out why he sounded so shaky on the radio. He and his RTO have been in country only 10 days. I gave him a pep talk; told him I was there to help him and since then he has improved.

"Our 1/5 Charlie company was securing the Rome plows but before they even got to the cutting area, they hit 4 mines. Fortunately, no one was injured very seriously but two vehicles were combat loss and the others pretty heavily damaged. When we extracted C 2/14 in the afternoon one of the choppers took some ground fire, so I got to do some shooting about 100 rounds and 'Issue' the FAC (forward air controller) did his thing with the jets.

"The Air Force is really something to see. As soon as I had the arty crank up, Issue was already on station and calling in (he usually says something like)

117

'This is Issue 25, just happen to be in the neighborhood, understand you've got something for me.' LTC Kurek identifies the target for him and then he works in as many jets as he can get on station with bombs and napalm.

"It is amazing firepower. We put C Company, 1/14 into the northern Filhol this morning and it was another good insertion and the prep was excellent. Charlie battery fired 91 rounds in three minutes which is the max rate of fire for a 105 howitzer (one round every 12 seconds) which is almost burning the paint off the barrel.

"Ron Taylor is the battery commander and he told me the other day that all indications are that I will take over 'Charlie' about mid-August. LTC Kurek told me the same thing. Now if LTC Crowe would tell me, it wouldn't just be rumor. I'm just going to hold what I've got and 'drive on' until it comes through.

"All indications point to either we have already broken the summer offensive or it never got off the ground. There was a lot of fighting last night. One of our AP's (ambush patrol) caught 15 of them in the open and chopped them up. If such is the case as far as the whole offensive goes, this ought to really drive the VC back underground (into phase II). It'll be interesting to see what history will have to say about this year. So far, the NVA has taken big losses.

"It has been a busy day and I'll try to 'tell it like it was.' We flew on a new operation called 'Eagle Eye' which is kind of cool. The Colonel, Major and I fly in the C&C (command and control) chopper and we have a light fire team with us plus 3 slicks loaded with our CRIP platoon. We fly around looking for ox carts and suspicious-looking people.

"We swoop down out of the sky and nail 'em. It got pretty dull as the first 3 or 4 were clean and we were about to go home when on the last one, this guy jumps out of his cart and runs like hell. The choppers kept swooping down and shooting in front of him but he kept going until the CRIP got out and stopped him.

"As they did that, they were right outside of a villa village, Trung Lap, when some clown stepped out of his hooch and fired an RPG at our chopper! Fortunately for us, he missed. They swept the area and got a couple of suspects; the guy running had two Chicom grenades and a bunch of blasting caps. He was a bad guy.

"Later, we went on one of the best operations I have been part of. We had an intel report of 20-25 VC or NVA who held up in a house every night. We had a good map grid and a picture of the house, checked it out and with the commanding general, the brigade commander and my battalion commander watching, we went in.

"Two gunships hit the hooch and knocked down part of it and then my prep went in. When the smoke cleared, there was only a pile of rubble left. In four minutes, we fired in 288 rounds of 105 mm, 155mm and 8". The slicks went in with no resistance and gradually the NVA started crawling out of their holes and running around.

"I fired in a total of 1,156 rounds. The end result was a 47 NVA enemy body count, 19 POWs, one machine gun, 7 AK-47's, a pistol and Chicom radio. We didn't get a scratch. The CG said it was the best operation he had seen in his Army career. Tonight, every ambush got into contact; maybe this is the beginning of the offensive, if so, they have lost big so far. One of the POW's said there were 20 people in the house when the first round hit and no one knew what to do. They all scattered but they didn't get far.

"We went back into the area with three companies and found a bunch of weapons, beaucoup rice and medical supplies. There were bodies lying all over the place. There have been people out here all-day asking questions and taking names. It seems the raid, its timing and fire coordination were a military classic. I might make the history books yet. I wonder what my 1,156 rounds will be inflated to.

"There were two outstanding events at 2100 last night. 'C' 1/8 fired its 10,000th round in support of 1/5 operations. That is 10,000 in 25 days or approximately 400 per day and that's a lot. While we fight, men land on the moon. Life is amazing. As I go out to fly my morning mission, the guys on the moon are preparing to walk on its surface. Somehow the lives of US citizens are worlds apart and it's nice we each find our own place.

"The lull in fighting reported in your news, never happened in our AO. As usual, we have been busy. We haven't pulled off any 'classics' lately but we have been killing NVA. We were on an 'Eagle Eye' operation and saw some suspicious 'eligibles' (any male from 6-60) in the paddies. We swooped in on them and NVA were running all over the place.

"Airstrikes, gunships and Artillery we had six body count and two prisoners. 'Eagle Eye' doesn't usually work that way but we just hit it lucky.

Things must be getting rough on the VC, as yesterday a VC company commander chieu hoi-ed. He is a big catch and gave us a lot of good info.

"It has been another crazy day. We found about 10 NVA again today, killed six and captured four. Our door gunner got one of them from our C &C chopper.

"My faith in God has been fully confirmed and justified. We had a two-battalion operation up in Bau Soi and since I wasn't the controller of the Artillery, I figured I'd have an easy day. It started out that way. In the end, it was not. It seemed all the FO's called in contact at the same time—two were moving in from the west and one from the east about a mile apart.

"Alpha and Charlie companies of the 2/12 ran into a bunker and the M60 machine gunner who was also the point man, got killed right in front of the bunker. The NVA grabbed his M60 and all his ammo. The colonel and I were bringing in some CS grenades to the 2/12 and that nasty guy opened up on our chopper with the M60. It was surreal.

"We were about 500 feet above the bunker and the pilot tried to turn to pull away. The engine roared and then nothing—silence. We crashed. The chopper was on fire right beside me. I yelled, 'This thing's burning. Let's get the hell out.' The colonel and the pilot were already making a quick low crawl back toward our troops. I tried to pull out my radio but it was stuck.

"Col. Kurick yelled, 'Forget it, I'll buy you a new one!' So I grabbed my map and got the hell out of there. Everything else burned up. Eventually, we got 47 body count and all kinds of equipment, including a 51-caliber machine gun. The prisoners were not VC. They were NVA from a regiment new in this area. That's why none of them quit or Chieu Hoied. They were all hard core and were either killed or dragged out of their holes. We won but we lost four guys KIA plus the chopper.

"The rest of this page gives me a chance to expound upon a bit of life and love in the midst of this madness. Don't waste any heartbeats. Some of mine have come too quickly lately and I have come close enough to death to realize how much I want to live. I saw a young medic lying dead and he was no longer a living, breathing person.

"Where he had been a friend, someone who laughed and fought with us, now he was just a body to be dusted off. In this place where death is just a heartbeat away, survival is the only law. I didn't phrase that properly. It isn't just survival; it is the yearning to live that makes men drive on even when the fighting is at its worst.

"It is even tied up in landing on the moon and letters from home but in that split second when you think 'God, this is it!' nothing else matters except. 'I want to live.' It is interesting and frightening but the lesson is to live every second of life and don't waste any heartbeats.

"When Gary was killed, I was angry. I started killing to avenge his death but being shot down literally brought me back to earth. I still did my job and protected our troops but I stopped killing for revenge. Gary would not have wanted that.

"The weather was bad this morning so our air-mobile operation was put off for three hours. Finally, I got the prep in and the choppers came in right behind it. The weather closed in again after the colonel and I set down with the center unit. We walked through Bau Soi, the place where we had killed so many the day before and it was deserted.

"The weather stayed bad but we finally got a break, so the Colonel and I flew out. The troops walked home. The brigade LNO, flew in and we laughed over the chopper being shot down. It's nice to be able to laugh over a close brush with death!

"LTC Crowe stopped by while I was out flying; calling him later he told me he just wanted to hear about the crash. I told him I'd make it in for a steak Saturday and give him the full story. I haven't been into Cu Chi in 1 ½ months. Another groovy day; not much happened except the donut dollies were here and when we were Eagle-Eying, one of the gunships took fire. I put out 74 rounds from 3 different batteries."

July 1969 became very reflective for me. War was about death. I was blinded into killing people for revenge after Gary was killed. My job was to protect my troops. So much of what I had written, I cannot believe I wrote to my mother. If she worried, she never let on. She prayed every day. Killing VC and NVA, being shot down and heavy combat for over 23 days out of 31—and then writing about it.

Putting that in context with the previous months and I was in combat for almost 100 days in five months. I read somewhere that the average soldier in WWII spent 44 days in combat in four years. 'The greatest generation' did not do as much fighting as the Vietnam generation. Some of our troops were under fire for over 250 days of their year here.

The obvious difference is that we flew into combat and the WWII guys had to walk. If we were wounded, med evac choppers (or 'dust-off') were on station and we were never more than 15 minutes from the best medical facilities. Does 60 to 70% of your time being in high stress take a toll? Yes, it's called PTSD today. Anyone in the Army may suffer from PTSD, not just the guys out in the bush but out there we felt the pressure.

July resulted in just under 800 US KIA. The number was down significantly from previous months but that did not help the young medic I crawled over when we escaped the chopper crash. Perhaps fewer deaths were the result of 'Vietnamization' of the war but we didn't see it in our area. At this point, I was about half way through my Vietnam tour of duty. At 180 days in country, the daily routine was clear.

"August 1. It was a wonderful day. I didn't go anywhere and nothing happened. Airmobile tomorrow.

"The prep and everything else in the operation went well. Then I flew into Cu Chi and got most of my affairs in order. I wanted to go in specifically to have a steak at 1/8. They really goofed me up! They had chicken, AHGG! I was so upset I threatened to take the next chopper back to the field. They appeased me by giving me two bronze stars (one with 'V') and my first air medal.

"I probably had enough air time for ten of them. That was ok, so I stayed and ate the chicken. It was good. Later Carl Savatiel, the brigade LNO and I went over to the 2nd Brigade officers' club. I got to bed at 0100 after the merry-making.

"I was awakened at 0300 and informed that the airmobile operation we had for 1200 was changed to 0700, so I went back to bed for three short hours, got up at 0600, was on a chopper at 0630 and back in the field by 0645. At 0700 we were up in the air again. LTC Kurek and I walked through the Hobos all day. Fortunately, no one was home.

"I shot a recon by fire with the 155 mm. They made a 100-mil quadrant error and dropped a round behind us. Pucker factor increased tenfold. Another airmobile but with a twist. We got the company in with no problem but on the way back to re-fuel, the gunships took fire just outside of Cu Chi. After we finished expending the gunships and dumping in 127 arty rounds, we put the troops in and got 11 body count. We have a crazy Baptist Chaplain who has a motto: 'KILL A COMMIE FOR CHRIST'.

"Airborne again today and it lasted from 0830 to 1330. My rear still goes to sleep. We put the troops in the Northern Hobos where only the 155's and 8" could reach. Then we eagle-eyed for 4 hours. During the Eagle Eye mission, the gunships spotted a camouflaged hootch in Bau Soi. We had spent days beating on the place and the NVA are back. We are going back in there tomorrow to clean 'em out again but after the gunships worked on the house without much effect, I turned the 8" on it.

"I hit it with the 11th round and destroyed it with #12. I prepped the area with 521 rounds. We had a combined operation with the ARVN and I thought they did a good job. They had the toughest and longest area of Bau Soi to go through. They got two body count but then they seemed to run out of gas after hitting a little heavier resistance.

"We brought in Artillery, gunships and an airstrike about 500m from our location and the ARVN soldiers went back into the area. They got seven body count, Artillery got 11 and jets and gunships got eight more but we had to walk home three miles through the paddies. Choppers picked us up about halfway back. We took a track from Patton to Devin. I haven't been so dirty since my FO days.

"Miss America, Judy Ford, was here today and there were a bunch of other girls with her. They were really great and quite a morale booster. They didn't do anything but stand around and look pretty but that was enough. Miss New Jersey everyone felt was beautiful. Miss Minnesota was the best built and Miss New York the coolest.

"LTC Kurek and I got flown into 1/8 for a steak supper; we flew in at 1945 and flew back out at 2230. That's not quite the jet set but it's at least the chopper set. Next day, I was shooting for Alpha company and the rounds were impacting about 300 meters from them. A piece of shrapnel splashed over and hit Bud Brown, the company CO, in the arm.

"It didn't seem bad at first but gradually he lost enough blood to require a dustoff. LTC Kureck reported it as a piece of junk from a booby trap. While I wouldn't have swung for it, I hate to shoot up the good guys.

"I took command of Charlie battery on August 22nd. The days before the change of command were hectic with checking over the 2 ½ million dollars' worth of equipment I am now signed for. Until the new LNO takes over, I get to do both jobs as the LNO and BC. The Bobcats managed to stay out of major contract today.

"The change of command was a brief ceremony. LTC Crowe gave Ron Taylor a bronze star for his 7 months as the B.C. and me my third one for my work as LNO of the Bobcats. Then we passed the guidon and I was officially a battery commander.

"Ron left to go on R & R, all the guests departed and I sat the troops down for a talk. I did all the talking, telling them about me and what I expected of them. Then I excused the troops and talked to the NCO's telling them what I expected of them. Then we all went back to work.

"In the past week, we finished three bunkers, put up an RPG screen, worked on ditches and shot a lot of Artillery. It appeared for a while that the rainy season had deserted us but in the last three days, it has been back in force. I continue to pull double duty as LNO and BC.

"August 1969: Six months in country and six to go. I took command of Charlie battery, celebrated my 24th b-day and earned a bunch of medals—what could go wrong? As I was to learn, a lot! I guess I was trying to do too much as both the LNO and the BC jobs. Combat command was my wish and it came true.

"The experience was not what I had expected. I shot over 20,000 rounds in the first six months and now we were going days without shooting a round. Inactivity and young soldiers is not a good combination. Too much pot around. US soldiers' deaths were under 1,000 KIA but up from last month.

"Saturday was a command inspection and very chicken. We did pretty well in most areas, so I'm not really worried. What does bother me is our battalion XO. I told him to get out of the unit. My chief of smoke was ready to walk out of here after that major got through talking to him. The base camp warriors come out here for two hours and expect the battery to stand on its collective head for them.

"I got Sgt. Blackburn cooled off and assured him that the only one he has to answer to is me. The battery had fired all night the day before the inspection. We fired about 700 rounds of the best shooting many people have seen around this country. After shooting all night, they expected us to get up smiling and happy for their stupid inspection.

"There has been a lot of pressure on lately with Artillery errors that have been fired. 'A' 3/13 dropped a 155 into base camp the other day which naturally increased the pressure. One of my guns fired a charge 7 when it should have been charge 6 and just missed some of our own troops. Natural pucker factor is tough enough but errors like that can kill our own troops. Fortunately, we haven't hurt anyone.

"I just spent the most miserable afternoon of my Army career. Last night, I was in Cu Chi for Col. Long's farewell party (he was 2nd Bde Comdr) and on my way back out to Devin, I was sitting, waiting for the division night chopper. I got a call that the battery had just dropped two rounds into base camp. Good Lord, what next!

"I got back to Devin and investigated the whole thing and found that two guns had indeed fired charge errors, so the next day I spent in Cu Chi. Thank God, no one was hurt and there was no damage. The rounds were actually outside the wire. Hope I never have to go through that again.

"September 1969: Mistakes can be lethal in this business and they can be deadly to one's military career. When I kicked the major out of the battery for chewing out my chief of smoke, I made a mistake. I violated Rule #1, 'Know who writes your performance evaluation.' Turns out it was not the battalion commander, LTC Crowe but the dumb-ass major I had kicked out.

"That mistake cemented my decision to get out of the Army. I was worried about my career while the guys I used to be with were getting killed. Deaths to US soldiers were under 700 KIA, their lowest since January of 1967. Ho Chi Minh died apparently of a heart attack. We did not morn for him.

"October 1969: We fired 1,100 rounds last night without a mishap and the action gave everyone confidence. The inspections continued. We were inspected today by Div. Arty S-4, Maj. McCord. He had nothing but good to say about us. It was quite a day for visitors. Colonel Whitehead, the new 2nd Brigade commander was here and Chaplain Galle was here today too.

"I went to his service to get reacquainted with God. The First Sergeant went on a 30-day leave, which leaves Dave Ackart, our fire direction officer (FDO), Sgt. Blackburn, our chief of smoke and me. Today, Dave went into Cu Chi and we got a fire mission, so I had to be the FDO. It was just like being at Fort Sill or Fort Bragg but shooting at people we were trying to kill. Last night we fired over 600 rounds and today we got inspected—again.

"We passed the inspection with flying colors. Just getting through the damn thing will make life easier to bare for the next few weeks anyway. The puny, chicken crap the battalion is putting us through is beginning to get us all down. The paper war has begun.

"I got back into Cu Chi to check out my orderly room and it isn't. It is a rats' nest of paperwork, which hasn't been followed up on. When the First Sergeant gets back, he is going to find someone in his chair—permanently. It'll take a month to straighten it out.

"General Camp, the ADC-S just paid us a visit. I was worried at first, as he wanted me to meet him at the chopper pad (as a rule the FSB commander, LTC Kureck would meet him) but he came to see the artillery us. I had to jump into my boots and shirt and I caught him just before he got to my area. I took him to base piece, the fire direction center, the ammunition bunker, the mess hall and gun number five.

"He left saying that the ammo bunker was the best he had seen in the division and that we had restored his faith in the Artillery. Apparently, he hadn't been too happy with what he'd seen before us. But our 'shit is in order', so I'm never really worried no matter who comes or how unexpectedly. We were in the middle of ammo resupply, so I just tell him he'll have to excuse the temporary mess. Lt. Owen called later and said he didn't know what we'd done but he'd never seen General Camp so smiling and happy.

"Got in to CuChi to straighten out the morning report and we've just about got it. The Div. Arty commander, Col. Stedham, showed up to congratulate me on Gen. Camp's comments. Apparently, Gen. Camp wrote a very complementary letter—every little bit helps. LTC Crowe came to visit us today. He didn't stay long and didn't have much to say.

"General Camp's visit turned out to be a life saver. With the slowdown in shooting we had spent a lot of time cleaning things up, so all the chicken-shit inspections didn't bother us. The AGI was a big deal and with the First Sergeant on leave, my XO changing jobs and no support from the battalion assholes, I was stretched pretty thin.

"November 1969: There was a meeting in CuChi about the AGI. The IG had inspected on the 10th and with the work SFC Blackburn, the clerks and I had put in, we passed—the best in the battalion. It was a lot of work but the results seemed worth it. I asked the Col if he wanted to see me before I went back to the field and he told me he'd call.

"He called later and told me that the change of command would be November 28. I was crushed after all the work we put in. He told me that I would go to 2/14 as LNO. I said no." This was another time in my career that opened my eyes to the lessons of experience. More importantly it showed that failure (or what seems to be failure) can pay big dividends.

"He couldn't believe that I said no and said he was doing it 'for the good of the battalion'. He pounded the desk and seethed that if I didn't like it, I could go see the Division Artillery Commander, Col. Stedham. I requested the meeting. After I left his office, I went to see LTC Kureck (CO of 1/5 when I was LNO. He was now G-3).

"I told him my story and asked him for a job on his staff. His words were, 'Bruce, I can always use a good man.' He said that he'd have an opening in a week or two. I was over-joyed and the next day went to see LTC Crowe again.

"I told him I had a better offer and that I wanted out of his command. He gave me his 'for the good of the battalion' talk again and I told him that I still wanted to see the Div. Arty Commander. My appointment was made for the next day and then put off until Wednesday. Bill Owen (my old XO now Gen. Henderson's aide) called in the meantime and asked if I wanted him to go to bat for me. He said he'd get me in to see the General if I wanted to. I said that I felt I should wait until after I talked to Col. Stedham.

"I got to Div. Arty about 5 minutes early and waited to see the Colonel. I walked into his office, reported to him and he said, 'Sit down, Bruce.' (Surprise #1, I didn't think he even remembered who I was.) I had come well-armed with General Camp's letter, the results of his staff's inspection and the AGI. I presented my case and he gave me a 'don't quit now, you're still good with a long way to go' talk.

"Then I told him that I couldn't see working for a man who gives me a battery, ruins my world by taking it away when we had performed well and then pats me on the back, saying go back to the field and do your usual outstanding job.

"I told him I wanted to work for the G-3. He said that he'd have me out of 1/8 as soon as possible. He must have called for LTC Crowe after I left. I went to see Bill Owen, telling him that I thought Col. Stedham had seen my side of things, so there was no need to see Gen. Henderson. Then I went out to 2/14 to see Dennis Crawford and LTC Crutchley.

"Dennis would be taking over the battery and Col C. was the 2/14 CO. LTC Crowe showed up that afternoon to chew my head off. Col. Stedham had seen my side. We talked (he did most of the talking). Now I wouldn't be 2/14

LNO but I'd stay at Patton to break in the new LNO and then go to work for the G-3.

"I had a formation to give some awards away the morning of the change of command and the guys in the battery gave me a plaque and a letter of appreciation signed by them. I haven't had such an experience before and leaving those guys was rough. The change of command was quick and almost painless."

November 1969 was great. Whatever questions I had about staying in the Army were answered. Looking back on all that happened, I probably assumed too much by doing two jobs when I took over the battery and the REMF's at 1/8 Artillery battalion could have supported me as a new commander better. My future path was unfolding and my toughest decision was whether to go to law school or business school—and where.

The yellow pages ended when I left the field. I moved into Cu Chi base camp and became a REMF. By the time I got back from my R&R in Hong Kong, it was the middle of December and I had about 75 days left in country. I was 'short', a two-digit midget and I was more than ready to go back to the world. Bill Moore, a roommate at West Point, had orders for Carson too, so we had made plans in Vietnam to get an apartment together. We both planned to get out of the Army.

The R&R was fun in HK. The interesting thing was that I fell in love with China. HK is not China but that is where it all started for me. It was the Christmas season and I was in a big department store. HK was a British Crown colony. The Brits were in control with a colonial governor and all that went with the colonial government including education. There was a choir of Chinese children singing Christmas carols in British-English and I was impressed with the beauty of it all.

Later, I took a tour to what the Brits called the 'New Territories', which was the land that buffered HK from Mainland (Communist) China. When I think about the history of the land that I was standing on both in HK and Vietnam, the facts are mind-blowing. The Chinese and the Vietnamese were fighting for their countries. They did not want colonial powers governing them. The US was supporting the claims of the Brits and the French—colonial powers!

Here I was a US soldier from the land of the free, supporting my government who was supporting colonialism. Was this a moral dilemma? Was

I a professional soldier or a mercenary? How does a 20-something deal with this? How does any soldier deal with this? I heard the distinctive sound of a Chicom AK47 and decided to hate the Chinese.

However, after visiting HK and viewing China from the New Territories, I was seeing the world through a differ lens. The Chinese were amazing and I think we made a mistake in Vietnam. I made mistakes in Vietnam but I was a soldier. Conflicting opinions can be tough to sort out at the moment and I had to return to Vietnam to finish my tour.

My assignment in the CuChi basecamp was in an air-conditioned office and my quarters were comfortable. I was getting over my anger at the lack of support from my Artillery battalion. We all had lessons to learn and their actions had convinced me the getting out of the Army was the right course for me. The staff work was not difficult and we got to see the Bob Hope Show. Soon it was time to go home.

A chopper flew a bunch of us to Bien Hoa and we drove to TanSonNuit. On the way back to the world, there were stops in Japan and Alaska. To set foot on US soil in Alaska was a mixed blessing. I was wearing a short sleeve uniform. It had been 95 humid degrees in Vietnam and it was 32 degrees and snowing in Alaska. I didn't care.

I wrapped a blanked around my shoulders and exited the plane. I had to touch the world again. When we landed in San Francisco, I caught the first flight back to Boston. People tell stories about being spit on and feeling unwelcome back in the States. No one spit on me and no protestors gave me any grief. I was just so glad to be home, it radiated and no one could break the spell.

After 364 days, I made it home and my friend, Gary, did not. Many friends and classmates did not. I was upset with the Army and all the stupid generals who put us into ridiculous situations that got good people killed and strategically meant nothing. I was angry and had made up my mind to get out of the Army.

My family felt that I had changed when I returned home. I never fully explained my bad attitude to them. They were just happy to have me back home in Rhode Island in one piece. I could not see any glory or justice in war. I took some time off and then headed west for my new assignment at Fort Carson, Colorado.

Together: Vietnam was not the end of our story. It was a part of the beginning. We couldn't explain what it felt like to lose close friends in war. It was a feeling of loss so deep and ugly that it took years to get over it—if you ever did. We thought of Tom and Gary every day. We carried their memories in our hearts.

We also carried those memories of others we fought with and fought against. Those faces were in our hearts too. The noise, the light, the dark, the tracers, the colors, the beauty, the impacts, the concussions, the smells, the fear—we often wondered how we survived but we did.

Something else happened when we came home. It wasn't the protestors but it was the so called 'greatest generation'. They didn't welcome us home. They had their own set of problems dealing with this situation they could not understand. Rather than sit down to grapple with and study the situation, they threw bodies at it, our bodies.

They never understood that in Vietnam, they chose to support the wrong side. Had they understood strategy, they might have learned from Korea and realized that this was not another World War II. It could not be won by 'body count'. Their stupidity and lies cost the United States over 58,300 lives and untold grief for the military and their families—not to mention the pain of the Vietnamese. That 'greatest generation' never truly understood what justice and equity meant.

We served our country with honor. We came home to friends and family who loved us and helped us move on but we still had to face what we had been through. The survivor's guilt, anger, racism and PTSD were just some of the battles we all still had to face. Those challenges were clearly part of why we were brothers.

Trauma, 'moral injury' and other difficult feelings or wounds were not the whole story. After Vietnam, we went different ways. Yet those different ways, helped solidify our brotherhood and we finally came together after almost 50 years. Vietnam brought us together. Combat experience cemented our bonds. Equity and justice woke up that brotherhood in us.

In Vietnam: Ray between flights

In Vietnam: Bruce between firefights

In Vietnam: Bruce with 105 Battery

In Vietnam: Ray with his UH1D

Chapter 5
Transitions-After the Vietnam War

Transitions are almost always signs of growth but they can bring feelings of loss. To get somewhere new, we may have to leave somewhere else behind.

– Fred Rogers from Mr. Rogers' Neighborhood

After being in combat for more days than most WW2 soldiers, we came home to a different world and chose different paths. We both had to focus to find our direction. Ray headed for a new assignment in Germany, got married and had a daughter.

Bruce completed his Army duty at Fort Carson and headed for graduate school. We took different paths but we both had to wake up to find our direction. Now we had to face other battles.

Ray: Getting back home to the United States, into the warm, open land of south New Jersey, was a little surreal. The land and the sky looked and even felt the same as it had been in my dreams, longing for home but I had changed. I looked at everything from a different point of view now. The sounds of the world around me were not like what I had experienced for the past year.

And the lights in the night sky in the world were altogether different. Looking up at the sky and seeing stars, the moon and streetlights at night, not seeing tracers of red and green going in every different direction and not having to wear a weapon.

New thoughts like not having to be suspicious of the people around me who were not in a US Army uniform, who might be a bad guy looking to kill me. When I went to bed now, I didn't have to think where the bunker was that I would have to run to from the next mortar attack raining in.

This was all very unnerving for a while, comforting but unnerving and I knew I could get used to the quiet! I was slowly but surely undoing the feeling of being hyper-alert all the time. Part of it was unwinding the fear of every situation that I had no control over. My ongoing emotional feeling was that I didn't really belong to this world in South Jersey.

My 'combat-reality' had developed very quickly over the last year, my reality had become what I had learned in Vietnam. I had changed from the dream of being a combat pilot to the reality of being one. I was not the same Raymond anymore. I was a professional soldier, ready for any emergency, hardened to the blood and gore that was the Vietnam War.

My mother was wonderful! She cared for me and took my every mood with her understanding and lots of love. She never pressed me. She just fed me and took in this new person who was her son. Besides my mother, there was my Aunt Callie and my younger brother. They sensed that I had changed and accepted all the extra baggage that came home with me.

My friends from my previous life could not or would not understand. They never asked what it was like for me to be at war and if I had been scared. One of my good friends that I went to college with asked me where I had been even though he saw me two days before I got on the airplane to go to Vietnam. My experience there was not real.

I found that I was not part of this world anymore. Somehow, I think I knew that I would not fit back into this lifestyle of South Jersey since my first days in flight school. Now I wanted and needed to find those people who understood my new world and the new me.

I did encounter a young woman who was not part of my past. She looked on me as what I was then and not what I had been. That love helped to smooth the edges of the world I was experiencing but even that relationship didn't make me want to stay in New Jersey. This was the old world as far as my thinking was concerned.

I had a life in the Army and I had another adventure waiting for me in Germany. I would be defending our country from a more powerful enemy, so I was going back to the military world that I had grown to love. I didn't run into war protestors or any real conflicts. Most of the folks in Salem County had to make a living the best they could and the war wasn't a real concern for them.

Their major concerns were just the daily effort of living and providing for their families. There were military funerals from time to time—too many really. But black folks like me made a bet with their maker, "God, if I live through this and get my ass home, I am ahead of the game of life. I have skills that I can use and I can use his experience to get a job. If I don't make it back, my family gets $10,000 and that's more money than most of us have seen at one time in our whole life."

What overwhelmed me was that none of my friends cared about the war. It was just a 10-minute segment on the evening news. We couldn't talk about how the war affected me, because nobody wanted to hear it. It seemed to me that it would all just be going beyond their comprehension. Even the woman who was in love with me didn't ask about Vietnam. I think she was just afraid of what I would say and what it would say about me.

I didn't tell my family about my experience. I wanted to spare my mother and Aunt Callie. I wanted them to feel that their prayers did their job and I was saved from the hard problems and effects of being in a war. The one thing that I knew was that I needed for my own sanity to get back to the Army.

The place where I knew how the system worked and the world would make sense somehow. To this day, I marvel how humans can embrace the horrors of war and think that we can become normal again. For a black man with the dream of being a Jimmy Stuart-like hero, respect for what I had become and what I had done was most important.

In 1971 back in New Jersey, respect for black men was not happening. In the Army, I was an officer and a pilot first. I had proven myself in combat and was not a little colored boy anymore. I was a professional soldier and a man. I did not forget about Vietnam when on leave. I watched the evening news looking for pictures and stories of my old unit.

I had trouble letting them go to war without me but I was half a world away. I was surprised at my loyalty to those guys still over there. I wanted again to share their danger, come back from a mission, go to the club and share stories over a beer about our day against the enemy.

For my friends at home, no one had any desire to get to know the new, real me. This person was different from the one they knew before I went to Vietnam. As the days of my leave came to an end, in my mind I began to become eager to go to my new unit, to get back into the Army and to see what service would be like in Germany.

I had never been to Europe, just as I had never been to Southeast Asia. New people with a new mission and a new unit awaited me. I was going to fly to protect my country once more. Just as important to me, I was going back to a military world that I knew and understood. People with the same mission, the same goals in our lives and daily duty. Men and women who thought more of others then of themselves. They would accept me as I am, an officer and a damn good pilot. A black man who is worth knowing—valued like everyone else.

The last few days at home were fun and exciting. My mother seemed comfortable with my new duty station in Europe. By this time, she embraced the fact that I had survived my time in Vietnam. She knew that her son had come home with a few changes from the boy that she had sent off to war the year before.

Then there was a young woman who saw the good in me. She was willing to explore what the Army had in store for me and wanted to share those experiences. We had found adventures around the New Jersey small towns and in family gatherings. It was good to see the world I had known from a little boy through her eyes and she accepted it.

When the day came that I was to depart for Germany, I was filled with excitement for another new adventure, what was on the horizon? I was going on a flight that was just half as long as the one that I had taken a little over a year ago. I was traveling into a country in Europe that I had some knowledge about from my studies in school.

Most importantly, I was going to be flying over a land filled with new things to see and no one would be shooting at me. My mother and girlfriend saw me off. This farewell felt so much different than that of a year ago when I was going off to war. Now I was going to stand guard against the evil Communist empire threatening the western world.

That's how I thought about it back then as a product of the '50s where the Soviets were the great threat, the Evil Empire. The Army now was a known element for flying and it was a peacetime environment in Germany. That was so appealing. These two women had big smiles on their faces without the fear that I was not coming back and the excitement for me in this new challenge in Europe.

I settled in my seat and looked out the window into the darkness. As the airplane was made ready for takeoff from McGuire Air Force Base, I got more excited. I was anxious to get going. My seatmate was going back to his unit in Germany and we got quickly acquainted for the eight-hour trip across the

Atlantic. I learned that wearing the same uniform meant more than hometown alliances, schools or color. We chatted about everything that we could think of and got well acquainted.

When we got to Frankfurt at about midnight, we hashed out plans for him to show me the city. I wondered what would be open this late and thought we wouldn't find much to do. I soon discovered that this was a first class, world city and just about everything was open. As soon as I got out of my uniform, we were on our way downtown and stopped at a gasthaus. I had my first half liter of German beer.

It was amazing and the food was wonderful! We went from night club to night club, eatery to eatery, until it was early in the morning and I just had time to make it to the train. I knew this was going be a great time in my life. Everyone we met was so friendly and they acted like they were glad to see me.

My new friends took me to the train station after I had changed back into my uniform in time to catch the train to Schwäbisch Gmünd, my new home. I didn't see much of the countryside on the train ride to my new duty station. I had been up for about 30 hours and slept most of the way.

I had read a lot about Germany in World War II and was looking forward to seeing the countryside. But all the beer the night before and the lack of sleep took its toll, so my arrival in this new town took me by surprise.

I got to the town in the early evening. No one was there to meet me. Since I had no numbers to call, I found myself at a loss as to what to do. I found a gasthaus, a bar, restaurant and hotel, to settle in for the night but I had no German money. The proprietor was willing to take American dollars. The owner of this establishment was truly amazing—he had a big smile on his face as he shook my hand and told me that I could stay there as long as I needed.

He also said he would help me find my unit in the morning. I was taken by the kindness of this very cheerful German, the first German I had a chance to get to know. It was clear—this was not Vietnam. When I was in flight school, it didn't seem so important to me that I was one of just a few black men going to flight school and that the only people of color I saw at graduation were three of us!

But I was so caught up in the excitement and sense of pride of making it through that maybe I really didn't even notice. When I got to Vietnam, there was one other black pilot in my company and I didn't think it strange that he did not have a roommate. When I arrived, I filled his two-person room. He only had a few months ago when I arrived and he was the pilot for an ARVN general.

We had long talks in our room and he helped me adjust to being in a war zone. I got the opportunity to fly with him, as his copilot a couple of times. As I look back on it, there was no big thing made of two black men being in the cockpit. But I was starting to awake to the more subtle institutional racism that was the US military.

After he left, when his Vietnam tour of duty was over, I was alone. When you are in a combat situation, thinking about the fairness of opportunity granted to people of color in the military does not immediately come to the forefront. You thought about each day's mission and surviving that day, completing that mission and getting back to base to have a drink and to write letters home before bed.

After my tour in Vietnam, I decided to stay in the Army, heading to a three-year tour of duty in Germany. I had never been further east than Massachusetts, so it was a big deal flying over the Atlantic Ocean to Europe. It was exciting. When I arrived at my unit, I noticed that there were no other black pilots. I was excited about this new adventure of being in a country on a continent that I had only read about.

I had flown through some of the key World War II parts of the Pacific and now I would get to see it from the Atlantic side. The next day, we made the phone calls and one of the men from my new unit came to pick me up. We headed out to a very small airfield and I was posted to the aviation section of the 56th Field Artillery Brigade. Our mission was to deploy Pershing missiles, the biggest nuclear arm of the United States Army.

In Vietnam, our company had 45 officers and now this aviation section had only 12 officers and 25 enlisted men. All of the pilots had served in Vietnam before coming here, so I felt comfortable with them. During my time there, we would share war stories of our adventures in Vietnam, our ups and downs, the times when we should have gotten killed and when we almost did.

We talked about many of the same emotions and experiences. This was good for me. I think these discussions went a long way to limit the PTSD that that could have tormented my life. I knew that in this company, I was truly home.

One of the things that had to happen right away was that I needed to get familiar with the mission of the brigade and flying around Germany. Also, I was required to get an instrument flying rating. The worst flying weather in the United States is better than the best flying weather in Germany, so we had to learn to fly in the clouds. Another new pilot and I were put into a unit training program that took about a month to complete.

We would go out almost every day and fly in the clouds. After we became familiar with the airports and flying around our local area of operation, we would fly to German, British and Canadian airfields. We would practice the different approaches at each field. We had to memorize the new rules and regulations of flying around Europe.

It was hard work but fun learning new skills and going to these different countries' airbases. After the training, I was ready for my check ride. Because it was winter, we had to wait until there was no icing in the altitudes where we were going to fly. The day came when I was doing an instrument take off, two or three holding patterns and four precision approaches. When it was finished, I passed.

The other thing I had to do was transition into the Army's new helicopter, the OH58. It was a small helicopter, fun to fly with a great view out the front window. At the end of my five days of training, I had to get eight hours of solo flight before I could carry a passenger. Operations told me one morning, bright and early to take the OH58 out and don't come back until I had eight hours. I had a mission the next morning to take a technician to five of our missile sites.

I went and looked at the map in operations and I decided on a route. I would go all the way up to the North Sea on the coast of Germany and then over to the Belgium border. After that I would fly to the French border on the Rhine River and follow it home and I would be done. It all went smoothly. It was fun. Imagine flying over countries I had only read about before!

I learned so much about Europe and all the airfields. Twenty-seven years earlier armies were fighting over the ground I was now flying over. I found out where to get fuel and food. I got home about seven in the evening with my eight hours logged and excited about my new mission.

The next day, I got to the airfield and picked up my passenger. When he got there, he was an older warrant officer with a load of manuals in a briefcase. He looked at me a little warily but gave me a big smile and introduced himself. The first site was easy to find because of the missiles sticking up in the air. I noticed that he was looking at the controls and watching what I was doing.

After that first location and on our way to number two, I asked him if he would like to fly a little. He looked at me and said he wasn't sure he could do it. I told him that flying is the easiest thing in the world to do. After an explanation of what the controls did, I said, "You got it, just hold this heading." He did an outstanding job, so I thought he must have flown before. I just looked out the window with one eye on what he was doing and enjoyed the flight.

It was lunchtime when he got done with his inspections, so we met in the mess hall. As we sat down, I asked him if he had ever flown before, because he did such a good job. He looked up at me and out of the blue said, "You're not the first colored pilot I've ever seen."

I gave him a puzzled look and said "Oh?" He then related the story that he had joined the Army Air Corps near the end of World War II and he was assigned to fly attack bombers in 1945. On his first bomb run, he was the last bomber to attack a railyard. It was filled with smoke and flames and debris. Diving through the smoke to drop his bombs, he was bounced around through all the turbulence.

When he came out the other side of this mayhem, he was alone. Training taught him to head west and go as fast as he could. By himself, he was an easy target and before long, German fighters caught up with him! Since he had no defenses, he put his head down and flew as low and fast as he could. As the German fighters closed in, he thought he was dead.

Out of the corner of his eye, he saw an American fighter, then two, three and now four fighters coming to his defense. They shot down one of the enemy aircrafts and chased off the others. He relaxed and said, "I made it. These guys saved my life." Then one of the fighters came up beside him.

The fighter pilot looked into his cockpit and said, "Come on white boy, we'll take you home."

The other pilot was so close, he could see his face. He could see it a man of color! He had never heard of a black pilot—never even knew that this was possible. When he got back over France, the escorting fighters peeled off and wished him good luck. When he landed at his base, he relayed the story at his debriefing.

The operations officer said that it was the 'Red Tails' and they had been operating out of Italy and North Africa for three years. They were the Tuskegee airmen who were the first African-American military aviators in the United States armed forces.

He looked at me and said, "Those boys saved my life and kept me out of a German prison camp!" We had a wonderful day. I let him fly and he shared more stories of flying in World War II. We had several missions to those missile sites. He told me what it was like to go through flight school in 1944, as a very young man and then take a boat to war.

He was discharged from the Army in July 1945 and he was recalled in the new Air Force in 1951 for the Korean War. We shared stories about flying in a war zone then and now. It wasn't just in our aircraft that we would chat. We also shared stories over drinks in the officers' club.

About six months after our first meeting, he asked me to show up at his office one afternoon for his retirement ceremony. He had accomplished 25 years of service to our great nation. I readily accepted his invitation and looked forward to seeing him get his last military honors. When I arrived, I noticed all the high-ranking officers.

I looked over to find him wearing the blue uniform of the United States Air Force and he was a lieutenant colonel. He kept on getting promoted in the Air Force reserves, so he would retire at this higher rank. I was so happy for him and for all that he had accomplished. I was grateful for all the wisdom and experiences he had shared with me.

When I first got to Germany, it was my first time in the real Army outside of a war zone. Here traditions, customs and decorum were strictly followed and it was difficult for me to get accustomed to this strict atmosphere. But the unit I was in, an aviation section for a very large Artillery brigade, was somewhat more flexible and tolerant.

All the pilots had served in Vietnam, combat veterans who did not put up with some of the nonsense of the peacetime Army. We were based on an airfield on a hill about five miles away from headquarters, so we had lots more flexibility. Since we all had just come back, we understood what it took to help each other readjust from the stress of war.

As an aviation unit, we flew the command staff, repair people and other members of the brigade around to the various missile sites. Since this was a very important brigade in NATO, we got to fly to some very important NATO meetings. There were basically two chains of command in the Army, officers who were in charge and responsible for the where the unit was going and the NCO's were responsible to see that the work was done to get us there.

The top NCO is the rank of sergeant major. A sergeant major has been in the Army for 20 years or more and knows all the ins and outs. One day, I flew one of the brigade sergeants major around to all the sites to give the troops inspiration to do their very difficult job. Since it was all day with many hours in the air together, we got to know each other.

He was outgoing, talkative and very inspirational. He told me about his career but more importantly, he explained to me how the Army really works. He gave me new insights as to how I fit as a young officer in the whole scheme of the Army. I liked him a lot and enjoyed his stories about joining the Army during the Korean War.

He invited me to call him anytime or visit, if I had a question or needed help. I took him up on that and over the next couple of months, I gained helpful information so that my Army life became much better. One afternoon, he called me and asked if I was free after work at 5 o'clock for 'bosses' night'. It wasn't formal but it was serious. The senior NCO's would invite officers over for a beer and discussion of the past month in the brigade in the NCO club.

I said that I would love to meet them and it was a great honor for me. When I got to the NCO club, Sergeant Major Johnson met me at the door. The first thing he did was give me a salute, shake my hand and bring me to the bar to buy me a liter of beer. I was one of the youngest officers there and as a W-2, one of the lowest ranking officers there.

He introduced me to all the important NCOs in the brigade. He told them that I was a good young officer and that I had a lot of potential and all I needed was a little assistance from time to time. I thoroughly enjoyed meeting everybody and knowing what they did, I quickly figured out that this was a change in my career.

I knew from then on that I could be a good officer when I found all the outstanding sergeants there were to support me. This is the kind of support that can make a young officer's career. These two men helped me and my career as friends and mentors.

One of the key military points about being in the 56th Field Artillery Brigade, was that we had missiles not howitzers. We had the largest, most destructive weapons in the United States Army. Our missiles could deliver nuclear warheads and there was a set of procedures called nuclear surety.

These protocols ensured that the right orders to launch the missiles, should they ever be given, came from the proper higher command and got to the individual units on ready status, on time and accurately. The brigade headquarters had an operations room manned 24 hours a day to ensure that all the procedures were followed for either a test or a launch of our missiles.

To become a duty officer, we had to study the procedures and we were tested to get the instructions 100% correct. With all the tests, everyone had to have a top-secret security clearance. Once at home on leave, some friends told me that the FBI had come through the neighborhood to check on me. I passed the FBI investigation as well as all my tests, so I was ready to be the duty officer in the command center.

It was interesting to pull a 12-hour shift during the week and a 24-hour shift on weekends. We had phones directly from the Pentagon in Washington DC and NATO Headquarters in Brussels. We couldn't leave the room, so we either had to bring our meals or have them delivered. During my time as duty officer, I usually only had training exercises to verify as authentic but one weekend when I was duty officer, I got a call saying that we had 25 new soldiers and they all needed quarters.

This was not covered in our book of procedures. It said nothing about finding quarters for new troops but with a few phone calls, the arrangements were made for quarters for all the new troops—except one. When I got to the lobby, to my surprise I saw a woman first lieutenant. I said to her that I didn't know there were women in the field Artillery.

She looked at me, smiled and said that a few weeks ago, the Army ended the Women's Army Corps and women were being integrated into every part of the Army. I looked at her, smiled back and said, "I know what you're talking about!" Being a black man, I knew what it was like to be excluded. It had only been 25 years since the US had integrated black Americans into all of the forces. Even by Presidential order, it took some doing. We found her some quarters.

During that first year in Germany, I saw many changes besides the end of the Women's Army Corps. The Army even started race relations training. There have always been race problems in the Army—segregation or black soldiers being in separate units from whites. Now having all races integrated in Army units created unique problems.

The Army is a microcosm of America itself and the country was in a race relations maelstrom in the 1960s and '70s. The Army had to do something about it. So the Army in their infinite wisdom made everybody go to classes on race relations to air out everybody's feelings and let them know where the Army stood on equal opportunity for all.

The first class given in my unit lasted for five days. The deputy brigade commander and I were the only officers in our class of 30. The colonel could not understand why we even had this class. It seemed a waste of time to him. The Army had made up its collective mind that we were all going to follow orders to be equal! But there were people with different problems than just following orders—issues like where they came from, their family background and training in their churches and towns.

Obviously, even five days of training was not going to change that but interestingly, it was a start. It gave those with serious problems with equality among races a setting to air their thoughts any misconceptions. Sometimes it turned into a shouting match and the goal of trying to change patterns of thought, I felt it had serious flaws. But the Army was trying and in my mind that was the most important thing—nothing changes in a day or a week—and this was a start.

In Vietnam, I wrote letters to my mother almost every other day making sure that she knew that I was OK. Now in Germany, I wrote her often but I had another young woman to write to also. She came over for a visit after I had been in country about three months. We had a marvelous time and by the time she went back to the States, we had decided that we would get married. When I got back home three months later, we were married.

Two months later, she came to Germany where we set up our first home. A year and three months after getting married, we had a beautiful baby girl, April, born in Stuttgart, Germany. Since both of her parents were Americans, she was an American citizen and because she was born in Germany, she could also claim German citizenship. What a gift of choice when she got older.

In 1973, the Arab nations decided to start a war with Israel. The US supported Israel and the Soviets supported the Arabs. We sent over tons of equipment and supplies from Europe to Israel. The Soviets wanted us to stop that aid, so that the Arabs would win. They had greater numbers but Israel had greater fire power.

The Soviets threatened to shoot down our supply planes and interfere with the war. The US said no way and to back up that threat, we took our Pershing missiles out to their war sites in the forests of Germany. We were told that this could mean a general war with the Soviet Union and to be ready for this eventuality.

Our families had to pack their bags, have half a tank of gas in the car and wait for the word to go to Frankfurt to get on Air Force transports back to the States. We were sitting in our tents out in the October weather of Germany and our families were waiting at home for the word to travel back to the United States. They were all terrified. We could talk to them to say we were OK but they could not communicate with us.

Terrifying scenarios filled our minds. But all-out war was not to be and within six days, we got the word that we could head back to our barracks. Everything settled back to the status quo. Israel had defeated the Arab nations with our massive supplies. The Soviets decided that nuclear war was not in the world's best interest. We took our missiles back to base and we settled in for a wonderful snowy German winter.

When I had about a year to go in the 56th Field Artillery Brigade, I was given the job as operations officer for the aviation section. For the year before that I had been assistant operations officer and when my boss left, I was given his job. It was another sign that I had found my calling, for I had reveled in this job.

Making sure all the flight records were up-to-date, being sure that everyone made their missions on time, assigning missions to the pilots and flying the ones that I really liked myself. I took the hardest missions, because I felt that I had the experience and knew how to handle them.

During this last year, I got word that my mother was in the final stages of cancer. She had contracted lung cancer from a respiratory ailment she had for many years. Today, I think it was from the harsh environment around where we lived. Factories of all kinds, mostly unregulated and spewing out toxins all over the place.

I came home for a couple weeks and found that she was in a tough place. I talked with the doctors and found out that it was only a matter of time. My mom was always in good spirits and looked to her religion for her strength. About four months before my tour in Germany was up, I found out that I was going to Fort Riley, Kansas.

I hadn't asked to go there, so I called the Department of the Army. I was told that I was needed there and I could go to flight instructor school on the way to my new duty station. I picked helicopter instructor pilot school, because

I had been a teacher before joining the Army. I thought this was a good way for me to build on those skills I had learned in college.

As the day drew near to move my family back to the United States, I felt a little twinge. I didn't really want to leave Europe. I had never been in the Midwest but there was a lot of history in the state of Kansas. I planned to explore it all. The family was excited about the new duty station, because my wife's parents were living in Wichita—not that far away.

So we packed up and flew home, looking forward to this new adventure. Three years away from Vietnam and I felt the transition back to the real world was successful. I made it. I was happily married with a daughter. We thrived during our three years in Germany and the Army offered new opportunities and adventures.

Bruce: My thirty days of leave after Vietnam was a fun time home with family, skiing with friends and avoiding the Army. But the good times had to end and I went back to work. I had been stationed at Fort Carson where I had served in an Artillery unit as a cadet in 1965, so I still knew people there. Also, Colorado Springs was a great town with the Air Force Academy and Colorado College plus the nearby ski areas—C-Springs was not your typical Army town.

My old roommate from West Point was also stationed there, so we rented a very comfortable apartment together. The high-rise building had an indoor pool, sauna and good restaurants and bars close by. We quickly realized that we were not in Vietnam anymore. The good life got better when I met a guy who played rugby for the Colorado Springs Grizzlies Rugby Club.

I had played hooker for the West Point Rugby Club and soon I was a Grizzly with a great group of guys. But the best part was teaching skiing at The Broadmoor. It was a small slope for teaching skiing but it paid off in free passes for the big Colorado ski areas.

There were a lot of great skiers in our group, so we were always headed to the slopes on weekends. If it sounded like I was ignoring the Army and just having fun, I was but it didn't last. The commander of my battalion, LTC Darrell Irvin, was a good man and he had given me the cushy staff job I had been looking for.

As his S1 (personnel officer) he pushed me to take over one of the six-gun batteries as its battery commander (BC). The current BC was a friend and a skier. I wondered how I could better support the current BC but Col. Irvin told me that he had made the decision and wanted me to command the unit. I asked the battalion CO if I could speak to the First Sergeant before I decided to become the BC. He told me that First Sergeant MacDonald was one of the best in the Army, so go talk to him.

'Top', as the top sergeant was known in each unit, was a black man who had been in the Army for over 20 years. This was 1970 and the order to desegregate the military had been issued in 1948. Racist officers kept it segregated pretty much until 1952 when Eisenhower became president.

I sat down with Sergeant Mac and explained that if he and I were going to work together, I did not want to be left hanging, as I had seen the former commander left flapping in the wind. Sergeant Mac was a big black soldier with a commanding presence.

He sat up straight, looked me in the eye and told me. "Captain, let me tell you something. I have been in this man's Army for over 20 years and there are 20 units on this street who know me and would want me as their First Sergeant. If you don't want me, you just say so and I will find another unit. But if we are going to work together, here is how it will be. If you want to make a decision that I don't think is right, I'll tell you once. If you still want to make that decision, I'll tell you again. If you still want to make that decision, I'll tell you the third time. If you still don't listen to me, I have not left you hanging. You have hung yourself." Sergeant Mac's language was much more colorful and I was smart enough to become his BC.

We became a great team. We did not always agree but each time I heard, "Captain, we need to talk." I knew I needed to stop and listen to him. If there was ever going to be equity and justice in the Army, in business and in life, it would pay big dividends to have a Sergeant Mac close by. He kept a quart of Old Grandad whisky in his desk drawer but his drinking never impaired his fair judgement with the troops. Occasionally, he would ask to use my office. He would simply say, "Captain, I need to council this young man."

One time, a young soldier in our unit stole some equipment from the motor pool and tried to sell it in Colorado Springs. The Army was an interesting place to operate. You could kill people but you couldn't steal from the unit—a unit couldn't live with a thief in its midst. I had the Military Police pick him up and put him in the Ft. Carson lockup. When I visited him in jail and talked to him through the prison bars, I saw a very different person from the swaggering troop he had been. I saw a very scared kid in some very hot water.

I could have given him an Article 15 (a slap on the wrist) but the First Sergeant and I took the stand that we had to make him an example, so the stealing would not happen again. In the Army, even a small-unit commander has power beyond his years—I was just 25. I had the power to put this young man behind bars. I could see in his eyes that he was scared.

The power I had and had used in Vietnam sometimes scared me. This soldier's dad called me and asked for me to reduce the penalty from the court martial to an Article 15. He said his son had learned his lesson. He had, so Sgt. Mac and I agreed to reduce the penalty.

As an Airborne Ranger to show how tough I was, I used some pretty foul language. One night, I went to the bus station to pick up one of our soldiers who had gone AWOL. I gave this trooper a rough chewing out. When I stopped, he told me that he had come back, because he had found Jesus. The next morning, he stood at attention as I gave him an administrative punishment. He saluted as he left and with a big smile said, "Captain, God loves you!" I told him to get the hell out of my office using more bad language but his words woke me up.

Later that week, I went to a church service. The Bible readings included the story of Peter denying Jesus. The verse in Matthew says that after Peter denied Jesus, he 'began to curse and swear'. I was embarrassed. This soldier had found the moral courage to accept Jesus in his way and had returned to face the consequences. He had also discovered that God loved him and he shared that revelation with me.

A few months later after this soldier left the Army, he wrote me a letter thanking me for understanding his situation. The letter ended with a PS, 'Have you tried to stop swearing quite so much?' I laughed, because I had tried and I was making some progress. Like Peter, I was learning to love the Christ. I started reading the Bible on a regular basis and attending services in a local church.

I did not change my language overnight but I was growing in my understanding of God's love for me. Over the years, I had cleaned up my language considerably and served my church in several capacities. The service I cherished most was teaching Sunday school children each week that 'God loves you'.

Field training in Colorado was a game. We'd go out for a day, set up the guns, shoot for a few hours and be back by the evening. There were times that we would stay out to shoot at night but that was rare. The great part was that when we did spend the night in the field, Sergeant MacDonald and I shared a tent with our driver. Sergeant Mac would tell us stories about the segregated Army. It was an incredible first-person history lesson.

As the commander of the unit, I decided that we could train for the Army in four days a week and volunteer in the community one day. I told my commanding officer that 'the Army was an instrument of social change'. He gave permission to take the troops, all volunteers, off post to work at the Colorado School for the Deaf and Blind.

Today, these children would be mainstreamed in classes with other learners but at that time, they were not. We helped in gym classes and coached the deaf kids' basketball team. I saw disabled children and education through a new lens. The editor of the *Colorado Springs Sun* heard about our unit and wrote an article about the good things we were doing in Colorado Springs.

As I prepared to leave the Army, Sergeant Mac got orders—not for Vietnam but for Korea again. We had a heart to heart talk and I told him how much I appreciated all he had done and shared. He wrote to me later from Korea that it was great to be back where there was no shooting but the women were 20 years uglier. Sergeant Mac had served in the Army when it was segregated. Black soldiers were in one unit and white soldiers in another.

When we were out in the field, Sergeant Mac enlightened me on how it was back then. He told me how it was and how much he hated the white privilege of those white officers to that day. I learned some lessons in empathy and thought back to how Oris, Miss Harry and Mr. Walker must have felt. I had been blessed my whole life to learn from these incredible people. What would it take for America to learn?

When I left Ft. Carson and headed to The Wharton School at the University of Pennsylvania, the new commander put an end to the volunteering in the community. I still believe that the Army is an instrument of social change—it's just that most people don't understand what an impact the military has had. Executive Order 9981 to desegregate the military was signed by President Harry Truman in 1948.

The history of black soldiers goes back to the Revolution and the Civil War. I learned from Sgt. Mac. Our volunteer foray into Colorado Springs did not have the impact that desegregating the military did but we all learned a little about the courage of children with disabilities. Those lessons have stayed with me to this day.

My roommate had applied to Wharton when I did. We agreed that we would room together at Penn but we got some bad news. I was accepted and he was rejected. He was disappointed and applied to Harvard where he was accepted at Harvard Business School. Now I say, if you cannot get into Wharton, go to Harvard.

I spent time at home before checking into grad school. My parents were excited for me to attend Penn, an Ivy League university. Neither my dad nor my mom were college educated but they had encouraged all of us five kids to go as far as we could. I was the first but not the last, to get a graduate degree. Near the end of his life, I asked my dad if he regretted not getting a degree. His brother had a PhD from Harvard. He said he was not jealous of his brother and he was proud that all his kids had college degrees.

Before I headed for Penn in Philadelphia, I went back to Boston to a church meeting of college students. I had flown from Boston to San Francisco on my way to Vietnam. The meeting was held at the Christian Science church, the Mother Church that I had asked the Boston cops to drive me to see back in February of 1969. I was in a small discussion group when a man sat beside me. As we shook hands, his nametag caught my eye.

I said to him, "We need to talk." I explained to him that before I turned 20, I had gone back to the Providence church to attend Sunday school for the last time with my favorite teacher, Mr. Docherty. After the class was over, Mr. D had given me the name of a new Christian Science Teacher and Lecturer, Charles Ferris and made it clear that when the time was right, I should seek him out and consider Christian Science class instruction.

He wrote down the man's name and address. I had carried that piece of paper in my wallet for the past six years including 364 days in Vietnam. He was the man and I felt I was ready to get closer to God. I told him that I wanted to take the two-week class instruction course but I still had an occasional beer.

"Was that OK?" Instead of just telling me no, he said that at social occasions when alcohol was served, he and his wife found alternatives like fruit juice or sparkling water. He suggested that we keep in touch and let him know how I was doing. I didn't have another alcoholic drink from that day on.

Wharton was hard work but fun. The GI Bill paid for most of my tuition and I worked part-time to pay room and board. I joined Penn's rugby club and we played all the other Ivy teams. It was a great way for me to transition from the military. After every rugby game, the opposing teams got together to drink beer and sing British rugby drinking songs.

As the 'hooker', it was my job to lead the singing and the drinking. With a mug of water in my hand, I led the singing. My favorite song was, 'I don't want to join the Army'. The real test came when I went back to Colorado Springs the following year to visit friends. At a party, my friend Jeff who was the Grizzlies Rugby Club right prop cried, "My buddy Bruce comes back to Colorado and won't even have a beer with me!"

Wharton's academics were challenging. In my first accounting class, I was surprised to find that about half the class members were already CPA's. I could not understand why these men and women would waste a class and the money on what was an easy course for them. The light dawned. Class standing and grade point average were on their minds but my mind was on transition. There were a number of veterans in my class and I usually hung out with them. They weren't much help in accounting.

I needed the help with accounting, so I got a tutor. I was surprised when Gus walked in the door, because he was a black man. He was also a CPA and a great teacher. My West Point education had nothing to do with business debits and credits. I had a lot to learn. During an early conversation with Gus, I asked him if he played basketball. Gus just looked at me and said very gently, "Bruce, not all black guys play basketball."

My equity education continued as did my accounting classes. I had to figure out why this basic business was so hard for me. From basic to intermediate accounting, I improved. Gus was so good a tutor that I passed the basic class and became an accounting and management information major. I also took every finance class I could fit in.

By the end of my first year, I could almost walk the walk and talk the talk of business. I had a great summer job doing market research, which had me traveling around the country and allowed me two weeks off to take class instruction. The man whose name I had carried with me for six years, became my Christian Science teacher and mentor. This relationship would pay great dividends over the next 45 years.

My second year at Penn, I became a dorm counselor in a freshman dorm. By this time the dorms were co-ed—a far cry from how things had been at West Point. The Military Academy would not even admit women into its cadet corps for another four years. The dorm was a great experience and I learned lessons from those young people. I would joke that I missed the '60s because I was at West Point and in the Army. Between the dorm and Penn rugby, I managed to catch up a little.

I had let my hair grow long and one day over lunch, a redneck from Georgia was surprised to find out that I had gone to West Point. I was wearing my Army field jacket, so he told me that with my long hair, sweatshirt and jeans, I was a disgrace to the uniform and the Military Academy. I neglected to ask him where his Purple Heart was. Or his DFC? Or how many friends he had lost in Vietnam? I just said, "thank you" and left the table.

During my second year, I took a portfolio analysis class from Dr. Harry Markowitz, a famous American economist. He came down from New York every Friday morning to teach the class. When I heard of his class, I jumped at the chance to spend a few hours each week with one of the wizards of the finance world. In 1989, he received the John von Neumann Theory Prize and the 1990 Nobel Memorial Prize in Economic Sciences for his work that helped create the Capital Asset Pricing Model aka in financial circles as CAPM.

However, in their summer 2004 review in the *Journal of Economic Perspectives*, economists Eugene Fama and Kenneth French wrote that 'the failure of the CAPM in empirical tests implies that most applications of the model are invalid'. Yet another financial theory bites the dust but it was amazing to read his book and sit in Dr. Markowitz's class to hear the theory. The business world awaited my newly discovered knowledge.

I looked at a few jobs before I left Wharton but the entrepreneurial bug had bitten me and my plan was to head west and start up a company with one of my mentors from the Army. As I was packing to leave, a box arrived from my high school English teacher—the same teacher who had tried to talk me out of going to West Point.

Inside the box were all the letters I had written to him over the past 10 years—four years at the Military Academy, four years in the Army including 364 days in Vietnam and two years at Wharton. On top was a short note which read, 'Now you tell me you weren't brainwashed!' I didn't have time to think about being brainwashed just then, so I headed west to start a new company.

Together: During the three years after Vietnam, we made big changes. We didn't have life under control, because control was difficult to apply to real life. We needed to settle down into a pattern that made sense to live within the situation where we found ourselves.

Ray spent three years serving in the Army in Germany and Bruce finished his Army service at Ft. Carson, Colorado and had gone on to grad school at the University of Pennsylvania. We were both still learning about what life after combat meant.

We had fulfilled our dreams to go to flight school and West Point. We were combat veterans who had lived our dreams. What was left to do? We discovered that we both still had a lot to learn and we were finding out that we were in a unique position to discover what that meant.

Ray was one of a very few highly decorated Vietnam black combat pilots. Bruce was a highly decorated Vietnam combat veteran who could use his 'white privilege' and West Point education to his advantage. As twenty-somethings in 1973, what did we still have to learn? We met both some interesting and unique men who brought new perspectives into our lives.

Ray had to work through one of the most racist times in our history. As one of only a few black pilots in the US military, he flew around Germany where he came in contact with a former Army Air Corps pilot who had met the Tuskegee airmen. They had saved his life and he expressed his gratitude.

Remember what those black WWII heroes faced when they came home—racism and very little gratitude. Ray also found a mentor in Sergeant Major Johnson, a Korean War veteran, who helped him understand better how the Army worked.

Bruce had the opportunity to work with one of the best First Sergeants in the Army. Sergeant MacDonald supported this young Captain and they became a team that no other unit could match. Sergeant Mac had been part of the segregated Army and Bruce respected and appreciated him. Bruce found business school support from a black CPA who helped him understand how the world of financial accounting. Ray and Bruce were working with people who had lived historic moments.

If you are 15 years old and looking forward to the next 10 years, there is high school graduation and college, jobs and maybe even graduate school—if you have the courage to look into the future. It may seem daunting but it does not need to be. All it takes is a dream and a plan. With that said, we agree that it's not easy.

How do you decide what your dream is? We recommend thinking first, which is hard work. Think about what you see as exciting. What wakes you up and gets you to say, "That's what I want to do!" Whatever that is for you, go for it. Take the chance no matter what anyone else says.

The Army was an excellent place for us to learn how to plan both tactically (short term) and strategically (long term). From our military training, we started with the squad concept. A team or a squad is an organization to help you get things done. Your dreams are the start but not the end. You need your squad.

We started by following good leaders—the best we could find. Who? Start by looking at teachers, clergy, coaches, friends and leaders in clubs, teams and other groups you belong to. You know who the leaders are who you admire. Then, begin taking on leadership roles yourself. Start small and build up the size of your followers.

Remember, you cannot be a leader without followers. Find mentors and coaches who can see you in depth and help you through the rough spots. Even when you become a leader, check in with your mentors. Keep in contact with them. Do not lose touch. Then implement your plan. Keep thinking both short term and long term. Review and renew your plan with your mentors. Take what's working and build on it.

Toss out what isn't working and don't be afraid to fail. It's important to remember that failure is a great teacher. We say that success is not always the goal—experience is. Unless the situation is life or death, failure is always an option. Keep trying, stay at the plan with its big goals and eventually you will learn how to get there—wherever 'there' is for you.

Build on your education and training. Build on the experiences life gives you. Get help from your squad members, mentors and teachers. Failure is a great teacher, so learn the lesson and move on. Never, never, never quit! You will start to see similarities in our experiences in using our Army training and leadership skills in combat and beyond. We both had to find our place within our combat units.

Ray had to prove himself as a skilled pilot and Bruce as a skilled Artillery officer. We were both successful but Ray more so. Ray handled the loss of his friend better than Bruce did. In addition, Bruce forgot rule #1. After Vietnam, we each found success in the Army. Ray in Germany and Bruce at Ft. Carson (when Bruce finally remembered rule #1).

Ray got married and added a daughter to his family. Bruce stayed single, rediscovered God and went to grad school. Both of us had to clean up our language and we started to see how much we had to learn.

We do not hold the key to all wisdom. We are experienced men and former professional soldiers who want to share with our family and friends so they can understand who we are and how we got here. We both had to understand what it meant to take that oath 'to protect and defend the Constitution'.

We took that oath and served with honor. We continue to be proud of our service to our country and we learned our first lessons in what it means to be a person of color in the military. Ray was learning firsthand and from history. Bruce was instructed by First Sergeant MacDonald. There was still more to learn.

After Vietnam: Ray promoted

After Vietnam: Bruce as Battery Commander

Part Three:
Awakening after War

And gentlemen in England now a-bed Shall think themselves accursed they were not here.

– Shakespeare

Chapter 6
Awakening to Be Leaders

There are no secrets to success. It is the result of preparation, hard work and
learning from failure.
> *– Colin Powell, former U.S. General, Secretary of State and National*
> *Security Advisor*

Ray's path took him back and forth to Germany and two more combat tours.
Bruce chose to go into business. They found different ways to serve and to
lead. Ray was married, divorced, remarried and left the Army after a 22-year
career, two more combat tours and two more helicopter crashes looking for
new challenges.

Bruce got married, became a CPA at KPMG and then left Honeywell after
10 years to find new ways to serve. He discovered that the public schools could
use his help. Both started to reflect and build on lessons learned.

Ray: When we returned from Germany, we found out my mother was
getting worse. This sad news dampened the enthusiasm of the return to the US
and the new place we were going. I had 25 days leave before I needed to report
to Fort Rucker, Alabama for instructor flight training school. My mother
seemed to be doing OK, so I thought that she would last the month to get the
family settled in Kansas. Then I could get back home to see her.

Instructor pilot school was fun and exciting, doing all the maneuvers that I
was going to teach other pilots to do. I found out again that I love being in
school. I loved learning and every day I seemed to do better and better at my
studies. Flying was my life and I was very good at it.

I talked to my mother almost every day but I could sense that she was
getting weaker. It really preyed on my mind. By the time I was getting down

to my final check ride, I knew that my mother wasn't going to last very long. It was difficult to concentrate but I passed the tests and went on to check out as an instructor pilot. Then I headed back to Kansas to get my family settled. That day, I called my mom and told her that it would be a few days and I would be home with her again. She rallied a bit but her voice was weak.

I jumped in my car and drove from Fort Rucker to Wichita, Kansas. I was determined to make it in one night to reunite with my family and then head back to New Jersey to see my mother. It was the longest drive that I ever had taken. I was determined to make it in 10 hours.

It was getting dark and I couldn't appreciate the beautiful countryside of the deep south and the mid-west. I made it safe and sound and was happy to see my wife and daughter. We got settled in and I told them what was going on. I was so tired that I fell asleep right away.

It was about one in the morning when my mother-in-law came in the door of our bedroom. She woke me up and said that she was so sorry. She handed me the phone. On the other end was the doctor from the Philadelphia Naval Hospital where my mother was being cared for. He told me how sorry he and the staff were and what a wonderful person my mother was.

He told me that she had died just an hour ago in her sleep and that she did not suffer. He asked me if I would approve an autopsy so they could fully determine what had taken her life. As I was fully comprehending the fact that my mother, the sweetest person in my life, who cared for me, loved me and encouraged me had passed away. I approved the doctor's request for the autopsy, hugged my family and prepared for the long trip back to New Jersey.

After a very difficult two weeks leave, burying my mother and settling her affairs, I took my family to my new duty station at Fort Riley, Kansas. I was assigned to the legendary First Infantry Division, the oldest division in the Army, the Big Red One. It was a long drive out to Kansas from New Jersey but I had never really seen the Midwest and it was wonderful.

We found an apartment in Manhattan, Kansas where Kansas State University was located. It was a lovely college town with lots to do. Looking out on the Kansas countryside was beautiful. The wide-open spaces, the rolling hills and the amazing amount of flowers on the prairie in the spring and early summer made it an idyllic place to live.

I arrived at my new unit, the First Aviation Battalion and found out that I was not going to be utilized as an instructor pilot. I was upset. After I had gone through all the instructor pilot training, I thought that I would be a very good instructor pilot and wondered again if it was because I was the only black pilot in the unit. I decided that I had to chalk this up to the needs of the service. I went out to try to be a good pilot in my new home.

What was happening here? In three years, I had gone from Vietnam to Germany, gotten married, my daughter was born and my mother died. This young officer could have used some support. What is the Army spirit? "Suck it up! Drive on!" Something had to give.

Like Germany, the people of Kansas were not very friendly to newcomers at first. I thought that when I was back in the United States, it would be like in New Jersey. I hoped there would be a lot of people of color but I saw very few. Even at the university where I would travel through the campus often daily, black and brown people were rare.

My new unit was not like the unit in Germany either. They weren't that welcoming. No one really offered to show me around and take care to make sure that I was settled in. I had to do that basically on my own. I did make two or three friends and they made the days very tolerable. I was a very social person, so friends were important to me.

I was flying a lot of scout missions. We would go out and practice scouting roads for the truck convoys and tanks that would be going out to the firing range. I would observe the firing ranges early in the morning to ensure that there were no farmers out near the impact area who could get hurt by the tanks firing. After flying around in Germany with all the wonderful historical sites to see, I found this stateside flying very beautiful but very boring.

Something had to give—me and I didn't know how to ask for help. For various reasons, my marriage was breaking up. Back then, I couldn't tell why. Perhaps I was trying too hard to be a good Army officer and not the husband and father I could have or should have been.

I spent a lot of time at work and didn't pay attention to what was going on at home or focus on how to take care of my family. I was immature. I didn't know how to balance home and work make these things work in my life. I focused on flying and my military duties. We decided to end the marriage.

I had met my first wife on my return from Vietnam. Looking back on it, I was not ready for anything like marriage. I was committed to the United States Army and all the things that it required from me. We had a four-week romance and decided to get married. I then shipped off to my new duty station in Germany.

We wrote to each other and she came to visit for two weeks. Two months later, I came home on leave at Christmas time thinking that this is the time that we were going to announce our engagement but no, we decided to get married right away. We got married in my mother's house surrounded by my family.

It was a fun year, being young and in love in Germany. Our daughter, April, was born at that time and gave our life focus and purpose. But Army life became more stressful. I was assigned new jobs, which took up most of my time. I did not know how to manage the time between the Army and family. 1974, I was transferred back to the United States to Fort Riley, Kansas.

As we set up our home there, things got increasingly difficult in our marriage. We got divorced and my wife moved back to the East Coast, leaving our daughter with me. It was a very important time in my life. I was a single father and I had to change my priorities. I put my daughter first!

About a year after her mother had moved back to Minnesota and worked on getting her degree, my ex went on to get a master's degree in education. She had gotten herself together and per our agreement, she took custody of our daughter.

So the Army became my wife, life and family. The Assistant Division Commander's (ADC) pilot was rotating out of the unit for Korea. They needed a pilot with solid qualifications. They thought of me, because I was an instructor pilot and I could meet all the requirements for that position. As I became the general's pilot, we got a new ADC. He was a brand-new Brigadier General and, in my mind, he was an atypical general. On our first flight before we took off, he squeezed himself between us pilots.

He looked me in the eye with a big smile on his face. He said, "Ray, I am General Johns and I am so glad to have you as my pilot." I knew then that we would have a perfect relationship. For the next year, I enjoyed flying him all over Fort Riley and eastern Kansas.

One of the First Infantry Division's missions was a training exercise called Re-Forger. It was an exercise to get American units back to Germany in case the Russians invaded Western Europe. It involved units flying from various airports in the United States on large Air Force transports and landing in Germany. There we would get our prepositioned equipment and pretend we were fighting a war with the Ruski's for two weeks.

During my time with the Big Red One, I did this training exercise twice. The first time as a pilot and the second time, I was a staff officer assigned to schedule helicopter missions and coordinate with the United States Air Force. We were nine days into this two-week exercise when my boss told me that a helicopter was in bound and that I could get some stick time going over to the Canadian sector to coordinate a move. I looked at this as a bit of excitement after being on the ground for nine days.

The helicopter came in and after greeting the pilot, two passengers got in the back and off we went. The pilot was assigned to a unit in Germany. He asked me if I wanted to fly the ship and of course I said yes. It was a cloudy day and we had barely 300 feet of ceiling with just a quarter mile visibility. I did not know this area at all from the air and the pilot was navigating.

We were flying through a valley and he told me to go over the ridge line to my left and then go straight down the next valley, as fast as I could. We were pretending to be at war and this is how you fly to keep the enemy from shooting at you.

When we got over the ridgeline, all I could see were high tension wires! I tried to turn but realized that there was nothing I could do. We hit the wires and everything started to shake. Things started falling apart, as I held onto the controls and looked at my instruments. I was trying to fly but there was no way that I could control the chopper.

We hit the ground, I think we bounced and slid for a good distance. I remember no sound but I could see everything very clearly. My head was on the ground sideways and I watched the ground go by. My armor seat was holding the aircraft up off my head just barely. Besides the ground and not hearing anything, there was the smell of burning grass and fuel.

For about a minute or so, I just hung there, upside down. All of a sudden, the sound came back in my head of the engine of our helicopter that was still running. I made a quick assessment of any injuries to my body and upside down, I unstrapped myself from the tangled mess of a cockpit. The next thing I knew, I had crawled about 10 meters away.

I stopped, looked back at the helicopter and focused on the rest of the crew. I ran back to the helicopter and saw one of the passengers crawling away. I went to where the other pilot was caught in the cockpit. He was OK with just some bruises. I got him untangled and away from the helicopter. I found the passenger who had crawled away.

He had a hurt leg, so I assured him that help would be coming soon. The second passenger was no longer in the helicopter. I panicked. He was nowhere to be seen. I started looking for him all around the helicopter in nearby locations. Finally, I found him. He seemed not to have a scratch on his body but he was unconscious. When I checked more closely, he was dead. I hadn't seen a body since Vietnam.

Rescue came quickly and all of us were taken to a local hospital. I had a leg compression injury and the long underwear I was wearing stopped the bleeding and sealed the cut on my leg. I was taken to an American hospital and put in a room after treatment with an Air Force pilot who had ejected from his fighter plane that afternoon.

When I got back to Fort Riley, I had a new assignment because the general I had flown for received a new assignment. I was back in the maintenance section again. One day, I was helping out with some maintenance, holding the tail rotor driveshaft when the blade was turned accidentally.

The second finger of my hand was cut off. I had never felt such pain. I went through many procedures to get my finger reattached and over the next few months, the doctors got it to work almost back to normal.

During this time off flight status, I was transferred to battalion headquarters and made the assistant operations officer for flight scheduling and projects. I hated the job at first but I started working with some great people. My boss, Major Ottiman, gave me all the things that I wanted to do. He helped me learn the things that I did not know how to do, so I learned a great deal about the United States Army and how it worked in those eight months. The leadership and support brought me back to life.

About this time, I did not think that I was going to get promoted. Consequently, I would be out of the Army and looking for a job and a new life. Because of my time flying the general around and his good words about me back to the Department of the Army, I was promoted to W3. Also, with all my flight time and experience, I became a senior Army aviator. I now had wings with a star above it. That promotion and the upgrade gave me a new spring in my step.

I went to the Army's airborne school not because I was gung-ho and wanted to be an airborne pilot. I didn't want to be one of those elite soldiers who jumped out of a perfectly good airplane to face the enemy all around them. I went to jump school because my boss in the S3 shop at Fort Riley wanted someone to go with him. He said it would be good for my career. He knew that it was going to be good for his career, because he was an infantry officer in a helicopter pilot billet.

We got down to Fort Benning on a Sunday and the school started on Monday. It's not the same school that the guys who make a career of being an airborne soldier began from the very start. Ours was a school to give other enlisted men and officers the experience, the expertise and knowledge to use the airborne elements of the United States Army. I had been in the Army for about 10 years, so I was right in the middle of the age group of my fellow classmates.

We started out by getting ourselves in proper physical condition. We had a physical training (PT) test to see where a baseline was and then the instructors proceeded to kick our butts. I had never done so much PT. We ran every place that we were supposed to go. In my whole life, not even the first half of warrant officer flight school, did we have to run everywhere. Basic training and the other schools were half as hard as this rugged training.

After going to classes from the history of parachute jumping through all the deployments of parachute troops through all the wars and even the proper way to fold a parachute, it was time for the big jump. We went up in a C130 and there were 30 of us. Everybody was very quiet on the way to the drop zone. We were filled with our thoughts and our fears and I was scared as hell!

What turned out to be a blessing was that I was in the middle of the stick and when it came time, I stood up, hooked up and shuffled into the position. When the jumpmaster hollered over the roar of the engines for everybody to go, I was just hustled along with the man in front of me and pushed along by the guy behind me. I closed my eyes when I went out the open door.

Then as the wind hit me, it was kind of amazing. The roar of the aircraft was gone, so it was very quiet. And the view! With nothing around me but other jumpers, the view was spectacular. My training kicked in. I looked up for my chute to open and I held onto my reserve. I had a feeling of great relief when my chute fully deployed.

Then I had to think about what I was going to do as the ground got closer and closer. Again, my training kicked in and I was all set. Luckily, it had rained the night before and the ground was like a cushion. Everything worked as the instructor had told us. We jumped two more times and I was awarded my jump wings.

I wasn't going to get paid for it, because pilot status was higher priority and more than airborne pay. I have never jumped since and probably never got any real career benefit out of it, except I did make it through that tough airborne training. It was a boost to one's self esteem and it added another set of wings to my uniform.

Within a few days I received new orders, because my time at Fort Riley was up. I had been there just over four years and had placed a request for transfer back to Germany. The orders came through. As a single man now, it didn't take long to pack my bags, sign out of my unit, clean out my apartment and get on the road back to New Jersey. I would have a few weeks to see family and spend some time with my Aunt Callie and my older brother.

I enjoyed my time at home seeing the family. I was excited about going back to Germany, a place where I had been so happy. It seemed like I had a mission and purpose there. It was going to be another adventure and this time I knew where I was going before I got there. I received a welcome letter from a pilot in the 59th Ordinance Brigade. I was going to a place very close to the French border. I would be discovering a whole new region of Germany.

Before I left my post as assistant operations officer for the First Aviation Battalion, I was detailed to be the announcer for the battalion change of command. It was an interesting assignment. I helped organize the band and helped them choose the marches that would be played.

I organized where each of the companies were to stand in the order in which they would parade in front of the new commander. An important part of this duty was to announce the chain of command, read the history of the unit in the Army and the biography of the new commander.

The day was bright and sunny, a perfect day for this important event. We had a flyby with the helicopters in the battalion and the band music was outstanding. I think all my life I have loved martial music. The ceremony went like clockwork. I was nervous but didn't mess up any of my speaking parts. I had never been good at public speaking before large crowds of people, so when the ceremony was over, I felt very proud of myself and our unit's performance.

As things were winding down and people congratulated me, a full colonel walked toward me. As he got closer, I came to attention, saluted him. He congratulated me on a fine job that I had done and then he said, "Are you from Jamaica? You speak the language so distinctly!"

I was taken aback, I looked him in the eye and said to him, "Sir, I am from New Jersey and everyone in New Jersey speaks exactly as I do!" His eyes got kind of big and then he walked away. I saluted him with good military decorum. For the moment, I thought, "There are still people in high places with very small minds." This high ranking, ignorant man probably did not even realize how offensive and racist his comment was or did he? I had to do something.

Being black and being in the Army in most ways was very comfortable for me. I saw many more people of color in this line of work than I did in other jobs. To me, there was a sense that all of America was part of this organization and all were playing a part in protecting our country. So in a sense, I felt it was a noble calling in since black Americans have defended their country since before it was the United States.

I had this great feeling of pride that even as such a small factor in this Army, I was one of its leaders, one of its officers and one of a very few black pilots with combat experience. But I still had to cope with American society. Individually, there were people who felt that I shouldn't be a leader because of my color.

I shouldn't be an aircraft commander. I shouldn't be ordering other men around. In the enlisted ranks, men of color had been sergeants and sergeants major from the Civil War on. Until 1948 when President Truman integrated the armed forces, a noncommissioned officer was the highest position of leadership for black men. Very few blacks were commissioned officers. I found that in some cases I was looked upon as an oddity being an officer and a pilot.

Few of us were inspired much less encouraged to serve in that capacity. There were many times when I felt that I was being examined and all my decisions were questioned about what I decided to do. My leadership was also scrutinized. I decided that I needed to keep a more even check on my emotions. I really couldn't display any anger or be truly upset with someone's performance.

If I did, my opinion would be disregarded, as I would be characterized as an angry black man whose opinions were irrational and not coming from knowledge or investigation. I had to learn to live with this racism and to employ strategies to show I was a truly thoughtful leader. That is what I did. I developed those leadership skills to be calm and patient when I spoke to earn the respect of those I led and those I had to follow.

There were senior officers who looked at me as an exception to the black population in America and most of my peers viewed me as an example of the people in this country we were committed to serve. As much as I enjoyed flying the UH1 helicopter with about 3,500 hours in the cockpit, I really enjoyed flying the Blackhawk.

Not only was it twice as big and twice as fast but also it had two engines and a cockpit filled with fun things to do. That was power! A year later, I was back in Germany and enjoying my life being a senior Army aviator and an officer in a very important unit. After a year, I got a call from my daughter's grandmother saying that my daughter, April, needed me take care of her.

Her mother was having difficulties and needed a break. I flew back immediately and picked up April, who was now seven years old. I took her back to Germany and enrolled her in school and in the daycare program. Once again, I was a single parent. That is not the same power as flying the Blackhawk but the power of joy to be her dad was great.

That was a wonderful, happy year that April lived with me. I enjoyed so much being her dad and the whole responsibility of being a single parent in the military. It was hard work making all the arrangements that had to be made but friends volunteered and it all worked.

At the end of that year, her mother was again in a good position to take her back. This is what I told her that I would do and I kept my word. I had become overwhelmingly attached to my daughter and wanted to be with her always, so the parting was difficult. About a year after, I brought April back to her mother. I was again transferred to Fort Riley.

Per our agreement, April came to see me during the summers and every other Thanksgiving and Christmas. I would drive up to Minnesota to attend parent teacher conferences and to see my daughter every other month. When I got back to Kansas, I bought my first house and took great pride in being a homeowner.

It was good to get back into the US and to have community around me. There were other benefits like having reliable electricity without hearing a generator nearby. Also, I had the opportunity to be around folks that were not in the Army. Being back on the rotation meant that we would be on standby alert. Our standby ran for 24 hours, from seven in the morning.

On this one day in June 1985, it was a very quiet day to start—no emergency runs and a bright, warm Kansas day. Then after about one o'clock, our operations got a request for transportation of a seven-year-old Army dependent to go to Kansas City Children's Hospital. He had fallen and injured his head.

It wasn't a difficult mission to plan and the weather was good—a direct flight of about 45 minutes. The young patient, a doctor and a nurse arrived at our aircraft shortly after two. We loaded them on board, the crew was all set, we started up and took off. The sky was clear with very little wind and you could see forever. It looked like a very uneventful flight.

About ten minutes into the flight, we all settled into what we thought would be a routine trip to Kansas City. Then my copilot, said to me over the intercom, "I see a shadow on the ground that just went under us!" I started to scan from the left side of the cockpit all the way across the front to the right. As I looked out the right-side cargo door, the sight that greeted me, scared me to death!

It was an airplane! All I could see was the engine and propeller. Immediately I grabbed the controls from my copilot, turned the helicopter hard left, reduced power and tried to dive for the ground. We were up about 2,500 feet in the air at the time, so we were just seconds from the earth. As I got the aircraft turning away and diving down, I felt a bump! And then the chopper started shaking! At that moment we were hit, a midair collision. No one I knew had ever survived this.

As we were heading down to the ground, with the nose straight down, I said to myself, "So this is what it's like to die!" Saying that seemed to calm me down. I started trying to figure out what I could do to right this aircraft. I would move one control and if nothing worked, I'd move another. Then I would move them in combination. With a certain methodical moving of the controls, the helicopter started to respond.

I righted the ship and the ground started coming up much slower. I picked a place to land and put the aircraft down. I shut off the engine and told the passengers to stay in the aircraft until the rotor blades stopped turning. I had made emergency radio calls on the way down, so I assured everyone that help would be here soon.

I got on my portable radio and contacted the helicopter inbound and made sure they knew exactly where we were and that we were all safe. When helicopter arrived, it picked up the doctor, the nurse and the patient and took them on to their hospital. The next helicopter that came in was the battalion commander.

He looked at my helicopter with one rotor blade severely damaged and said, "Raymond, you did a wonderful job. You saved their lives!" That meant so much to me. I just about got teary with the stress leaving my body.

In late October 1984, I was the standardization officer for the 82nd Medical Detachment. My boss, Major East, got orders to send two full medevac flight crews plus maintenance support to Honduras. The aircraft would already be down there and we would be replacing a team from Fort Hood, Texas. Our team would consist of a maintenance officer and a mechanic, four pilots, two crew chiefs and two flight medics.

We were going to depart in two weeks and the Army expected that would be enough time to get our affairs in order. We had to prepare to be there for six months. I was single at that time and had to arrange for someone to take care of my home. I had purchased my first home about two years before. I was just getting settled in the house and had to deploy.

I was lucky enough to have a retired sergeant major as my backyard neighbor. We had chatted many hours over the back fence and he had become a good friend and source of information. He readily accepted the responsibility of caring for my home. I gave him a key and my APO address. With his looking after things I felt that my new property would be safe.

About five days before departing, I was called up to division headquarters. I did not know what it was about. I had done nothing wrong and all I was told that I was supposed to meet a person from the Department of the Army. I showed up at the proper time, walked into this conference room and saw a gentleman who was as round as he was tall in a business suit and a tie that didn't quite match.

He stood up as I came in, shook my hand and showed me his identification. I studied his ID card, looked at him to match the picture to the man and said, "What can I do for you, sir?"

In all my encounters, going up to division headquarters had never been a good thing. So in my mind, this meeting created some tension. The gentleman was from Army Intelligence. He told me that because I had a top-secret clearance and was a fairly senior warrant officer, they had a mission for me during my time in Honduras.

Right away, I thought but did not say, "Why do they want me? And what can I do for Army Intelligence flying medevac helicopters?" He assured me that I would not be doing anything dangerous or outside of my normal duties. Army Intelligence wanted me to observe and report on all that I could see during my travels around that area of Central America.

We were supporting the contras in Nicaragua and there was a small revolution going on in El Salvador. What I could see and report about the military operations and the local situation would help them evaluate the entire situation. I would just be one little piece of information to help make the big picture clearer.

After his briefing, first he told me that I could not tell anyone about what I was doing and that if I accepted this assignment, to call his office when I returned and he would come out and debrief me. He also said that I could decline this assignment without prejudice to my career. I thought about this for about one minute. I looked into his eyes as I thought about what he had said. Then I told him that I'd be happy to be of service.

He smiled, shook my hand and said thank you. I left the conference room— in clandestine spy mode. I was a little excited about the whole idea of my being a secret agent. I had seen a couple James Bond movies but this assignment seemed rather docile.

When I got back to my office, the other pilots asked me what the meeting was about. Everybody knew that I was called up to division headquarters. I smiled a little and said, "Can't tell you," and went about my business with a little smile on my face.

After we got to the hospital area in Honduras, we met the soldiers that we were replacing. They were a medevac crew from Fort Hood and they were glad to see us. They were going home. We dropped off our bags in what is known as a sea hut, a wooden barracks with screens halfway up to the ceiling and a corrugated iron roof. We had three of these barracks for the aviation section. One was for operations and our supplies, one for officers and pilots and one for the enlisted personnel.

Since this was not my first deployment, I found an empty corner, set up a bunk and made myself at home. After that the guys that we were replacing took us over to this little all ranks club. There I met many of the doctors and nurses and corps men and women of the 47th Army Field Hospital. Since I had been a medevac pilot for two years, I expected to be part of a group of men and women that would be fun to be with. I was not let down; we were greeted with big smiles and hearty handshakes and a couple of beers apiece.

If you had ever seen the movie *Mash*, the surroundings would be very familiar. We had a dental unit and the dentists became some of my best friends. There was every surgical specialty doctor and nurse that you could possibly think of. We even had a hospital veterinarian. His team lived right next door to us and he became a good friend trying to educate us about the animals in the area. We all ate in the mess hall and most of the time, the food was really good.

From time to time we would get local food that would really spice up the meals. There was no running water, except for the communal shower. Of course, one side was for females and one side was for males. About 6 o'clock every evening, there was a parade of all the personnel to the showers.

We had a water tanker that had to be filled every week or so. We took small tanks, filled them up from the large tanker and used that for drinking water, washing our faces and brushing our teeth in the morning. We had ten out houses where underneath of the seat was a 55-gallon drum cut in half. Every day the local personnel would drag the drum out, pour diesel fuel in it and set it on fire. That was the origin of my flashbacks when I first arrived in Honduras, the smell of burning crap filled me with memories of Vietnam.

During my six months in Honduras, my main job was to ensure the high standards for flight proficiency for day, night and inclement weather flying. Since we only had two crews, I would be on standby every other day. Our mission varied quite a bit but our primary mission was to provide air ambulance service to all US and allied military personnel in Honduras. This area included the border with Nicaragua, El Salvador and Guatemala.

Also we had a humanitarian mission of providing medical support to the local Hondurans. The hospital ran a weekly clinic for local people. They would come from miles around to get treatment. Twice a month, we would take a medical team to more remote spots in the country and spend the day treating hundreds of local residents.

Because this was an Army hospital staffed by members of the Air Force and Navy, we got to do some extraordinary things. I got to work in the medical clinics. I made friends with the chief of surgery, the hospital dentist and the veterinarian. During my days off, when I wasn't flying, I would go over to those clinics to learn and help out as much as they would let me.

You might be surprised to know—they let me do a lot. I helped prepare the operating room for surgeries and got to observe them! When the hospital conducted clinics for the local people, I was trained to do triage. This was a very fulfilling time for me. I got so interested in the medicine that I would help out during surgeries. I learned how to help set up the surgical theater and clean it up afterward.

I found this was a very rewarding and exciting time to be an Army pilot. Most days I was doing continuous training for my guys, keeping my pilots sharp in instrument flying and night vision goggles. Not only did I do the training but also the real missions could get very exciting. We had Americans come down and parachute in for training and of course some would get hurt.

We had an ongoing insurgency in Nicaragua supported by the United States government, so there were times when I flew very close to, if not across the border to pick up wounded individuals. It was an important time in history and I was a part of it. One of the highlights of those months in Honduras was that I was notified that I was on the promotion list for Chief Warrant Officer 4.

At that time, it was the highest rank for warrant officers and within a few months, I would pin on my new higher rank. I was very proud of my progress in the Army but I never did become the black James Bond. When our time was up and we came home, we didn't have a big parade or anything like that. We got off the airplane at the Air National Guard ramp in Topeka, Kansas and took buses back to our detachment area at Fort Riley.

Our commanding officer thanked us and gave us the weekend off. Three of us who were single went out for pizza and a beer, talked about our time in Honduras and then went home to settle back to our regular Army lives. When it was time to go back to Germany in my heart, I wanted my daughter with me. I talked to her mother and she was not involved with anyone. I thought we would give our marriage another try and she agreed.

So again, we were married and we headed off to Germany as a family. April was in junior high school in Germany and we took trips as a family all over the continent. However, it became apparent that I still had not learned how to prioritize my family.

When I got my orders for Germany, I knew I wasn't going to a medevac unit. I would be a UH60 pilot and would be going to a front-line field unit. The new unit I was going to was the First Armored Division! A unit with a lot of

173

history from World War II fighting in Europe. Except for the First Infantry Division, I had been in support units, very important to the cold war effort but not on the tip of the sword.

When I got to Ansbach, Germany, near the city of Nuremberg, I found that I was the senior warrant officer in my company. There were only three other officers who outranked me and they needed a platoon leader. I was given first platoon with command of five helicopters, 10 pilots and 12 enlisted man. I was amazed at how fast I took to the responsibility.

These are my people and my aircraft and I signed for them all—literally $15 million of equipment and 22 men. We were going to be the best platoon in the company—if not the battalion. I had a new family. I took the time to know every man, his full name, his background, where he was from and if he was married or not. We started a program in the company, so everyone that did not have a GED, would get one.

Also for all the mechanics who wanted one, we would help them get an FAA mechanics license. Even before all that was completed, our aircraft were the cleanest and the most mechanically fit in the company. I was so proud of my platoon. I loved my job as the platoon leader. Taking care of my troops and getting the mission done was exciting to me.

Then one day, after about a year in the unit, the company commander asked if I wanted to go back to Fort Rucker to become a Blackhawk Instructor Pilot (IP). I didn't remember that I had told him when I first got to the unit that was my goal. I wanted to be a UH 60 instructor pilot.

Within two weeks, I found myself on an airplane flying back to the United States. When I got to my training unit, I was excited about being an IP. I had flown the UH 60 for a little over a year. It was the best aircraft I've ever flown, so I was really excited about the school. The school was well run and my instructor was just outstanding.

For an old guy, I found that I could regurgitate the information readily and that information stayed in my head. Four weeks later, it was time for a check ride. For the first time in my flying career, I was not apprehensive. I met my check airman. He was a no-nonsense pilot and off we went to the aircraft. The trick about being an instructor pilot over a pilot, is that you have to describe each maneuver as you do it. I found that the information flowed from my brain through my mouth with ease. This was the best check ride that I had ever flown.

I loved teaching in the Blackhawk. It is a complex helicopter but so logically laid out and fun to fly. I was the only IP in the unit, so I did instruction for all procedures and new procedures at least two times a week. The rest of the time I was on the First Armor Division missions. Support for that mission, we did sling loads of ammunition and fuel for the tanks and for the division's attack helicopters.

Another mission we had was training to rescue downed pilots in case of war. Attack helicopter pilots and utility pilots had pick up points throughout the division's battlefront area. We trained to fly low level and pick up downed pilot at those designated areas.

The training that I really loved most was instrument flying. I enjoyed flying in the clouds, talking to aircraft controllers and flying approaches when the weather was really bad. There was a lot of rain, snow and low clouds in Germany. Having instrument flying skills was something that gave you peace of mind and confidence that you could perform any mission in any conditions.

After our three years in Germany, I had 20 years in the Army, so it was time to think about retiring. I could have left the Army in Germany but I thought that I needed time to figure out what I was going to do to find a place to live and what civilian work to do.

My family wanted to live in California so I applied for a permanent assignment change to Fort Ord on Monterey Bay. I couldn't think of a more wonderful place to be for my last two years in the Army. When you make a permanent change of duty station, you have to give the Army two years of service.

Little did I know at the time that I would spend over half that time in Panama. We moved the family to Sacramento and I did a two-hour commute to Monterey. I came home only on the weekends. We were a family but again the stress was mounting.

Fort Ord was a great place to do my last bit of duty. The beautiful California coast near Monterey and Carmel was spectacular. I was assigned to the Ninth Infantry Division. Not knowing too much about that division and their mission, I decided to let the anticipation build the excitement. When I got there 30 days later, I was happy to find out that I was to be the battalion standardization officer.

I would have 10 instructor pilots reporting to me and would be charged with maintaining the high standards of flying for three companies of

Blackhawks. The other thing that was not so great were the regular trips to Panama. The assignment was three months there and three months at home. We were in support of the operations in Panama to show American strength and presence. I wanted to spend more time at home, being a regular Army officer and planning out my future as a civilian.

I thought that I had given enough with ten years overseas, in the twenty years I was in the Army. That was not how the Army saw it. The need was in Panama. I soon learned that going to Panama was exciting and fun. It was like the days when I was a brand-new pilot in the Army—roughing it in many of the craziest and exotic places in the world. I found that it was much like flying in Vietnam—lots of jungle with lots of amazing animals to see and many different missions to fly.

In 1989 when we were back in the US, central California had one of its biggest and most damaging earthquakes. I had never been through an earthquake before. When it first happened, I was conducting a meeting of my IP's and this giant hanger we were in started to shake. I looked around, wondering what was going on. In the blink of an eye, all of the guys were running out the door. Not wanting to be left alone, I followed.

There we were in the parking lot, looking up at the hanger as it shook with the shock waves but nothing fell down. San Francisco was especially hard hit. Later that evening, we got missions to take Army engineers to the Presidio of San Francisco. I did a run and when I got there, you could see the damage. It was tremendous. When I got back to the airfield, I was done flying for the evening.

It was quite late and I went to my room to get some sleep. All the lights were out, because there was no power. As I climbed into bed looking for a good night's sleep, all of a sudden, an aftershock hit us. It shook me out of bed and when I came to my senses, I ran outside to the parking lot with the other residents. After waiting for more aftershocks and nothing happened, we went back to bed.

Then the political situation in Panama started to get tenser. Our missions took on a new sense of urgency. We were moving field Artillery around the canal zone and we were doing night vision goggles training with special operations forces. Then in December 1989, I was at Fort Ord planning on going home for Christmas to see my family when we deployed.

'Just Cause' was my third time in combat. First, of course, was Vietnam, then medevacs on the Honduran-Nicaraguan border and now Panama. Six months before I retired, I was sitting in my room, planning on going home for Christmas. The phone rang and the guy on the other end was the operations officer for our battalion. He told me it was an emergency recall and we all had to report to our duty station. I got to airfield operations and we were told that we had an emergency action in Panama.

We were to fly our Blackhawks over to the Monterey airport to be loaded into Air Force C5 cargo jets. I said to myself, "I have only six months to go in this Army and I've already been in war—twice." Then I said to myself that it was my duty, so I take the money and go where they send me. I helped figure out who was going to fly with whom and on what aircraft.

I briefed the six crews on where we were going to go at Monterey airport to wait for the C5's. In the early morning hours, we took off in formation and flew the ten minutes to the airport. Once there, the mechanics were driven over to the airport and helped us fold all the rotor blades, so they would fit into a C5 aircraft. About an hour after we got all that done, the Air Force showed up with their magnificent cargo airplanes.

Once they were in position, we loaded up our helicopters and waited for takeoff time. We had food brought out to us and settled in for takeoff. Our colonel, the CO of the battalion, came by saying hi to all of us and seeing how we were. When he got to me, I stood up and shook his hand.

I looked him in the eye and half joking said, "Sir, I have six months to go before retirement. I've been in combat in Honduras and in Vietnam, do I really belong on this trip?"

He looked at me with a smile and said, "Ray, another chance for a good man to excel!"

We landed in the dark and taxied to the ramp of Howard Air Force Base, rolled our helicopters out, unfolded the rotor blades and did a maintenance run up to make sure that everything was correct. We had a final briefing and prepared to pick up a company of Marines. We had five Blackhawks to pick up 100 Marines.

We had no seats in the back of our helicopters and just cargo straps across the doorway. We got over twenty Marines inside of our helicopter. It seemed like they were sandwiched in all over the ship with their feet dangling out the door and hands hanging onto the cargo straps. This is where I found out that the Blackhawk is a marvelous combat helicopter.

The Huey could only carry eight troops and we carried almost three times that many. We flew in close formation with night vision goggles. It was so smooth like sitting in your living room chair! As we reached our objective, we inserted the Marines next to a Panamanian defense force base, between them and an American housing area. We had Air Force C130 gunships for support.

We started taking fire from the base, green tracers coming up at us, so flight lead called for gun support. Within a few moments, a whole host of red tracers magically coming from an invisible place in the sky eliminated the fire! When we landed there were a few troops that opposed us but the Marines charged out and ended all opposition.

After dropping off the Marines, we took off and headed back to Howard Air Force Base to learn what our next mission would be. The rest of the war was not as exciting as that first night. We did mostly support missions bringing supplies to the infantry unit as they moved through the country. Actual combat lasted about 10 days and after that for another week or two, we helped move troops to occupy Panama all the way to the Costa Rican border.

We stayed at a Panamanian Army airfield where there were not a lot of amenities. We had to fly in our food and make arrangements for showers and latrines. All in all, our lives as flying infantrymen were mostly enjoyable. The tours in Panama were not heavy combat but there was a tension between the government of Panama and the United States who at that time still owned the Panama Canal.

I would go down there every three months for three months to conduct exercises with the United States Army. It showed the government in Panama we could not be pushed around. There was one crazy event that I want to share. I was a check pilot most of the time, doing training on instrument flying and giving training in night vision goggles.

We were stationed on Howard Air Force Base and the airfield was really packed. We were parked right next to the fence and on the other side of the fence was the thickest jungle I had ever seen. On the other side was a myriad of creatures, things that flew, crawled, ran and slithered.

On one particular day, I was assigned to do training and give an instrument check ride to one of our pilots. We did preflight of the aircraft, planned the mission and got ready to go early that morning. Both of us pilots had done a thorough pre-flight and we were confident along with our crew chief that the aircraft would fly perfectly. We got our clearance to takeoff and hold at 6,000 feet at a nearby VOR beacon.

The clouds were pretty low, at about 1,500 feet and as we climbed out, at 4000 feet, we were on top. As we finished our climb to 6,000 and were about to enter holding at the Beacon, the other pilot saw something coming out of a hole in the instrument panel. When the three of us recognized that it was a snake and most likely poisonous, the copilot became unnerved. He was trying to get out of his seat and couldn't, so I took control of the aircraft.

During this time, the crew chief was trying to kill the snake and had brought with him between the seats the biggest knife I had ever seen. I told him to watch out that the knife didn't short out any of the radios and I called approach control to get us clearance to land. I told them that we needed to land very quickly.

He said that we were number two and would have to wait our turn. Things were getting really bizarre in the cockpit. The copilot was becoming more and more panicked and the crew chief was wielding that knife around, trying to kill the snake.

I called back to approach control, told him that I would have to declare an emergency. He came back with name type of emergency and I said, "Snake in the cockpit." He said without hesitation that we were now number one for the approach and cleared to land. He vectored the other aircraft out of the way and we were on the ground seven minutes later.

Once we landed, we were told to park next to flight operations. When we taxied in and came to a stop, there were a bunch of people waiting for us, one of whom was the Air Force veterinarian. The crew chief got out of the aircraft, holding this five-foot-long snake just under its head and handed it to the veterinarian. The vet secured the snake and talked to my crew chief for a short time.

The crew chief got back to the ship and we moved across the airfield to a parking area. The crew chief told us that it was a very poisonous snake and if it had bitten any of us, we would have been very sick. The vet also said that they usually found their way into the aircraft to warm up during the coldest part of the night. It had happened before and would probably happen again.

Once operation 'Just Cause', was completed and Noriega was safely in a Miami jail, we started heading home. My crew and two other flight crews were on the last couple of airplanes out of Panama for California. I got back in the middle of the night and it was good to be home. Panama would be my last deployment.

It was the end of January 1990 and I was a little over five months from retirement and had lived through 75 more hours of combat flying time. I had a choice now of wearing the Ninth Infantry Division patch on my left shoulder or staying with the First Aviation Brigade patch I earned in Vietnam. I decided that I would honor my time in Vietnam, it was a whole year of being shot at, mortared and supporting troops in the field.

I was a young man in Vietnam. That was where I had to grow up, where I lost my best friends and my youth went. It lived in my heart. As the last months of my assignment at Fort Ord rolled on, it wasn't your typical light duty and good weather before I retired. Forest fires raged in California and we were called on to help fight them.

The first thing we had to learn to fight fires was to put a big bucket that held 400 gallons of water and hang it under our helicopter. We learned how to collect the water from a reservoir, fly it over to the burning area and drop it on the fire. I had that opportunity. It was exciting and a big high to help the citizens of California.

The last three months were taken up with normal duties—paperwork, inspections, check rides and teaching. When I had about a month to go, I started out-processing paperwork and at the same time, I sent resumes out to about 30 different companies. I was too young just to sit on my butt and do nothing. I decided that I had to find work and Army retirement pay by itself was not going to cut it.

So my last days in the Army, I researched companies and made cold calls. Out of all those resumes and cold calls, I received three offers—one in Pittsburgh to fly for a hospital, another to fly in the Marshall Islands in the western Pacific and the last for a teaching job at Northwest Airlines. My wife and I decided that Minnesota would be the best place to be.

It was the summer of 1990 and I did some phone interviews and one personal visit. I would be teaching classes in the flight simulator and my aircraft would be the Boeing 757. I took the job, thinking that it would be a great new adventure.

A week before I retired, my boss came up to me and said my retirement day parade will happen next week. I looked at my boss and said with great respect, "I don't want a parade. After 22 years in the Army, I have been in at least 50 parades. I don't want all the battalion to go through all that work just for me. I came into the Army without a parade, so I can go out the same way, it was an honor to serve."

Well, my boss looked at me and said, "Ray, you have no choice. This is an order. After 22 years, you get a parade." When that day came, I stood out on the large green quad. I was moved by the pageantry, the music and my fellow soldiers marching with military precision. There were seven of us retiring that day. I was the highest-ranking retiree and the longest served. I got to review the battalion and give the command to pass in review.

My whole military career played through my mind, as I watched the Army band and the battalion march by. I knew that it was tradition. I was grateful to be part of that tradition and I was honored by the whole event and to have served my country for all these years!

After two more helicopter crashes and two more combat tours, I retired from the Army and we moved to Minnesota where April's mom wanted to be. I got a job at Northwest Airlines and it was just as stressful as the Army. I had to learn a new way of doing things in the airline business. This situation put more stress on our family and April's mom and I divorced again.

Bruce: There was a lot to say for the entrepreneurial spirit but startup companies required money from people who believed in your idea. The idea for our new company, Rendezvous Industries, was to set up campgrounds on large plots of land in some of the most beautiful spots in the western US.

With an associate from West Point who had been my tactical officer, we convinced investors that we could make it happen. In eight months, we raised $1.5 million and I headed to Colorado, Wyoming and Idaho to find the land. I was convinced we could make it work and now my job was to convince others.

The theory was that people with recreational vehicles would buy into a tour of the campgrounds in the most scenic western locations like Pikes Peak and Rocky Mountain National Park in Colorado and Jackson Hole and Cheyenne, Wyoming with scenic stops along the way. It would be like the old days when the mountain men, fur trappers and traders would rendezvous to trade their goods.

Now campers, trailers and other recreational vehicles (RV's) would be the transportation. The concept was close to brilliant and the execution was almost flawless. Colorado was difficult to operate in but Wyoming and Idaho were more hospitable to the concept.

We found beautiful ranches where the owners contracted with us to underground the electric hookups for the RV's. We would truck in the water they required and truck out the sewage as needed—we would joke, not in the same truck. The idea was to preserve the land and give the RV owners a unique Western adventure. From our Army experience, we knew how to move in, set up and move out without destroying the land.

The concept was excellent but the timing could not have been worse. Problems in the Middle East, as Ray mentioned, created a gas crisis in the US. As the price of gas soared, gas lines grew at service stations and supplies dwindled, the gas guzzling RV's stayed home.

In the meantime, I had met the love of my life. Audrey was an elementary school teacher with a master's degree in reading education from Chicago. Something happened when I met this woman in the Minneapolis Public Library where we both had taken a class. I'm not sure what it was about her. She was beautiful but it was not her beauty that attracted me.

It was something deeper. I was still traveling all over the West, putting the land deals together but when the snow hit, there were camper RV shows to attend to build business. One of the biggest RV shows was in Chicago where she lived, so we set up a date. I had to drive to a western suburb to pick her up. It was raining like Vietnam and I almost turned back.

When I reached her apartment and she answered the door, something told me she was the one. That was our first date in January. She visited me in February and I proposed by the falls in Sioux Falls, South Dakota. She said yes.

I met her brother and his family in Chicago and she met my mother in Boston. But I had a feeling that something was missing. I had not given her an engagement ring. We had decided that our love was all we needed but now I needed to buy the ring. It was not a big diamond but it was the biggest I could afford. I flew to Chicago to give it to her.

She met me at the gate in O'Hare Airport and as we walked through the airport holding hands, she felt the ring on my pinky finger. She asked, "What is that?" We stopped. I got down on one knee and re-proposed in front of the Eastern Airlines ticket counter—very romantic.

We were married in June in Chicago and had a one-day honeymoon at the Drake Hotel. I had to get back on the road, so we packed up her apartment and she moved from Chicago to Sioux Falls. I took this young woman from Chicago to Sioux Falls—and from the Drake Hotel to a trailer in Cheyanne, Wyoming. She really must have wondered what she had signed up for.

The company did have a unique success during Cheyanne's 'Frontier Days' celebration. It was not easy for RV's to find a space during Frontier Days, so we convinced a rancher to let us use his land to prove our concept. We set up in a field just outside of the city and ran our campground. The concept worked beautifully.

This test gave us a lot of confidence to keep moving forward. My new bride and I spent our honeymoon in a cramped little trailer with paint peeling off the ceiling in Cheyenne, Wyoming—we survived this first test. The company, however, did not survive. We went bankrupt. We went through the $1.5 million in a year and a half. A great idea failed, so what did we learn?

Sometimes even the best ideas fail. Sometimes even the best execution fails. Sometimes there are just some things like a gas shortage that are totally out of your control. When the company went bust, Audrey wanted to move back to Chicago and I wanted to ski in Colorado. We compromised and settled on Minneapolis where we met and where we both had friends.

I interviewed at two CPA firms and went to work at KPMG (then it was Peat, Marwick, Mitchell & Co). I chose KPMG, a large CPA firm, because they had the best clients in Minneapolis. Audrey got her teaching credentials for Minnesota. With Audrey's teaching job and steady promotions at the CPA firm, we bought our first home in South Minneapolis.

A new neighbor, Walter 'Rocky' Rockenstein, was the only Republican on the Minneapolis City Council and I worked on his campaigns for several years. Audrey and I were Republicans at that time and we voted for Richard Nixon for President. Friends today are surprised if they find out that fact. Rocky was a Yale Law School grad and a Marine Corps veteran. One day, he was helping me move some furniture in our home.

My West Point class ring was rolling around in the drawer of the bureau we were moving. He asked me why I didn't wear the ring. Rocky, as a former Marine, understood my answer. I told him that with all I saw and did in Vietnam, I had no interest in any connection with West Point or the military.

He thought for a minute and replied, "There's more to West Point than Vietnam." He was right.

Rocky's statement stopped me in my tracks. West Point had been my dream since I was five. Now, 28 years later and ten years since graduation, I had to think about the facts. West Point was a great experience for me. My classmates, my best and closest friends, were from there. The great traditions, the world travel, the education—they were the highlights of my life so far and I was blocking them out. Why? What was going on? At the time, I did not know what PTSD was. Rocky's words woke me up.

Institutional racism was alive and thriving at the CPA firm. There was one black CPA in a firm of over 300. When the black CPA decided to leave the firm to move back to Texas, I was assigned the task to talk him into staying in Minneapolis.

After a brief conversation, this young man said to me, "Bruce, I am going back to Texas where I will work in a black CPA firm. How would you like it if you walked into work every day and never saw a face that looked the same as yours?" It was a great question for which I had no answer. I wished him the best and he left the firm.

Interestingly, I had never thought how that would feel to be the only white person in a firm. I would learn more about that in China. I had never even considered how my black kindergarten teacher or my seventh-grade social studies teacher felt in all white workplaces. It never crossed my mind how Oris felt, how he must have struggled being around so many white kids at camp. We were friends. It just never dawned on me what struggles he faced.

As a senior auditor, I was in New York City training to become a statistical audit specialist. I have always loved math and wanted to find better ways to complete business audit assignments. Statistics seemed like an answer, so I was selected for the program and trained in statistical methods applied to specific audit problems.

The two-week training often ran into the late evening hours at the firm's New York office on the 14th floor of the building. One evening all of a sudden, the lights went out. It wasn't just our office but the whole city had gone dark. During the two days of New York City blackout of 1977, it was interesting because we went down on the street and talked to some uniformed police with their great New York accents.

They were walking the streets because without lights, there was some street crime going on. As we parted, one of them said, "Watch out for youse-selves, there a lotta scumbags out on the street tonight!"

We even had to improvise the study of audit statistics. After I left the Army and became a CPA, I thought what's the worst that could happen? Maybe a heavy general ledger could fall off the shelf and crush a foot, so this was pretty exciting being in the middle of eight million people with no electricity. The whole city rallied and became friendlier. Do you know the difference between an introverted CPA and an extroverted one?

The introvert looks at his shoes when he talks to you. The extrovert looks at your shoes when he talks to you. Everyone seemed to open up—even our statistics instructors. We also got more exercise walking up and down fourteen flights to the class and twelve to the hotel room. Who says being a CPA isn't as tough as being a soldier?

In Ranger School when you took over running a unit, the sergeant running the exercise would say, "What you gonna do now, squad leader?" It was fun to see that statistical nerds can improvise.

Passing the CPA exam and being promoted into the management group in four years at the firm were big milestones in my business career. I was auditing several excellent manufacturing companies including Tennant, Toro and Cargill. From being tutored in accounting at Wharton to auditing the records of major manufacturing firms was great progress in my understanding of business finance and accounting.

I was offered a job as controller of an ad agency. I accepted the offer and later found out that I had made a mistake. It was a difficult workplace and I left to join Honeywell at their corporate headquarters in Minneapolis a year later. Honeywell was a place I thought I could better serve. Ray and I had discussed what 'service' really meant.

I did not know him at this time but given the different paths we had chosen, I too was gaining new insights on what real service was all about in business. I knew several people who worked at Honeywell and it seemed like a great fit and an excellent culture.

The change to a major Fortune 100 company became a big growth step for me. Besides making the move to a new company, our daughter, Molly, arrived on the scene. I was in the room as she was delivered. When everything had settled down and Audrey, Molly and I were alone, I held that beautiful child in my arms and sang 'Edelweiss' to her.

Then I gave my 'Ranger' tab to Audrey. I assured her that carrying that child for nine months and giving birth to a seven-pound baby was tougher than anything I ever had done in Ranger School. On top of all that I was elected Reader in our church. It was a great opportunity to get closer to God, the Bible and the church I cherished.

At a Honeywell management dinner, a woman manager repeated the litany of changes I had just been through and declared, "You're going to die! That's too much change for a body to endure." I did not die and as a family, we thrived. Honeywell was also one of the best manufacturing companies in the world. My manufacturing audit background helped me on the job.

I started at the corporate headquarters in Minneapolis as part of the Controller's office. Because of my manufacturing inventory audit experience, I was given an assignment to examine the impact of converting Honeywell's inventory from a FIFO to a LIFO basis. The technical difference doesn't matter to our story but my expertise did. This assignment would end with a presentation to the Honeywell Board of directors.

It was a great opportunity, became I traveled the country with my new boss touring plants and understanding their inventories. I put the final presentation together and rehearsed it over and over at home. At breakfast on the day of the presentation to the board, I said to Audrey that I wanted to rehearse one more time.

She said, "No! Give me those slides." She took the slides and presented them flawlessly. I was ready. It went well. My boss became a mentor and friend and soon I was promoted to be controller of the Solid-State Electronics Division (SSED). This division had been losing money for years and I was tasked by the Corporate Controller to stop the bleeding—not an easy task.

The powers that were gave me a year of grace but then expected results. After the first year, the division lost $5 million. The Corporate Treasurer was jokingly philosophical. In a private meeting with the Corporate Controller, he quipped, "Bruce, five million here, five million there, pretty soon we'll be talking real money."

We only lost $2 million the following year but I was feeling the pressure. Half of SSED was located in Colorado Springs where I had lived during my last year in the Army when I was stationed at Fort Carson. It was always fun to visit old rugby buddies there. When I first got the job, I hoped to ski with my old friends but the pressure was big—I skied one time in four years! With a new boss we broke even the following year but all was not well. I was becoming a serious workaholic.

This business was new and dynamic and I had so much to learn. We found ways to sell our expertise to other companies. We also created a unique photo product called the through camera lens (TCL). It was an incredible technical innovation for the camera industry. After our engineers introduced it, every Japanese camera manufacturer bought the concept or we ended up suing them for patent infringement.

We had to buy the creative talent to invent it from Silicon Valley. The PhD we consulted with to create the technical aspects of the lens cost us $1,000 an hour. I was impressed with this genius as well as the salary he could command as a consultant.

During this time at SSED, our son was born prematurely. With complications, he passed away that first day. I held him in my arms for eight hours and did not want to let him go but he did not make it. This was a tough time for Audrey and me. I was angry at God and everyone else. Nothing seemed to help—friends, words, flowers—my bitterness just grew. The one shining moment in all of the sadness was the smile on Molly's face when we came home.

Going back to work was difficult with a boss who basically said, "Get over it and get back to work."

Nothing at work helped until one day a friend put his arm around my shoulder and whispered, "You'll see him again someday, you know." I finally awoke to the fact that I did know that. I started to forgive myself and grow and stopped being angry with God. This was the second time a close death experience had made me angry with God. Not since Vietnam and Gary's death had I had such bitterness in my heart. The feeling was not pleasant. I still put in too many hours at work.

After four years at SSED, I was promoted to Controller of the Residential Division. SSED was a relatively small division at Honeywell. Residential was big, profitable and it was fun. The famous Honeywell round thermostat was manufactured in our plant in Golden Valley, Minnesota along with other products and there were still other products we bought from Taiwan. So other than an occasional trip, my travel time was much less. My boss was a dynamic vice president who gave me the opportunity to take some risks.

By this time, our daughter was going to the local public school. A neighbor called and asked if I would serve on the school's site council. I had to ask what a site council was. After understanding that this was an experiment in local control for the school, I joined the council. Our school district was (and still is) one of the best in the state.

Like other school districts the superintendent ran the district. The chain of command ran from the superintendent and his staff to the school principals and then to the teachers. We had five elementary schools with grades K-6, a junior high school with grades 7 and 8 and a senior high which covered 9-12.

With Minnesota's open enrollment laws, there were many changes going on. The fifteen council members were divided between district employees and community members, eight to seven. The principal was a man and all the teachers were women. Of the seven community members four were women and three of us were men. Of the guys, one was an attorney, one a salesman and I was the finance person.

When the superintendent and his team put together a plan to move grades and students around the district, the principal and the teachers were not happy. They came to us as council and community members and asked for our help. We didn't like the plan either, so we decided to see if the council really did have any power. The group was appointed by the school district but no one was elected, so the council had no legal power.

We formulated what we thought was a better plan. I will never forget the look on the superintendent's face when we, the community members, told him that we had changed his plan. After some consideration by his staff, a few days later they agreed to follow our plan. I continued to serve on the council for thirteen years—long after my kids were out of that school. The principal, his staff and the teachers ran a great school and it was fun to make a contribution to change the system.

I attempted to change things at Honeywell too. There was a new accounting method called activity-based management (ABM) and the division GM gave me the opportunity to check it out. ABM was the new cost accounting. I worked with two professors from Harvard Business School in the early days of the concept. Cost accounting is a lot like West Point, two hundred plus years of tradition, untouched by progress.

ABM was a better way to do accounting but the old controllers at Honeywell were not buying it. As a young upstart controller, it was made clear to me that if I wanted to play in their game, I had to play by their rules. They made it crystal clear that while I was playing war in Vietnam, they were doing the hard work of being Honeywell controllers in military divisions.

With a wife and child to support, this was not the time to challenge their 'my way or the highway' mentality or their view of Vietnam. ABM would have to wait to be implemented by someone else at Honeywell—if ever. In 1986, the movie, *Platoon*, was big and I reluctantly agreed to go with a friend. Early in his tour in Vietnam, the character played by Martin Sheen and his soldier buddies were doing something but from the camera shots the audience couldn't quite see what they were doing.

All the viewer could see was heat rising, a little smoke and occasional flames. The theater was quiet but I burst out laughing. I couldn't help it. My friend whispered, "What's so funny?" I was almost out of control.

I said through my laughter, "They are burning shit." I could almost smell the diesel fuel burning the crap and hear my battery First Sergeant telling an FNG to 'burn the shithouse down'—which to the First Sergeant meant burn the crap in the 55-gallon drum. The FNG took the First Sergeant literally and set fire to the new outhouse.

I'm not sure if this was a flashback or not but I swear I could smell that burning shit and still see the look on our First Sergeant's face as the outhouse was ablaze. Later, my friend didn't think my explanation was nearly as funny as I thought it was. He thought I had totally lost it. He was right and I can still smell that burning shit.

After four years building thermostats, I became controller of the Undersea Systems Division. This division was part of the military side of Honeywell's business. We built torpedoes in Hopkins, Minnesota and shipped them to the Navy in Seattle, Washington. The Mk46 torpedo was a basic anti-submarine weapon in the Navy's arsenal and the new Mk50 would improve their capabilities.

These weapons were key to the US Navy's anti-submarine warfare. Who knew that the Navy used torpedoes against submarines fired from submarines or airdropped and had them built in Minnesota. Winning the Mk50 R&D contract was a big deal for us but winning the production contract was an even bigger.

We won them both and it was a great feeling to build my team over those four years. I started with a relatively small accounting staff and grew the group to over 100 people picking up contract administration along the way. Especially during the long and difficult contract negotiations, the hours were brutal. The contracts meant jobs and a billion in revenue over several years.

Audrey and I wanted another child but were having trouble. We decided to look at adoption and got better acquainted with friends from Molly's preschool who had adopted two girls from South America. We went through all the requirements of the adoption agency and then found out Audrey was pregnant. With all that she had been through, we decided to wait until the end of the first trimester, to make a decision.

On the first day of 1987, we received a call from Chile. The voice at the other end said, "We have a little boy for you!" Everything was going well with Audrey's pregnancy, so we decided to go with our baby and called off the adoption process. Jonathan was born six months later. He brought a whole new dimension to our family.

Molly was in first grade and thriving. At six years old, she became a second mom to Jon. Molly always had a friend or two at the house, so Jon got a lot of attention from all the girls. Jon was not a great sleeper. I was pushing him in his stroller one day and a neighbor said, "Bruce, God is punishing you." I was taken aback by her comment.

Then she said, "Molly slept through the night from five weeks. She was so easy and Jon never seems to sleep." I don't think to this day Jon has ever slept through the night but both of our children have been a great blessing to our home and family.

I was proud of USD's contribution to the defense effort and money was no longer an issue for us. I had been a Honeywell controller for almost ten years but now I was ready to search for other opportunities. As I started looking, an opportunity opened up that I had not expected. Residential Division's management team decided that the timers, lights and smart switches that they were building in China would be dumped from their product line.

A marketing guy was adamant that this was a bad move and called me. We had an engineer friend from SSED, so we teamed up to create RBC, Inc. We bought all the inventory that Honeywell had and went to work building new timers, lights and smart switches for the US home market—in China.

After the relative comfort of a Fortune 100 corporation, this was a big step for us. Our plan was to take the existing inventory, sell it at a profit, raise $1 million of venture capital, improve on each of the timers, lights and smart switches, go public with the new products and all make some money. We had a great plan. The question was could we pull it off? I wasn't sure but we took the risk. What had I learned in the twenty plus years of my career plus two years of study for an MBA at Wharton?

My experience was teaching me to put my family first. I wasn't practicing it yet but the lesson was becoming clearer. If I ever lost Audrey and our children, I would have lost everything of value in my life. I had to figure out how to put my family first. I had seen too many men put their careers ahead of their families and the result was divorce.

In the Army, the deployment separations were difficult or destructive on families. In the CPA firm, there was a running joke that you could not make the partnership without being divorced at least once. It was no joke—it seemed to be reality. I had to change but I didn't yet understand how to change my workaholic ways and still make a decent living.

Vietnam had changed me and I still had a bitter feeling in my gut. I needed to get over the survivors' guilt and PTSD and heal myself. I knew I was a better leader for having served in combat. I proved that at Fort Carson but how could I channel that into business success. The military had not prepared me for that—but Wharton had.

The military and entrepreneurial spirit said, "Never quit. The only time you truly fail is when you give up." Failure is always an option, quitting is not. Failure is truly the great teacher. I had become a business and community leader. I could analyze situations and make sound decisions. I was learning to better listen to others and use that input to make better decisions.

I was learning to see the greater good of our community and how I could influence others to join in school and community projects to improve everyone's situation. I was learning about myself and to deal with what I had been through. Rocky was right. West Point was not just about Vietnam. I put the West Point class ring back on and put my medals up on the wall of my office.

I found that hard work was good for me but I had to learn to balance that with my family, my church and my community. I was not a good debater but I was finding the words to stand up to the business bullies who were not good to others. I was learning.

Together: When we talk about racism, we think there are two main types and many other lesser ways to show prejudice. The first is individual racism or what a person learns from their experience, their hometown and their families. Then there is institutional racism, where the whole fabric of the workings of our society, businesses and organizations stand against black and brown people for no reason but for their color or where they came from.

Racism in the military, in our schools and the workplace is institutionalized by policy. We would like to think that Ray's experience with the ignorant and racist colonel was just an individual case of racism. Unfortunately, it was not. Institutional racism was alive in the military just as it was in the rest of society. What can one person do? Ray faced that discrimination his whole life.

Bruce faced discrimination in a different form but after a certain point in his career, he could hide his poverty and use his 'white privilege' to advance. This is what 'white privilege' is about. It isn't that white people don't work hard, I did. I could change my status but Ray could not change the color of his skin and the racism that followed him throughout his life. Bruce had some different lessons to learn.

Ray was very fearful of traveling down south back in the early days of 1969. He was a young man in the late '50s early '60s when the news on television and print told of murder, intimidation, beatings and jailing for no reason but asking for your rights as a human being. After his reception in the United States Army and all the things that his family had told him and all he had seen about the south, he made up his mind that he would not leave the Army installation.

He felt safe there. He was from the north and did not know the rules and customs of the south. He was afraid. Twenty-two years later, Ray was no longer afraid. The country had changed. Ray had changed and he was still learning. When Bruce first drove into North Carolina and saw the billboard with the Klansman on a white horse and a burning cross, he was afraid of what he had gotten himself into. It was all so new and different as he saw it.

As a white man, he did not have the same fears for his life that Ray did but North Carolina was not Rhode Island. For this Yankee, the south was a different world. Twenty plus years later, Bruce was no longer afraid. He had matured and grown and he was still learning. Both Ray and Bruce were learning what courage meant. Combat tours and helicopter crashes will do that. The stress of business and family can help too.

What overcomes fear? The confidence that comes from education, training and experience can teach us to handle almost any situation. Does it take 20 years? We don't think it has to take that long but for some of us, the answer is yes. It may take a while until we really listen to the voices of leaders and learn to blend our voices with theirs—to stop the racist policies that are holding us and our country back.

We had to look at ourselves. We want to make sure we can address racism, justice and equity. To start, we looked at definitions. This is not a research project. It is our story but we did go the dictionary on the internet.

Here is what Merriam-Webster had to say on Merriam-Webster.com: The definition of racism is a belief that race is a fundamental determinant of human traits and capacities and that racial differences produce an inherent superiority of a particular race. The definition of equity is justice according to natural law or right, specifically: freedom from bias or favoritism.

Justice is defined as the maintenance or administration of what is just especially by the impartial adjustment of conflicting claims or the assignment of merited rewards or punishments. What is just? Just means having a basis in or conforming to fact or reason or acting or being in conformity with what is morally upright or good.

Ok, lots of words—how can each of us put those concepts into action that we can live by, so we can use them when we need them? Listening to others is important. We were growing but we weren't finished. We were finding our own voices to take on racism with brotherhood.

Chapter 7
Building Our Communities

True peace is not merely the absence of tension; it is the presence of justice.
— Dr. Martin Luther King

Ray became a civilian and continued to serve as a leader in his community by mentoring veterans who were in trouble in the justice system. Bruce grew into new roles as a leader in his community by serving for 16 years on his local school board. When they met, they discovered that they were brothers and shared their stories with their communities. They wanted poor students of all colors to see that they needed to fight for their dreams. They both reflected on race, justice and equity.

When Ray left the Army in 1990, he was 44 years old. He was ready to take on new challenges but when you have been with the same large organization for 22 years, it was more than a job change. It was a life changing move for Ray.

Bruce's change from ten years of working for Honeywell was not quite as radical for him. At the same time, it was a change going from an organization doing over $1 billion in sales to one doing under $1 million. They both had a lot to learn.

How do we learn to build community? In the military, there is often instant community in units as both Ray and Bruce experienced several times but some units are more welcoming than others. Communities can be like that too. A survey of troops leaving the military reported that over 85% wanted to serve their communities—the follow-up survey showed that less than 20% actually found a way to do so. Why?

Fitting into a community is not always easy and veterans' experiences can put them in conflict with how things are done in civilian or community groups. An FNG in a combat unit is isolated at first and if he isn't killed in the first week, he is usually accepted in the unit. It is almost like that in communities but the time to be accepted is usually more than a week.

When they moved to Minnesota, they found that they had to make it through their first winter there before anyone would even say hello. Once they survived the bitter cold and still stay here, then they were considered one of them. Look at life and at how Ray and Bruce took on the community challenges. Listening to others is important. They were finding their own voices and discovering its strength.

Ray: Before I moved to Minnesota and took the job at Northwest Airlines, I found out about an opening for a helicopter pilot at Stanford University Hospital. They were flying a really neat looking advanced helicopter. I wanted to be a part of that organization, so I applied to the parent company and went up to their flight operations at Stanford.

I interviewed at the operations center with their chief pilot. He was a nice guy and the operation was very interesting. It looked fulfilling in my way of thinking giving back to this community as I had given back to America by being in the military. The chief pilot was optimistic about my background and experience. He said that I would get the job.

As chief pilot, he had approved of my job application and I had to have an interview with the hospital staff. I met this young woman from the transportation division of the hospital. She was pleasant and conducted a thorough interview.

As I asked her questions, I found out that she wasn't a pilot but was in the personnel department. I thought the interview went well and I was very hopeful that I would get this job. It was almost a dream job for me. I had grown to love California and wanted to make it my home.

Right after the interview, I checked in with the chief pilot and he told me that it would take maybe two weeks to get a decision from the hospital. I told him that I would check back then with him. In two weeks, I checked back in and still no word. I gave it another two weeks and called him again; still no word.

I called him a week later, I was getting anxious and with that he told me I did not get the job. He said it was given to a younger pilot with less than half of my flight time and less than a quarter of my experience. He went on to tell me that the interviewer thought that I did not have any experience in flying in the civilian environment!

I said that I had told her that I had worked in a program to help civilian hospitals and law-enforcement in Kansas for four years. Anyway, military aviation has always worked in the ATC environment when flying VFR and IFR. The chief pilot knew all this and could not explain to me why I was not hired.

I felt that the only thing that kept me from the job was racism as a part of the hospital. I was surprised at Stanford and felt just like I did all those years ago when I was trying to learn how to fly. I thought that the past 20 years of experience this nation would have gained more equality but I was wrong. After serving my country with all those sacrifices, I was not judged on my ability and experience but on the color of my skin.

In July 1990, when I retired from the United States Army. I had been looking for work and had some unique possibilities. But as things were going slowly, I got an offer to apply for an instructor pilot position at Northwest Airlines (NWA). I would be working in the simulators and teaching new pilots in the classroom.

I heard about the teaching job at NWA from my father-in-law who was a mechanic at Northwest. He sent me an application and after filling it out, I sent him back a resume. He hand-carried it to the training department and I got a call for an interview. The teaching job wasn't my first choice, because it didn't have anything to do with actual flying.

Flying would be in the classroom in a simulator. The simulators are almost but not real flying. In the Army, I was used to the latest simulators but Northwest Air had even higher, better quality. In the classrooms, they were state of the art. Part of my interview was teaching a class to NWA staff members. All my college teacher training and Army instructor training kicked in. I did well and was offered a job in the 757 department.

Most of the people that I met were very friendly. One in particular was a guy, Terry Marsh. He was a big man with a big smile and a big laugh. He gave me a great welcome and every day that he was in the training department, he would come over to say hi, how you are doing and ask how things were going. He was in the 747 section.

But there were just a few people in my new section and some didn't seem so warm and friendly to me. During the training, I was given all the books I needed but no real guidance on how to study or what it was like to be in a civilian training mode. I got through the training, basically on my own. Talking to other new instructors at the time that was the way things worked in the civilian world.

Like all businesses during the early '90s, there were ups and downs. NWA started to get a downturn in revenue and needed to cut back. With my background as an instrument instructor in the Army, I was offered an instrument instructor position. I would be moving to the orientation and annual recurrent training department. The airline was cutting back on aircraft instructors and I was fortunate to be offered this position.

When I had accepted the NWA offer and moved to Minnesota, it was a beautiful time to come to this wonderful state. In my new position part of my duties, besides teaching in the classroom, was to refine and develop new course curriculum for new pilots and annual recurrent training. This was unlike anything that I had done in the Army. There our training was developed from on high and passed down to us to instruct.

At Northwest, we had an instructional design section. These people would help us with the technical aspects of developing coursework to very high standards. Users of the instructional design section would be subject matter experts. We would give the instructional designers the technical information and they would format it into teaching materials.

This was where I met Kathryn (Kit) Eastman. She was one of the instructional designers and I came to find out, she was an expert in developing courseware. She had a master's degree in the subject from the University of Minnesota. We worked together for many hours to update the new hire program and every year, we would work for months to fulfill the FAA requirements for annual recurring training.

It became obvious that my military training did not fully prepare me for this type of instruction. Kit was very kind and patient in giving me advice on how to proceed with any given subject. With what developed into an outstanding working relationship, we also built a friendship. Over coffee, we shared various aspects of our lives including our children and families. I found Kit to be a caring person with great insight of all things around her.

I valued her friendship. As things progressed, we were both in difficult marriages. We tried to work them out but it didn't work out for either of us. At the same time, Northwest Airlines was going through some financial difficulties. Everyone got a pay cut and for some people, this pay cut was too much. This was the case for Kit and she went looking for a new job. Before long, she found one and left NWA.

During her last days at Northwest Airlines, we decided that we would have lunch someday after she got settled in her new position. Not too long after that, we contacted each other and made arrangements for lunch. By this time, we were both single people again and we decided to give our friendship a chance to grow into something more. Our thoughts about each other had been growing in a pleasant, caring way.

Our friendship became a romantic relationship over a two-year period. I found out all these amazing things about her. She was the mother of a wonderful son. She was a person with progressive ideas and an accomplished artist. I felt that she was a strong person making her way in life and after the two years, we decided to face life together.

I was excited about these new jobs. I loved helping people fly better and working in the instrument department, gave me the opportunity to do that and fly almost all the aircraft in the Northwest fleet. As a new hire instructor, I got to see all the new pilots that came into Northwest and I taught them for two weeks.

They were all excited about their new jobs of flying and eager to learn everything about this world of airline flying. And I got to teach it to them, so I was very excited. With a great job and a wonderful new wife, this was the happiest I had been since I left the Army.

Being at Northwest Airlines in the training department was a good bit like being in the military. Almost all of the instructors had served at one time or retired from one of the branches of the military. One of my good friends was the navigator/bombardier, flying A-6's in the Navy. There was another Army pilot who worked in the DC9 program.

We had fun conversations sharing war stories and they both helped me to adjust to the airline business. Since I was the only rotary wing guy, I took some friendly joking. After another year teaching in the basic indoctrination course, I decided that I should get the rest of my ratings in airplanes. I wanted to fly again.

I found myself a course in a flight school at Saint Paul airfield and went on to earn my multi and single engine commercial licenses. I loved going to school, meeting all the young people who were just starting out on their careers and learning something very new.

Northwest Airlines had an internal hiring program and I very much wanted to be a line pilot to fulfill one of my oldest dreams. But this was not the Army. The people I reported to didn't seem to have any restraints from customs or the idea of fair play like the Army. My boss was from the south and while my experience had taught me that not all southerners are prejudiced, this guy would not endorse my application to be an NWA pilot.

I had to wait until he departed. My new boss was much fairer. He was a reserve Navy commander who believed in the advancement of the people who worked for him. On the day of my job performance review, he asked me what I wanted to do. Did I want to be a line pilot? I told him that was exactly what I wanted. He set the wheels in motion and I was transferred from basic indoctrination training to the 727 program.

I learned to teach the systems of that aircraft and before I knew it, I was in the captains' training course. I would become a first officer. The company wanted all internally hired pilots to be at a high level. Completing the captains' training proved you were a high-quality pilot.

The training was four weeks long and it was rigorous. The instructors were high caliber and they enjoyed their work. Most importantly, they passed on that enjoyment to their students. It was a difficult course with both learning to fly this amazing airplane and being in command of a crew. Two other pilots had been flight instructors and I had commanded crews before. I was excited when my check ride came.

I had studied hard but I was still very nervous. There was so much information to share with my check pilot. I passed the check ride with flying colors. That was a cause for celebration! About two weeks later, I got the word that I was to be a member of the new hire pilot class to start in October. This was August. I would be happily teaching in the classroom until that day and then it would be my turn to again be behind the student's desk.

The date was 10 September 2001. The next day, my oldest dreams of flying jet aircraft were put on hold. The events of the world brought them to a halt. The attack on the twin towers of the World Trade Center in New York and the Pentagon in Washington, DC, put the whole airline industry in a tailspin. But when the hold was over, I did get to fly those big, fast jets.

I got to teach 727 systems and to be a first officer on 727 ferry flights. It was amazing flying those aircraft across this country. I would be a part of the crew that either dropped off an aircraft in Seattle for maintenance or picked it up. There were times when they needed an aircraft to replace another one that had broken down and I would get that assignment. I loved to fly that marvelous old aircraft. It was like being a part of Northwest Airlines history.

Within a couple of years, they retired the 727 and I moved to the 747. I loved teaching systems and I enjoyed being a ferry pilot on that incredible aircraft. However, I was getting older and the federal regulations put an age limit on airline pilots of 60 years old. I had to make a decision at 59, to find another flying job.

I decided that I would go back to helicopters. So I retired from Northwest Airlines after 15 years and sought a job with a medical helicopter program in the area. I found a job with Lifelink. It brought me back full circle to be a medevac pilot. I had done this when I was in the Army, using my skills to help people in need. It was very rewarding.

I flew for Lifelink for eight years and enjoyed the company of really great people who are dedicated to helping citizens in need of emergency medical care far from their home. I am honored to say that I was a part of that team. I loved flying and at this point, it was fun to fly into small towns just to see the look on their faces when a black pilot stepped out of the aircraft.

Serving others gave me pride, so serving as a volunteer mentor in the Ramsey County Veterans Court system became a natural step for me. The county's website describes the Veterans Court as a joint effort designed to recognize that veterans may be struggling as a result of their service to our country and those collateral consequences may have contributed to their contact with the criminal justice system.

The court collaborated to identify eligible veterans who had been charged with a crime and connected them to the services they'd earned to address any underlying problems they may be experiencing. To graduate, the participant had to complete all of the program requirements, including an aftercare plan, a minimum period of continued sobriety, a high school diploma or GED and employment or enrollment in school.

The mentee must also be in a recovery support group, live in a sober, stable residence and pay all program fees and restitution or have a judgment entered. All participants are assigned a volunteer veteran mentor. The role of the volunteer veteran mentor was to act as a coach, guide, role model and advocate for the individuals he or she worked with. The mentor encourages, guides and supports the participant as she or he progresses through the Veterans Court program by listening to the participant's concerns, making suggestions, assisting in determining where his/her needs may lie and acting as a support for the participant at a time when she or he may feel alone in a way that only another veteran can understand.

In early 2017, I had been mentoring at Ramsey County veterans' court for almost 2 years. Bruce and I got in contact and set up the day and time to meet. I was looking forward to meeting him and exploring what 'Minnesota Remembers Vietnam' was all about.

Bruce: With a new start-up business, raising money and traveling to China, I learned an interesting lesson while I was in Hong Kong. Each morning, I would run in the park near my hotel and one day, I saw some people doing Tai Chi in the park. There was a man on a platform leading the movements, so I stopped and got behind the group to follow the moves.

After a few minutes, an older woman in front of me noticed that I was there. In a low voice, she growled to the woman next to her, "Gweilo!" Eventually, the buzz made it all the way up to the leader of the group. He greeted me at the break and said that I was welcome to participate. Later that morning at the plant where our products were manufactured, I asked the Managing Director's son, who was a student at Harvard, what the word Gweilo meant.

He laughed and said, "To you, Bruce, it means honored foreign guest." Actually it meant 'white devil' and is used to refer to anyone who is not Chinese.

The Hong Kong people used it to refer to their British colonial masters and the Japanese during their occupation during World War 2. It is generally considered a derogatory racial slur. It was one of the few times that my 'white privilege' did not make me feel welcome in China. It made me think back to my CPA days when Archie was the only black man in our office. I was the only white person in the park and I realized that I would never be part of the Middle Kingdom.

Audrey supported me in each entrepreneurial venture but made it clear that if we lost the house, I would lose her and our family. She was not happy with

RBC's financial situation but we didn't lose the house, so the family and our marriage were safe. RBC had to declare bankruptcy. It was not easy facing those investors who had put in over two million dollars. I had failed again. The experience did not feel good but it woke me up to the fact that I was not walking my talk.

I had preached to the people who I worked with, "The family comes first." But every day, I was putting in more hours at work than at home. This was not the model I wanted to live. For Christmas that year, 1994, my family gave me the book, *First Things First* by Stephen Covey. I had been reading his Seven Habits of Highly Effective People for several years and sharing it with people I worked with. Now Audrey was adamant that I practiced what I preached. I was burning out and not putting the family first.

I really had to hustle to figure out how to rebuild my career. I worked to start a financial consulting business but the economy was not strong. I had to take a job that required a 65 mile commute each day and they would not take me on as a consultant. But the ABM experience and financial expertise I had gained at Honeywell paid dividends and I was able to consult part time. Even the commute paid a surprising dividend.

One evening as I was driving home, an accident happened right in front of me. There was a car at a stop sign, waiting to pull out. Apparently, the driver did not see the car coming on the main road I was on and she pulled out right in front of the oncoming car. The car swerved but hit the one pulling out, just missed my car and careened off into a cornfield. I pulled over and made sure the people who had caused the accident were ok and ran into the cornfield to check out the other car.

After all the action, there was silence as I approached the car, except for the high-pitched whine of the engine. The two people were not moving in the front seat. As I ran up to the car, the engine was screaming because the driver still had his foot on the accelerator. The dry corn stalks under the car were catching fire. It was the first time I remember having a 'flashback' to Vietnam.

The scream of the engine and the fire took me back to the day we were shot down. I stopped. Then it was like being in a slow-motion video. Normally, I think my Army training would have kicked in and said jump in there and rescue those people. But at that moment, the voice in my head was saying, "You have a wife and two children at home. If that car blows up and you are killed, what happens to them?"

I could hear the whine of the chopper and see the fire next to me. Then the Army training did kick in and I ran to the car. The old sarge's voice was saying in my head, "Ranger, you better move!" The two people in the front seat were out cold, so I reached into the car and switched off the ignition. With the car switched off, I stomped out the fire.

The people in the car were still not moving but I saw no blood. By this time, emergency med techs were running toward us down the path in the corn mowed down by the car. They took over and moved the two out of the car and into the ambulance.

After I gave my statement to the police, I drove home very cautiously. I pondered what had made me hesitate and why I had the flashback. Since I left the military, I had been so focused on business, marriage and family, I had not given Vietnam much thought except for my conversation with Rocky about my West Point class ring—which I still wasn't wearing—and the *Platoon* movie burning shit smell.

When I left the military, service in the Army Reserve was an option but I made the choice to stay as far away from the Army as I could. I had to do two years of inactive reserve but I made it my business never to put on a uniform again. I wondered why I was so bitter and angry. Now I had to take a hard look at myself. I knew that there was more that I could do—more that I had to do.

As the economy regained momentum, I built the consulting practice. I was able to quit the commute and consult full time. Our family prospered. Molly was our star athlete and I coached her basketball team until she made the traveling squad. When she was in high school, her AP history teacher asked me to address her class about Vietnam.

Something woke up in my heart and head. This was 1997, thirty years after I had graduated from West Point and 27 years since I had returned from Vietnam. This class was something I had to do and I had to think. I prepared for talking to these students more than even talking to the Honeywell Board. I had to—my daughter would be in that classroom.

Molly and I had a great father-daughter relationship. She, of course, knew that I was a West Point grad, a veteran and that I had served in Vietnam. I had not talked very much about my service there with her or her mother. Neither of them knew me when I was in the military but when Molly was considering colleges, we took the whole family to West Point. I wanted her to at least consider the Military Academy.

We walked all over the campus, saw the museum and looked at classrooms. As we walked around the parade ground, known as the Plain and I saw a woman cadet drilling her platoon. I called to her and she came over. There are places cadets can take visitors that even a grad cannot enter. She took us into the mess hall, a cadet room and Central Area where I had lived for four years.

The Academy started admitting women in 1976, so this young woman was part of the first ten classes of trailblazer women graduates. She was a senior and a cadet lieutenant and she sold West Point better than I ever could have.

After the cadet left us, I gushed to my daughter, "Molly, wouldn't you love to go here?"

She gave me her best teenage eye roll and said, "Dad, you have to be kidding!" She had other ideas on what her college experience should be. She would choose a great course and she would find it—her way.

While I was in Vietnam, I took some pictures and I used them to frame the discussion in Molly's class. I started by explaining that when I was five, I saw the West Point Story at the movies. How many people can grow up and live their dream? I told them how I had worked all through school to get the grades to go there. I explained what the Military Academy's motto, 'Duty, Honor, Country' meant to me—both before and after Vietnam.

In combat, we stopped fighting for our country and fought to protect the guys we were with. The focal point of the story was about my friend, Gary and how losing him was so difficult. I kept the story factual but I still get emotional when I speak about him. A girl at the front of the class cried about Gary's daughter losing her dad. She blurted out, "That can't be the end of the story!"

I answered, "It's not," and finished with a picture of Gary's daughter, her husband and their son, Gary. War is about death but life is what happens after war for those of us who make it home. Telling the story that first time helped me. Then the questions started. The students in the class knew Molly and many of them had been in our home, so they knew me.

The question came up, "Would you do it again?" It was the first time but not the last that I got that question. The simple answer is yes. But the answer is not so simple. This first time speaking to a classroom of students in 1999, led to other classes and other schools. Speaking to history classes also let to speaking to English classes where the students had read Tim O'Brien's *The Things They Carried* gave me a chance to reflect. The students were smart and their questions made me rethink my Vietnam experience.

After Molly graduated from high school, she went to Whitman Collage as a political science major. For a summer job, she worked for US Senator Paul Wellstone. After Senator Wellstone was elected to the Senate, he gave a speech at the Vietnam Memorial. This anti-war speech upset many veterans including me.

Meanwhile, my consulting experience was building and I had run a successful campaign for a friend who ran for the school board in our city. So when I got the call from another friend about running for the school board myself, I had to give it serious consideration.

The school board is the lowest elected body in our country's electoral system. Since I had been working for the school district as a volunteer, I checked in with the principal of our middle school. He and I had done a lot of work together. He assured me that my work was appreciated and I could continue to do that.

But being elected to the school board was different. That election gave one a seat at the table and a vote. The vote mattered because with a $60 million budget, the board-controlled policy and the future of the district. He urged me to run.

Another friend was also considering running for a seat on the board, so we talked about how we could support each other. We agreed that if she ran, I would run her campaign and if I decided to run, she would run mine. She called me back just 10 minutes after we hung up and volunteered to run my campaign. We won. She put together a great team and the strategy was simple.

I had been a volunteer in the schools and on the site council for over a dozen years. One of our kids was a graduate of the district and the other was in the middle school. Also, my wife was a teacher with a master's degree in reading education and what I didn't know about education, I could ask her.

So on a sunny morning in September 2001, I registered as a candidate for the school board election. The date was September 11th. I was listening to the news and the report was that there had been an accident in New York City. By the time I got home and turned on the television, I knew that nothing about our future would ever be the same.

I was also concerned because my wife and daughter were in the air, flying to London. I didn't get comfortable until they called home. My son was at school. I talked with him too. I was on my way to a consulting meeting later and when the first tower fell, I almost drove off the road.

The school board election is non-partisan, so on my campaign literature, I had the endorsement of a Republican friend on one side and a Democrat on the other. One day, I was door knocking and a woman answered the door. She took one look at the brochure, recognized the Democrat and said, "Good, you are a Democrat, I'll vote for you."

I explained that the school board is non-partisan and the other picture and endorsement was from a Republican. She said, "That's good." I asked why that was good and she explained, "My husband is a Republican, so he will vote for you."

The learning curve for a newly elected board member was steep but we had a great board and a great superintendent. Other than some people who wanted to be on the board but lost the election, the community supported us and our schools. Our district, St. Louis Park, is right next to Edina which is one of the wealthiest suburbs in the US. The contrast between the districts was stark.

Our 'free and reduced lunch' student population was over 40% of the district. Edina's was under 10%. That simply meant that we had a lot more work to do for students with special needs and many who were behind their grade level. I vowed that I would do everything in my power to close 'the gap'.

When Rosa Parks passed away in 2005, Reverend Al Sharpton spoke at her funeral. At the end of his eulogy, he asked everyone listening to make a 'Rosa Resolution' to do something about the injustice and lack of equity in our world. I did. My Rosa Resolution was to close the gap. This was not an easy task. Some educators said it was impossible but to start, we needed to figure out what the gap was.

These was no agreement, so in St. Louis Park we decided to define it. We focused on three areas; reading at grade level by third grade, test scores and graduation rate. The gap was the difference between black and brown and white students. What we discovered was that it was not an 'achievement' gap. It was an opportunity gap and it was racist.

We did some interesting things during the next 12 years. We defined equity and differentiated it with equality. We took down barriers to learning with the International Baccalaureate® (IB) program in all our schools from elementary to the high school. We knocked down the barriers to black and brown students taking AP and IB classes.

Reading scores improved, test scores improved for black and brown students and the graduation rate improved but wiping out institutional racism in our schools was a much bigger problem. Finally, in my last year on the board we passed a capital improvement referendum for $109+ million to improve all our schools. I had hoped that we could create a school district where if we had 10 National Merit Scholars or valedictorians that three or four of them would be black or brown.

At the last graduation I attended as a board member, one of our eight valedictorians addressing her class chewed us out because all of them were white. I wanted to protest but she was right. We had made some progress but I had not accomplished my Rosa Resolution.

Ray wrote about not having test anxiety and I wrote that I was a professional test taker—with my own set of anxieties. How could we help students work through this anxiety situation? Where could we build equity into this system? Was there an answer here? We could not close the achievement or opportunity gap in a school district of 4,500 students. So what could we do?

We could keep working at it. We could make sure all students were reading at grade level by third grade. Then they had a chance to score better on the tests that would make a difference in their future. They didn't all need to be National Merit Scholars but they could approach each hurdle with confidence, knowing that they had antiracist mentors who supported them.

As I finished my time as a CFO, I wanted to see if I could do something to stop veterans' suicides and I was invited to speak at a meeting of the legislature to tell my story. After I finished, a man came through the crowd and introduced himself. He said he was the CEO of the Minnesota Humanities Center. I didn't know Minnesota had a Humanities Center much less what one was.

He invited me to participate in a discussion group called 'Echoes of War'. As we moved into the community with literature to share as discussion leaders, I observed an interesting phenomenon. Most of the veterans in our group were from the Vietnam era and while many would share their stories, some would not at first.

I spoke to a group about the story of a nurse who served in Vietnam. The story was entitled 'A Piece of my Heart' and she told how she went through bouts of PTSD after she returned home. I wondered how anyone who was not in combat could experience the same symptoms I had experienced. She went on with the story that every patient who left her hospital ward in Vietnam took a piece of her heart with them.

That got me thinking that it is probably not just combat veterans who feel the trauma of wartime experiences and military service. As I explained the story and my reaction to it, I noticed that the guys who sat there with their arms folded, relaxed and started to share. One daughter came to me in tears that her dad opened up in the meeting. He had not spoken about the war in 50 years!

This sharing led to working with the Humanities Center and the Twin Cities Public Television station, TPT, on a project called 'Minnesota Remembers Vietnam'. We spoke to large and small groups of veterans using the Ken Burns and Lynn Novick's 'The Vietnam War' documentary.

I was doing breakfasts for veterans at the Humanities Center and noticed that there were no black veterans attending. We put out the call to a few VSO's and got a good response at the next breakfast meeting. That's how Ray and I met.

He couldn't come to the breakfast meetings, so we talked on the phone and agreed to have coffee. He was mentoring a young man at the Ramsey County Veterans Court, so we met at Dunn Brothers Coffee on Lake Street by the Mississippi River Bridge.

Together: Building communities is not easy. Ray became a civilian and continued to serve as a medevac pilot and volunteer mentor for veterans in trouble in the community justice system. Bruce grew into new roles as an educational leader and learned new lessons about equity on the school board in his community.

He began working with veterans to learn more about justice. The quote by Martin Luther King at the start of this chapter gives us insights about what justice can do. We were doing good things in our communities but we knew there was more to be done.

Each time Bruce was elected and reelected to the school board, he raised his right hand to solemnly swear that he would 'support and defend the Constitution of the United States' just as he and Ray had done in the military when they enlisted and when they became officers.

Bruce almost laughed the first time he took the oath as an elected school board member, because he understood 'support and defend' in the military—

but as a school board member? Hell, yes! As we said in chapter 1, education is the way out.

When we met over a cup of coffee, we discovered we were brothers. The discovery had bigger implications than finding a new friend. Dr. King said it well, *True peace is not merely the absence of tension; it is the presence of justice.* Two men discovered that a black man and a white man could find peace through brotherhood.

When two people met, there was always some tension. It did not take long for the tension to dissolve for us. We quickly saw that it was equity and justice we both were striving for and we found our path to peace. It was just never easy.

Chapter 8
Brothers

The best arguments in the world won't change a person's mind. The only thing that can do that is a good story.

– Richard Powers

What could they do for students preparing to serve their country and for soldiers leaving the military to serve their communities? Their story wasn't about combat, it was about growing leaders. They want to contribute to leaders who could change their country.

Leaders who were antiracist and who shared common bonds of equity, justice and brotherhood—black and brown leaders who were strong and white leaders who were aware of their privilege. They both wanted all leaders to understand what it meant to be brothers and sisters.

Ray: The story of Bruce and I meeting each other began early in 2017. It is a mystery why people become friends. Bruce and I were from different sides of town. That is literally true. Bruce lives in St. Louis Park on the west side of the Twin Cities and I live on the east side in St. Paul.

But common ground is a good starting point. We were both from the East Coast. We both had higher education and military service in Vietnam. That was a big starting point but there was more. We have shared beliefs about how our government should be run—with justice and equity. We started out at different points politically but through our experiences, education and years of life, we have come to walk the same path.

Like our education after high school, Bruce went to the Military Academy to fulfill his dream and I went to a teachers' college but always dreamed to fly in the military. We believe in equal justice in all things and in the worth of every person. The one most important thing we share is the respect for everyone on earth on a basic level.

There are other things that make us friends and brothers. An important part of our friendship is an interest in each other, a curiosity of the other's point of view of the world around us. The other important thing is that we care for each other's well-being.

We both have activities that we are passionate about and we share that too. Bruce was a longtime member of the St. Louis Park school board. He is passionate about the education of all children regardless of their background. I feel that the education of our youth on an equal, equitable basis is our highest priority.

We go to different schools to teach students about our experience in Vietnam—yet another thing that we share together with those young minds. My passion is that equal justice should be given to all veterans. Because of their training and the very intense situations that they have had to endure, drug use and the legal problems can overwhelm a veteran.

So I am a mentor in the Ramsey County veterans' treatment court. Bruce shared his passion with me and now we are both board members on the Veterans Defense Project. This is a board whose goal is to get veterans treatment courts in every county in Minnesota and eventually in every state in the United States.

These are just a few of the reasons why Bruce and I are brothers. We have experienced the same traumatic situations in our lives and come through with a bit of dignity. We are brothers because we understand what the other has gone through. So if you look at it in the space of time we've only physically known each other for about three years.

But that's only if you do not count the histories of his life and mine. I think in so many ways, once we met with such similar lives, upbringing and dreams that we had to be brothers. In early 2017, I had been mentoring at Ramsey County Veterans Court for almost 2 years. The head of the mentors, Donn and I always had lively conversations as I waited for my turn to go up in front of the judge with my mentee.

This day, Donn told me about a guy who wanted to meet me for a program called 'Minnesota Remembers Vietnam'. He thought that I could tell a story that would be interesting. I told him that I would be happy to meet with a fellow

Vietnam veteran and tell my story. We set up the day and time and I was looking forward to meeting Bruce and exploring our stories.

The day came that we are going to meet and I walked into the Dunn Brothers' Coffee Shop. When I looked around, I spotted Bruce right away. As we had agreed, he had his West Point hat on. He was sitting with one of the TPT producers. He introduced me to her. She had another appointment and left us to drink coffee and talk.

Like veterans of all wars in our age group, we asked all the familiar questions that soldiers have been asking each other for millennia. Where are you from in the world? 'The world' is the United States when you're in a war zone or just overseas. Most soldiers, sailors, airmen and Marines think of the United States as the biggest and best part of the world.

First, we found out that we were both from the East Coast and just over 300 miles apart. I also found out that we both chose the Army. Bruce wanted to go to West Point to get a college education and I wanted to fulfill my dream to fly and become a combat pilot. Then to top that all off, we were in the same place in Vietnam. For our generation who served in the military, Vietnam was a defining event of our lives.

We were a year apart. Bruce got there before me but we were in the same area in and around CuChi. This area in the southern part of South Vietnam was very active with Communist forces headed for Saigon from the Ho Chi Minh trail. Bruce was an Artillery officer out of a fire base in the bush and I was a pilot flying out of Bien Hoa. If we had been there at the same time in country, I would have surely supported his unit.

And from his side, he would have supported with Artillery fire all the troops that I had flown into dangerous landing zones. Bruce flew a lot as an observer, so he knew what my life was like as an aviator. We had to face the same uncertainties that happen every time you takeoff in a war zone!

We are both open to new encounters with people of all kinds, always looking for the good side of a person and having them prove otherwise. As further meetings for coffee and sharing of ideas about the world today in about our history went on, we started developing a real friendship. We both had difficult beginnings in life, we weren't given much of a chance to for fill our dreams by some of those around us.

We had to work hard for what we accomplished through our lives. I think a big thing that created our friendship was that we fully respected each other's journey and had an eagerness to learn about each other's successes, failures and difficulties in life. Because of that shared upbringing, the hardships of our early life and the fact that we faced the same hardships, challenges and the dangers of war, we are brothers. Building on that relationship, we share much of our daily lives, our ups and our downs, with shared compassion Bruce and I want the best for each other.

We also found out that we both have a deep and abiding love for fellow veterans throughout our community and the nation. Bruce is really into veteran suicide prevention and I wanted to help veterans in the county justice system. With each of these goals shared between us how can we not be brothers.

We share the same ideas about love of country in the debt that this nation has to its veterans. We want to make sure that every veteran has the opportunity to serve his community and live a fulfilled life. As we shared our stories in the classroom with students, our bond deepened. The story improved as we grew together.

We shared more and our bonds grew. We wanted those students to feel what we felt from 50 years ago and now. We weren't two old guys telling war stories. We were brothers who wanted them to understand what those stories meant for us.

Bruce: I received a phone call from a Ray who had heard about the breakfast meetings but he was mentoring a guy in the Ramsay County Veterans' Court on Wednesday mornings. He couldn't make the breakfasts but could we have coffee? He lived in St. Paul and I lived in St. Louis Park.

Minneapolis was half way between us, so we agreed to meet at the Dunn Brothers' Coffee Shop near the Mississippi River on the Minneapolis side. I told him since all white guys look alike, I would wear a gray hat with USMA on it, so he could pick me out of the crowd.

In the meantime, I received a call from a friend at Twin Cities Public Television (TPT). She was active in the veteran's meetings at MHC and had a colleague, Amy, who was doing a 'Minnesota Remembers Vietnam' documentary called the 'Telling Project' about Vietnam veterans. Since I was already going to be half way to their office, Amy and I agreed to meet at the Dunn Brothers the hour before Ray and I were to meet.

The meeting on the 'Telling Project' was educational for me. Amy explained who she already had as presenters and asked. "What are we missing?" The show had already recruited Navy, Air Force and Marine veterans and a Hmong family member, so I thought it was a simple answer. After I recovered from my disappointment that TPT didn't want me for the show, I said that they were missing a black Army officer.

Toward the end of our meeting, I told her that Ray and I were meeting there, so I had to put on my 'USMA' hat because Ray and I had agreed that since all white guys look alike, he would recognize me by the hat.

About that time, a tall black man who looked like Danny Glover walked in the door. Amy said, "I think your guy just walked in."

I took one look at Ray and replied, "No, *your* guy just walked in!" After their original meeting, Amy recruited Ray for her project and Ray became a star of the show telling his story. After Amy departed that day, over those first cups of coffee, we discovered how much we had in common. Both of us were poor kids from the East Coast.

Both had a dream from the time we were five years old. We both fulfilled those dreams and they landed us in Vietnam—in the same place, CuChi. We shared war stories about being shot down in helicopters and losing good friends. It didn't take us long to realize that we were brothers.

I was giving a talk at a local high school and invited Ray to speak with me. As we integrated our Power Point pictures we shared with the class, even our tough-guy combat poses were similar. We still laugh about that. If we needed proof that we were brothers—there was the proof. My presentation was good but Ray's contribution made it great.

Later, we were invited to speak together in a 'Minnesota Remembers Vietnam' show called 'We Gotta Get Outta This Place'. We talked about being brothers. I told the audience that we always got the question, "How can you be brothers? Ray is so much taller than Bruce!" We got a good laugh, so we use the question each time we speak.

When we speak, our presentation does not change very much. We tell our stories of Vietnam, because that's a big part of what made us brothers. We do not glorify war. We share our stories of who we lost there. We want it understood that war is ugly and protecting and defending the US Constitution is the highest service there is. That defense keeps our families safe. We speak about our dreams, education, mentors and equity.

We ask each student to find a veteran and listen, really listen to his or her story. We think that if everyone did that, we can decrease the number of veterans' suicides. We urge everyone to find their own brothers or sisters who are black or white in this world and let them know that they care, support and love them.

Together: When we talk about what makes us brothers, the obvious similarities jump out. Poor kids from the East Coast who each had a dream, working to make our educations a reality were facts that made us laugh together. We may have crossed paths at Grand Central Station or the bus terminal in New York City but if we did, it didn't register.

So 50 years later, we met in a Dunn Brothers Coffee Shop in Minneapolis and found an incredible bond. That bond was made up of service to our country, equity for all people and justice.

When we discussed our military service, the similarities hit us right between the eyes—CuChi, Vietnam, helicopter crashes, the loss of friends in combat, command and leadership. These events are important in our lives and telling them to students, other veterans and anyone else who will listen became a part of growing as friends.

One day, we realized that we were brothers. We found a solid foundation over shared values like service, equity and justice. Bruce struggled with the concept of equity until a third-grade teacher put it into an example he could share with others. Ray and many black and brown teachers helped Bruce work through the concept of 'white privilege'. Equity we discovered had to include justice.

Justice may be easier to understand but more difficult in practice. George Floyd, a black man, lived two blocks from Bruce's home. When he was killed by a white Minneapolis police officer, riots broke out—not just here in Minnesota but around the world. When your brother is a black man, justice hits closer to home than ever before.

With a pandemic around us, we did not take to the streets but we decided to write about how we could save the world. How could we look at racism in a new way and stop it now? How could we bring about change in America that had resisted change since the first slaves were brought here from Africa?

Our answer was to *declare brotherhood*. Our solution was to do what we did. Find a brother and make sure that brotherly love prevails, protects and educates your brother—both ways. Are we our brother's keeper? Damn right we are. We brothers and sisters must stick together. Here's how we can start the process.

White people need to show the courage of their convictions and use their white privilege to challenge others when they speak untruths or racist words about people of color. They must tell these ignorant people their story about their brother as gently but forcefully as possible that they are wrong.

None of us can stand quietly by when they use their racist words. They are not only lying but also cheating black and brown people of their rights to life and liberty with their hate filled words.

Black and brown people need to take the risk to engage white people and then listen to what they have to say. As hard as it may be, they have to be patient with those they engage and as they tell their story about their brother, they need to correct the lies and incorrect ideas they are hearing.

That is no easy task as some of these people may harbor false ideas that have been passed down for generations through their families and towns. People of color have to make it clear that racist words and actions cause pain.

We think that we should share this brotherhood initiative with every citizen in the US. Each of us must realize that the history of our country shows how we have mistreated our citizens of color. We need to do the right thing and work to see the humanity, the brotherhood, in everyone. This is our action to save our world.

If we take action, we will attract good people to serve our country with equity and justice. When their military service is complete, then they will continue to serve as leaders in their communities. Equity and justice will continue to grow if we all *declare brotherhood!*

Printed in the USA
CPSIA information can be obtained
at www.ICGtesting.com
JSHW010918191123
52089JS00005B/33